International Journalism
and Democracy

Routledge Research in Cultural and Media Studies

1. Video, War and the Diasporic Imagination
Dona Kolar-Panov

2. Reporting the Israeli-Arab Conflict
How Hegemony Works
Tamar Liebes

3. Karaoke Around the World
Global Technology, Local Singing
Edited by Toru Mitsui and
Shuhei Hosokawa

4. News of the World
World Cultures Look at Television News
Edited by Klaus Bruhn Jensen

5. From Satellite to Single Market
New Communication Technology and
European Public Service Television
Richard Collins

6. The Nationwide Television Studies
David Morley and Charlotte Bronsdon

7. The New Communications Landscape
Demystifying Media Globalization
Edited by Georgette Wang, Jan Servaes,
and Anura Goonasekera

8. Media and Migration
Edited by Russel King and
Nancy Wood

9. Media Reform
Democratizing the Media, Democratizing
the State
Edited by Beata Rozumilowicz and
Monroe E. Price

10. Political Communication
in a New Era
Edited by Gadi Wolfsfeld and
Philippe Maarek

11. Writers' Houses and the
Making of Memory
Edited by Harald Hendrix

12. Autism and Representation
Edited by Mark Osteen

13. American Icons
The Genesis of a National
Visual Language
Benedikt Feldges

14. The Practice of Public Art
Edited by Cameron Cartiere and
Shelly Willis

15. Film and Television After DVD
Edited by James Bennett and
Tom Brown

16. The Places and Spaces of
Fashion, 1800–2007
Edited by John Potvin

17. Communicating in the
Third Space
Edited by Karin Ikas and
Gerhard Wagner

18. Deconstruction After 9/11
Martin McQuillan

19. The Contemporary Comic
Book Superhero
Edited by Angela Ndalianis

20. Mobile Technologies
From Telecommunications to Media
Edited by Gerard Goggin and
Larissa Hjorth

**21. Dynamics and Performativity
of Imagination**
The Image between the Visible
and the Invisible
Edited by Bernd Huppauf and
Christoph Wulf

**22. Cities, Citizens, and
Technologies**
Urban Life and Postmodernity
Paula Geyh

23. Trauma and Media
Theories, Histories, and Images
Allen Meek

24. Letters, Postcards, Email
Technologies of Presence
Esther Milne

**25. International Journalism and
Democracy**
Civic Engagement Models from
Around the World
Edited by Angela Romano

International Journalism and Democracy

Civic Engagement Models from Around the World

Edited by Angela Romano

Routledge
Taylor & Francis Group
New York   London

First published 2010
by Routledge
270 Madison Avenue, New York, NY 10016

Simultaneously published in the UK
by Routledge
2 Park Square, Milton Park, Abingdon, Oxon OX14 4RN

Routledge is an imprint of the Taylor & Francis Group, an informa business

© 2010 Taylor & Francis

Typeset in Sabon by IBT Global.

Library of Congress Cataloging-in-Publication Data
International journalism and democracy : civic engagement models from around the
   world / edited by Angela Romano.
      p. cm. — (Routledge research in cultural and media studies ; v. 25)
   Includes bibliographical references and index.
   1. Citizen journalism.   2. Journalism—Social aspects.   3. Journalism—Political
aspects. I. Romano, Angela Rose.
   PN4784.C615I36 2010
   070.4'3—dc22
   2009045293

ISBN13: 978-0-415-96110-3 (hbk)
ISBN13: 978-0-203-85204-0 (ebk)

Contents

List of Tables and Figures   xi
Acknowledgments   xiii

PART I
Deliberative Journalism

1   Deliberation and Journalism   3
    ANGELA ROMANO

2   American Public Journalism Versus Other International
    Media Models   16
    ANGELA ROMANO

PART II
Public and Citizen Journalism

3   Public Journalism in South Africa: Experiences and
    Experiments with Local and Community Media   35
    BRETT DAVIDSON

4   Civic Journalism Initiatives in Nigeria   49
    TOKUNBO (TOKZ) AWOSHAKIN

5   Sustaining Public Journalism Practices: The Australian
    Experience   63
    ANGELA ROMANO

6   Public Journalism, Kiwi Style: Lingering Echoes of a Big Bang   75
    MARGIE COMRIE AND DAVID VENABLES

7 Public Journalism in Japan: Experiments by a National Paper 91
YOHTARO HAMADA

8 Civic and Citizen Journalism in Germany 105
KLAUS FORSTER

9 Public Journalism in Finnish Mainstream Newspapers 121
LAURA AHVA

10 Citizen Voices: Public Journalism Made in Colombia 136
ANA MARIA MIRALLES
(TRANSLATED BY ANGELA ROMANO)

PART III
Other Deliberative Models for Peace, Participation, Development and Empowerment

11 Britain's *Big Issue*: Street Papers as Social Entrepreneurs 153
ANGELA ROMANO

12 Inspiring Public Participation: Environmental Journalism
in China 166
JIANNU BAO

13 Peace Journalism in Indonesia 180
GITA WIDYA LAKSMINI SOERJOATMODJO

14 Traditions of Public Journalism in India 194
PRADIP THOMAS

15 In the Hands of the People: Citizen Media for Revitalizing
Puerto Rico's Poor Communities 208
ANGELA ROMANO AND ANETTE SOFÍA RUIZ MORALES

16 Viração Magazine: Consciousness-Raising Media
for Young Brazilians 222
PAULO LIMA AND MARIA IZABEL LEÃO
(TRANSLATED BY ANGELA ROMANO AND ALICE BARONI)

PART IV
Conclusions

17 **Ongoing Issues for Deliberative Journalism**   231
   ANGELA ROMANO

Contributors   243
Index   247

Tables and Figures

TABLES

6.1 Issues Most Referred To: Comparison Between 1996 Conventional Coverage and Public Journalism   77

6.2 Problematic Situations for Conventional and Public Journalism Coverage   78

6.3 Aspects of 2001 Local Government Election Coverage   82

6.4 Aspects of 2007 Local Government Election Coverage   85

8.1 Aspects of Political News Coverage   109

8.2 Percentage of Articles with Sources of Direct and Indirect Citations   111

8.3 Formal Variables in Readers Edition   113

8.4 Percentage of Articles with Sources of Direct and Indirect Citations   116

10.1 Summary of Citizen Voices Projects in Colombia   147

13.1 Peace/Conflict Journalism and War/Violence Journalism   186

FIGURES

8.1 Issue-centred news coverage, percentage of given codes.   115

8.2 Non-issue-centred news coverage, percentage of given codes.   115

8.3 Mobilizing news coverage, percentage of given codes.   116

13.1 Stages of intervention.   187

Acknowledgments

I would like to thank Sam Chege Mwangi of Kansas State University for his support for this book. I first crossed paths with Sam when he contacted me about research he was doing on public journalism for the Kettering Foundation in Dayton, Ohio. At that stage, my plans to edit a book on public journalism in South Pacific nations had failed to eventuate. A few years later, Sam had visions of editing a book about public journalism initiatives from around the world, and although he progressed a little further than I did, his book plan did not reach fruition either. I am enormously grateful to Sam for putting me in contact with two of the contributors from his planned book, who have written chapters on Colombia and Japan for *International Journalism and Democracy*. He also kindly read early drafts of six of the seventeen chapters in this book, offering encouraging words to the authors. His enthusiasm and commitment to the principles of deliberative journalism have helped to provide me—and, without a doubt, countless others whom he has taught, worked and talked with—with oxygen as we try to breathe life into a relatively new way of understanding and practising journalism.

Part I
Deliberative Journalism

1 Deliberation and Journalism

Angela Romano

The news media are not merely mirrors of society or passive, impartial conveyors of information about social and political affairs. The news media's influence on public agenda setting and communities' understanding of issues and events makes them a major social power in their own right. The authors who have contributed to this book continue a long history of media practitioners, scholars and observers who have asked whether journalism's power might be wielded to help societies recognize and resolve their problems. They remember the adage of playwright Arthur Miller, who wrote that a good newspaper is 'a nation talking to itself'. In these days of globalization and multimedia proliferation, journalism should help the various publics that the print, broadcast and online media serve—whether they are small neighbourhoods or cross-national communities—to have meaningful conversations among themselves about issues that affect them. In other words, the book explores how journalism might support the processes of social deliberation.

Deliberation must be clearly differentiated from conversation, debate, argument and other forms of dialogue, although one or more of these types of discussion will always be involved in deliberation. Deliberation is the discussion and consideration that is undertaken before a decision or action is made. John Dewey's classic definition is that 'deliberation is a dramatic rehearsal (in imagination) of various competing possible lines of action. . . . Deliberation is an experiment in finding out what the varying lines of possible action are really like. . . . An act tried out in imagination is not final or fatal' (Dewey 2007/1922: 190). David Mathews further notes that deliberation does not guarantee that action will happen, but 'it creates the possibility that an action will be taken mindful of the consequences. Deliberation helps us to look before we leap' (Mathews 1999: 182).

The capacity of the media to mobilize a community response is not always a force for good; it may equally unleash an inferno of tyranny and injustice. The 1994 Rwanda Genocide is an example of the living nightmare that journalism might give rein to. Rwanda's local radio and print media were used to incite hatred, dehumanize members of the 'rival' ethnic group, and provide directions to killers on how to locate victims to butcher. While an estimated 800,000 to one million people were being systematically slaughtered, the international media corps might have alerted the world community and provoked an effective external intervention. Instead they largely overlooked, downplayed or misunderstood the events (Des Forges 1999, Thompson 2007).

Many types of conversation may lead to action, but for the purposes of this book, not all will be considered as deliberation. Both Rwanda's hate-mongering media and the sluggish international media contributed to the ways in which their respective communities crystallized a particular vision of the country's circumstances, and their decisions about whether and how to act. However, the conversation initiated by these media was not inclusive of a full range of perspectives. Nor did it provide information that would encourage reflection on the viewpoints, needs and values of other social groups or re-examination of each group's own positions. This chapter will explore the premise that deliberation must permit the participation of all relevant community stakeholders, including the minorities, the marginalized, the disadvantaged and even those deemed as 'deviant'. This enables the exercise of what John Rawls (1993; 1997) calls 'public reason'. This is inclusive, critical deliberation by a society that includes diverse and even unpopular views about the common good and has processes for enabling the expression of plurality.

DELIBERATION

The ability of communities to achieve great feats through self-governance has been noted for centuries. Observing American life in the early nineteenth century, Alexis de Tocqueville noted that a government might perform the activities undertaken by companies and private individuals. However, he also asked 'what political power could ever carry on the vast multitude of lesser undertakings which the American citizens perform every day, with the assistance of the principle of association?' (de Tocqueville 1945/1840: 108). De Tocqueville expressed the fear that if 'individuals lost the power of achieving great things single-handed' or the 'the means of producing them by united exertions', then the people 'would soon relapse into barbarism' (1945/1840: 107).

De Tocqueville's comments illuminate both the importance of deliberation and its underlying premise. Politics is not something that only happens in the realms of government or formal political processes. Politics occurs whenever individuals act alone or with others to identify and resolve issues, both minor and momentous, that affect their community. Community-driven politics usually transpires after deliberative talk, which helps individuals to establish the common understandings about the nature of their problems and how to deal with them.

Deliberation is different from mobilization. Deliberation may assist communities to marshal the labour, finances, physical resources or force required for such politics to occur. However, the mobilization of action usually requires a range of other activities and resources beyond those involved in deliberation. For journalists, this is an important distinction. Several chapters in this book indicate that journalists are more comfortable with the tasks involved in supporting deliberation than they are with becoming community mobilizers.

The difference between communities and publics also needs to be clarified. A community is a collection of people with some common attribute that gives them a loose or intense shared identification. Communities may be based on geography, such as the small-scale communities of suburbs and villages or the large-scale communities of nations or cross-national alliances. Others are communities of interest, whose members may be physically distant from each other but who are linked by common social and political characteristics. Every individual thus belongs to various communities of interest that are based on factors such as shared ethnic background, gender, sexuality, common concerns about a political issue or the environment, workplace activities, sporting or leisure interests, or other attributes. Communities become a 'public' when people turn from their private and individual affairs because they perceive a common interest in fixing shared problems or controlling the consequences of others people's activities and exchanges (Dewey 1991/1927: 126). The public is not just people who experience or assess the words, actions and policies of others. The public is 'a shared political space for people to assemble, speak their minds, and record their extended conversation so that others, out of sight, might be part of it' (Carey 1997: 14).

THE UNRULINESS OF DELIBERATION

In comments that have become more pertinent with time, Dewey has observed that individuals are distracted from public issues by popular entertainment, the demands of corporate capitalism, a focus on lifestyle and personal concerns, and the impact of industrialization on social structures and networks (Dewey 1991/1927: Ch. IV). Dewey also suggested that each individual's time is absorbed not just by many competing activities but also by the numerous publics that they might potentially join with. He noted that there are innumerable potential publics within a community, each with different, overlapping or opposing sets of issues and concerns. This makes it hard for individuals to focus on one issue, or to evaluate the far-reaching consequences that various courses of action may have for the various publics that they belong to (Dewey 1991/1927: 131–7). These factors weaken the possibility that individuals will form a public that will last long enough to engage in deliberation, decision making or action.

Given how muddled and confusing the processes of public life are, many of the procedures that have been consciously designed to promote public deliberation—such as deliberative community forums—invest a considerable amount of time and effort trying simply to understand what the nub of the problem is. Deliberation also involves recognizing the different stakeholders who may have an interest in the issue, incorporating their knowledge and perspectives, and identifying not just the differences but also the commonalities in each stakeholder's experiences, values and opinions. From there, the participants frame different ways of responding to the issue, appraise the consequences of each response, the resources needed for action, and the ways in which communities might be organized so that their disparate efforts contribute to mutual goals. These deliberative processes help to create and nourish a public, as well as help to achieve its goals.

Outside carefully planned exercises such as deliberative forums, the processes of deliberation rarely occur in a tidy, linear progression. However, most of these steps described previously are usually required to some degree if deliberation is to occur in everyday life. Mathews notes that processes and institutions that support deliberation can be easy to dismiss because they are often fluid with little coherent structure—such as informal gatherings, ad hoc associations, and the banter of people who mull over the meaning of their everyday experiences. He compares them to the wetlands of America's Gulf Coast, which were filled in or dug out for property developments and shipping channels by those who saw them only as acres of mud and matted vegetation. 'The consequences were disastrous: sea life that bred in the swamps died off, and coastal cities were exposed to the full fury of hurricanes' (Mathews 2009: 60). Thus many seemingly inconsequential interactions in daily life may potentially contribute in major ways to organic politics. For this kind of organic politics to be successful, societies need to master the art of civic or collective learning, in which citizens are both the agents and objects of learning (Mathews 2009: 61). The nature of collective learning has been identified in many different political traditions.

It can be seen in Paulo Freire's concept of conscientization (*conscientização*), which originated in Latin America but which has influenced many political movements elsewhere. Conscientization means that the public establishes a critical consciousness. To do this, people must become aware of the internalized 'myths' (or ways of understanding our world) that they learn through social communications, including the mass media (Freire 1993/1970: 121). These myths can shape and limit the ways in which we view social power relations, a community's potential, and capability to be self-determining actors. Freire opposes the 'banking model' of education in which someone acts as a traditional teacher, simply transferring preselected information and insights to the student (1993/1970: 52–60). Journalists also conform to the banking model if they see their role as only to transmit facts to an uninformed audience. Freire proposes that people who act as 'educators' must establish a reciprocal relationship with learners in which their joint engagement allows each to establish new ways of understanding the prevailing conditions and new priorities about which problems are worthy of study and action (Freire 1993/1970: 61–7).

Similar concepts of collective learning are visible in Mahatma Gandhi's still-influential principles of *swaraj* or self-governance, which promotes self-assessment and self-reliance at both the individual and the community level. Ghandi believed in bottom-up governance, and was concerned by people's propensity to assume that politics occurred only in formal government institutions and that there was no way for them to achieve change (Gandhi 1921). He said that *swaraj* could be attained 'by educating the masses to a sense of their capacity to regulate and control authority' (Gandhi 1925).

Ganhdi's proposed system relied on *satyagraha*, or adherence to the truth, whereby people must constantly put aside vested interests and accepted conventions in order to check their reality, admit to their mistakes, and adjust their behaviours accordingly (Gandhi 1982/1927). *Satyagraha* involves people fighting for principles rather than fighting other people, and recognizing that each viewpoint contains some truth within it. Gandhi also promoted *sarvodaya*, or welfare/empowerment for all, recognizing that the search for common good should not harm the individual, and that each person's contributions should be valued equally, regardless of their position (Gandhi 1982/1927: Ch. XVIII). Another important part of Gandhi's system was *ahimsa* or nonviolence, which employed strategies for putting aside antagonisms, obsessions and malicious impulses and seeking peaceful outcomes that benefit all. Gandhi's principles of peaceful self-governance are thus another example of the use of collective learning to promote mature and inclusive deliberation.

This is not to suggest that all deliberative theorists presume that decisions made by governments, corporations or elites and top-down political communications are always undesirable or inferior. Nor does it suggest that all horizontal communications between citizens are the repository of virtue. Processes of deliberation occur within parliamentary and other elite spheres as well as the less formal networks of the public sphere. My key point is that citizens can play a powerful role in defining issues and devising or supporting solutions to social problems. Even if the government is the primary actor in addressing those problems, when citizens are involved in deliberation, they are more likely to contribute their resources and work in mutually reinforcing ways towards collective goals.

DELIBERATION AND DIVERSITY

Anne Phillips argues that deliberators need to consider not only what topics and ideas they discuss. They also need to pay attention to the people and voices that are 'present' as participants in the public sphere. In analyzing the 'politics of presence', Phillips recognizes that it is possible for particular individuals or groups to champion the views of minorities, even when minority interests are counter to their own. However, she contends that social or economic minority groups must still have a direct presence in policy-making processes rather than have others speak about or on behalf of them in their absence. This is because people's values, beliefs, opinions, preferences and goals are very strongly linked to their personal experiences and social identities (Phillips 1996: 140). When discussions and decisions are 'worked out *for* rather than *with* a politically excluded constituency, they rarely engage with all the relevant concerns' (Phillips 1996: 147).

Every nation faces challenges about how to conduct deliberation or reach resolutions among community participants with intensely different identities, backgrounds, resources and needs. In the face of such diversity, Jürgen Habermas critiques the liberal traditions of discussion and decision making for focussing on the rights of one citizen against another rather than common solutions. He criticizes the republican tradition for seeking an 'articulation of a common good' and 'creation of solidarity among citizens' (Habermas 1996: 21–3). The problem with appeals to 'unity' is that 'the perspectives of the privileged are likely to dominate that definition of that common good'; less privileged people are likely to be asked to put aside their claims of entitlement 'for the sake of a common good whose definitions may be biased against them' (Young 1996: 126). Habermas argues in favour of a communitarian model, which focuses more on deliberation among plural groups, the identification of commonalities and differences between the parties, and the questions of 'who we are and who we would like to be' (Habermas 1996: 24).

Exploring a different element of this issue, Iris Marion Young finds that 'most theorists of deliberative democracy assume a culturally biased conception' about what is a 'better argument' (Young 1996: 121). People of certain cultural, educational or social backgrounds can be disadvantaged in public conversations because they feel intimidated by the formality and rules of such discussion. Such people may rely on exploration of emotion and ideas rather than the logic- or reason-driven arguments that are seen as superior in such settings (Young 1996: 123–4, 133). Thus 'they do not speak, or speak only in a way that those in charge find "disruptive"' (Young 1996: 124).

Furthermore, in public conversation, differences are often discussed only in order to find ways to transcend those differences, which are seen as partial and divisive. Instead of assuming that discussions must begin with mutual problems, shared values or collective understandings of the common good, Young presents the concept of 'listening across differences'. 'Listening across differences'—by expressing, questioning and challenging the knowledge of different individuals and groups—can transform people at three levels:

- Encountering differences of culture, needs and social position can help participants to realize the bias and predispositions in their own perspectives;

- It can lead participants to understand that collective policies are not always about shared interests, and that they may need to recognize and accommodate the unique needs of people in special or different situations,
- Participants are exposed to a wider picture of the factors that have shaped their perspectives. While they are not expected to abandon their old perspectives, it may increase their wisdom for reaching just solutions (Young 1996: 127–8).

Deliberation thus requires an examination not just of facts but of personal experience and emotions, which are inherently subjective. It also asks us to identify the various and conflicting values that affect our decision making, and consider how to reconcile them. For example, in deciding during a time of economic recession whether or not to help disadvantaged individuals or communities, we might have to balance our 'value of helping those in need' against our value of 'looking after our own first'. Reason and emotion are not separate, because the emotions play a role in all forms of assessment and judgement (Hall 2005; Nussbaum 1995; Rorty 1985). Compassion, solidarity and many other emotions are essential for publics to be committed to the often lengthy and challenging processes of deliberation. Arguably, publics themselves do not arise because of an objective set of facts or physical circumstances, but because of people's emotional response to conditions that may be seen as a problem, threat or issue. Despite this, emotion is often 'viewed as a villain in public discourse and decision making, undermining a "rational" approach to conducting public affairs' (Harwood Group 1993: 23).

Lynn Sanders suggests that these issues might be resolved by including more accessible ways of communicating, most particularly what she calls testimony, or telling one's own story to a broader group. Sometimes the process of testimony might need careful moderation or management to create the conditions in which people can freely share experiences and opinions without demeaning others or damaging their well-being. Overall, however, in testimony there is no assumption

> of finding a common aim, no expectation of a discussion to the resolution of a community problem . . . Testimony encourages the democratic consideration of the worthiness of perspectives not obviously rooted in common ground and not necessarily voiced in a calmly rational way. In other words, testimony could open the possibility of reasonable, collective consideration of novel, if disquieting, perspectives (Sanders 1997: 372).

Societies also clearly need to work more systematically at a social level to develop the capacities of people or groups that are usually left out of public discussion so that they are better positioned to share their perspectives. These various forms of deliberation can help to create what James D.

Hunter calls a 'substantive democracy', or a democracy in which a fractured culture can still reach working agreements. The priority is not to find 'the "middle ground" of fast moral compromise but rather a "common ground"' where 'people's beliefs are indeed recognized as sacred to the people who hold them . . . but common problems can nevertheless be addressed' (Hunter 1994: 34–5).

DELIBERATIVE JOURNALISM

The news media play a far-reaching and substantive role in public deliberation, and have done so for centuries. De Tocqueville described the mass media of his time, the newspaper, as an advisor that:

> talks to you briefly every day of the common weal, without distracting you from your private affairs. . . . To suppose that they only serve to protect freedom would be to diminish their importance: they maintain civilization. I shall not deny that in democratic countries newspapers frequently lead the citizens to launch together into very ill-digested schemes; but if there were no newspapers there would be no common activity. (1945/1840: 111).

De Tocqueville overstates the significance and power of the news media, but he presents a broader truth about the role of journalism in most nations. It is exemplified in the role that the news media have played in independence movements and nation-building processes around the world throughout the twentieth and twenty-first centuries. Gandhi, for example, was a prolific reporter and also editor of four weekly newspapers, and saw journalism as a service. 'I believe that a struggle which chiefly relies on internal strength cannot be wholly carried out without a newspaper,' he said (Gandhi 1928: 142). Gandhi's editorials, commentaries and investigative reports were an exemplification of de Tocqueville's description of journalism as a 'beacon' that helps isolated individuals, who feel 'insignificant or lost amid the crowd' to find each other and unite towards 'common designs' (1945/1840: 111–12).

All types of journalism have the potential to support deliberation to some degree. Individuals might find great and unexpected use in future years for a fragment of information that seems irrelevant to their lives today. People have great potential to weave together apparently unconnected shreds of information to create meaningful tapestries that provide a complex but coherent picture.

Certain forms of journalism, however, have greater potential to serve deliberation than others. For example, many scholars have noted that the liberal Western media are structurally impaired in facilitating an authentic deliberative discourse. Despite the rhetoric that journalists are the neutral conveyors of competing perspectives, in practice they largely broadcast the outlooks of eloquent political elites or others who have the resources to voice their arguments most effectively (Couch 1975; Habermas 1991; Voltmer 2006). Decades of research also shows that most work at mainstream news organizations is based on routines and standardized practices, which again favour elite sources and institutions rather than engagement with the general public (Bennett 2005: 180–207; Cottle 2003: 3–23). This model is insufficient for forms of politics that value popular decision making.

If one was to take the concept of deliberative journalism to its extreme, it would place an enormous demand on journalists. Journalists would need to bring issues to public attention, but not too many issues or they might create an information overload. Their reports would need to be sufficiently engaging to capture public attention, but also be incisive, comprehensive and balanced so that the public can frame issues and understand the background and implications of those issues. Journalists would then have to appropriately identify and include the insights and contributions of all relevant stakeholders and actors in the situation. Journalists would also report on communities as they evaluate potential responses, and then investigate whether and how they have acted upon the resulting decisions.

Described in these terms, the task sounds impossible. It should be understood, however, that the news media is only one of many social actors and institutions that work together to support deliberation. Journalists can help to plug the gaps in deliberative processes occurring in society more broadly. They can check *rationality*, by checking whether significant ideas and policy positions are being included; *accountability*, by drawing attention to attempts to manipulate public opinion; and *inclusion* and *fairness*, by inquiring into barriers and inequalities that may hinder participation (Dzur 2008: 168). Theodore Glasser and Stephanie Craft reassure us that 'deliberation does not formally require journalists to accommodate an unrestricted dialogue among citizens'. They stipulate that 'it does require that the day's news be written in a way that invites each citizen's judgement. At a minimum, this means framing topics as issues rather than events and then soliciting debate and commentary without regard for the speaker's power or privilege' (Glasser and Craft 1998: 213).

DELIBERATIVE JOURNALISM AROUND THE WORLD

Attempts in different countries and regions to cultivate deliberative journalism models must be rooted in local sociopolitical and economic realities. Jay Rosen has reiterated this point in response to questions about whether American public journalism concepts might be successfully uprooted and transplanted elsewhere.

I believe that public journalism should be homegrown, rather than imported. Of course, that ought to be true for journalism in general.

Each country has its own social history, political culture, press tradition, party structure—and its own problems. There is nothing wrong with taking inspiration and ideas for the movement in the U.S. But for the idea to develop, we need not only more laboratories, but different ones. . . . As a democratic art, journalism should serve the particular democracy in which it is embedded. (Rosen 2000).

After studying a range of public journalism-style initiatives outside the United States, Tanni Haas concluded that 'these projects have resembled their US counterparts in almost all respects. Indeed, the only substantive difference is that news organizations in some countries have promoted more direct interaction between citizens and government officials than has typically been the case in the United States' (Haas 2007: 117).

By contrast, Mwangi notes that a study of public journalism outside the United States presents certain methodological and conceptual problems. Mwangi argues that the idea of public journalism is universal, if one considers the core notion that journalists should 'involve citizens in democratic practice by providing them with information that they can use to act as citizens'. However, he concurs with Rosen that the best public journalism adapts to each country's social history, political culture, press tradition and party structure (Mwangi 2002). Thus, it may be that journalists and scholars attempting to study international public journalism may overlook many deliberative journalism ventures because their differences from US models and practices may render them invisible to those who have become habituated to American styles and standards.

This book explores how journalists in different countries have attempted to employ practices that promote deliberative democracy in ways that reflect and enhance local media and political cultures and traditions. This book does not summarize all the public journalism-style or deliberative journalism initiatives that have been conducted around the world. Countries and examples have been selected to explore different elements of deliberative journalism. Each chapter attempts to offer some insight about deliberative journalism that might potentially be used to enlighten, critique or improve deliberative media practices. This task commences with Chapter 2, which describes some of the main models for deliberative media.

Chapters 3–10 examine attempts in a range of countries to employ public and citizen journalism strategies, largely influenced by US models. Chapter 3 explains how some South Africans have selected and adapted American concepts of civic mapping to boost the performance of the community media in covering local issues. Chapter 4 indicates that Nigerian journalists have overlaid public and citizen journalism practices onto local 'guerrilla journalism' cultures in ways that continue and extend the country's traditions for promoting political action. Chapter 5 shows how some New Zealand newsrooms have achieved some short-term successes in adopting American public journalism practices 'wholesale', but experienced longer term problems because of insufficient understanding of the concepts or how to integrate them into local settings. Chapter 6 studies Australian newsroom experiences and explores issues affecting the sustainability of public journalism projects in mainstream news organizations. Chapter 7 describes how American public journalism concepts have meshed well with elements of Japan's newspaper and social cultures. Chapter 8 suggests that public journalism values exist in German newspapers, even though the concept never gained widespread currency in the country, but indicates mixed civic outcomes from the burgeoning citizen journalism movement. Chapter 9 discusses how Finnish journalists have domesticated American public journalism concepts, and how this has led them to reconsider the positions of the public and themselves in news making and political life. Chapter 10 looks at how public journalism in Colombia has relied on a university–industry collaboration, drawing from the strengths of both sectors and transforming journalistic processes.

Chapters 11–16 point to many other models of deliberative journalism that promote participation, peace, and personal and community development. Chapter 11 investigates the street press that aim to help homeless and other disadvantaged people, and the tradeoffs that result from these publications' role as social entrepreneurs. Chapter 12 explores how environmental journalists in China have exploited gaps in the constrictive political culture to provide a stimulus for citizen awareness and action, and how they have achieved noteworthy political successes in the process. Chapter 13 describes the practical application of peace journalism principles during a bloody conflict in Indonesia. Chapter 14 uses case studies from India to explore deliberative journalism as a spectrum that spreads across a wide range of activities, from investigative journalism to reporting inspired by Gandhian philosophies to community journalism. Chapters 15 and 16 reflect Freirian models of communication in Puerto Rico and Brazil. The Puerto Rican chapter highlights the conditions that enable citizen-created media to contribute to the social and economic regeneration of poor communities. The Brazilian chapter illuminates how community media can develop citizenship and community participation among young people.

The concluding chapter explores ongoing issues for deliberative journalism that may limit its sustainability or challenge its potential to play a significant role in public deliberation. It offers a pragmatic understanding that deliberative journalism models are generally new, and resolution of the many problems surrounding its theory and practice will only occur incrementally.

BIBLIOGRAPHY

Bennett, W.L. (2005) *News: The Politics of Illusion*, 6th edn, New York: Longman.

Carey, J.W. (1997) 'Community, public and journalism', in J. Black (ed.) *Mixed News: The Public/Civic/Communitarian Journalism Debate*, Mahwah, NJ: Lawrence Erlbaum, pp. 1–16.

Cottle, S. (ed.) (2003) 'News, public relations and power: Mapping the field', in *News, Public Relations and Power*, London: Sage, pp. 3–24.

Couch, C.J. (1975) 'Constructing social life', in C.J. Couch and R.A. Hintz (eds) *Mediated Communication*, Champaign, IL: Stripes Publishing Company, pp. 65–79.

Des Forges, A.F. (1999) *Leave None to Tell the Story: Genocide in Rwanda*, New York: Human Rights Watch and Paris: International Federation of Human Rights.

De Tocqueville, A. (1945/1840) *Democracy in America*, vol II, Phillips Bradley (ed.) New York: Alfred A. Knopf.

Dewey, J. (1991/1927) *The Public and Its Problems*, Athens, OH: Swallow Press and Ohio University Press.

Dewey, J. (2007/1922) *Human Nature and Conduct: An Introduction to Social Psychology*, reprinted edn, New York: Cosimo.

Dzur, A.W. (2008) *Democratic Professionalism: Citizen Participation and the Reconstruction of Professional Ethics*, University Park, PA: Pennsylvania State University Press.

Freire, P. (1993/1970) *Pedagogy of the Oppressed*, revised edn, M.B. Ramos (trans.) NewYork: Continuum.

Gandhi , M. (1921) *Hind Swaraj or Indian Home Rule*, Madras: Natesan.

Gandhi, M. (1925) 'Interrogatories answered', *Young India*, 29 January. Available at the Collected Works of Mahatma Gandhi Online, http://www.gandhiserve.org/cwmg/VOL030.PDF (Accessed 1 September 2009).

Gandhi, M. (1982/1927) *An Autobiography, or, the Story of My Experiments with Truth*, M. Desai (trans.) Harmondsworth: Penguin.

Gandhi, M.K. (1928) *Satyagraha in South Africa*, V.G. Desai (trans.) Ahmedabad: Navajivan Publishing.

Glasser, T.L. and Craft, S. (1998) 'Public journalism and the search for democratic ideals', in T. Liebes and J. Curren (eds) *Media, Ritual and Identity*, London: Routledge, pp. 203–18.

Haas, T. (2007) *The Pursuit of Public Journalism: Theory, Practice, and Criticism*, New York: Routledge.

Habermas, J. (1991) *The Structural Transformation of the Public Sphere*, T. Burger (trans.) Cambridge, MA: MIT Press.

Habermas, J. (1996) 'Three normative models of democracy', in S. Benhabib (ed.) *Democracy and Difference: Contesting the Boundaries of the Political*, Princeton, NJ: Princeton University Press, pp. 21–30.

Hall, C. (2005) 'Passion and reason in deliberative democracy', Annual meeting of the American Political Science Association, Washington, 1 September. Available at http://www.allacademic.com/meta/p39866_index.html (Accessed 1 September 2009).

Harwood Group (1993) *Meaningful Chaos: How People Form Relationships with Public Concerns*, Dayton, OH: Kettering Foundation.

Hunter, J.D. (1994) *Before the Shooting Begins: Searching for Democracy in America's Culture War*, New York: The Free Press.

Mathews, D. (1999) *Politics for People: Finding a Responsible Public Voice*, 2nd edn, Urbana: University of Illinois Press.

Mathews, D. (2009) 'Afterthoughts', *Kettering Review*, 27(1): 58–63.

Mwangi, S. (2002) *A Survey of International Media and Democracy Projects*. Available at http://www.imdp.org/artman/publish/article_86.shtml (Accessed 25 February 2004).

Nussbaum, M.C. (1995) 'Emotions and women's capabilities', in M.C. Nussbaum and J. Glover (eds.) *Women, Culture, and Development*, Oxford, UK: Oxford University Press, pp. 396–401.

Phillips, A. (1996) 'Dealing with difference: A politics of ideas, or a politics of presence', in S. Benhabib (ed.) *Democracy and Difference: Contesting the Boundaries of the Political*, Princeton, NJ: Princeton University Press: 139–52.

Rawls, J. (1993) *Political Liberalism*, New York: Columbia University Press.

Rawls, J. (1997) 'The idea of public reason revisited', *University of Chicago Law Review*, 64(3): 765–807.

Rorty, A.O. (1985) 'Varieties of rationality, varieties of emotion', *Social Science Information*, 24(2): 343–53.

Rosen, J. (2000) 'Re: [BlueEarBooks] Jay: International public journalism'. Email to blueear-books@egroups.com, 2 September.

Sanders, L.M. (1997) 'Against deliberation', *Political Theory*, 25(3): 347–76.

Thompson, A. (Ed.) (2007) *The Media and the Rwanda Genocide*, Ann Arbor, MI: Pluto Press.

Voltmer, K. (ed.) (2006) 'The mass media and the dynamics of political communication in processes of democratization', in *Mass Media and Political Communication in New Democracies*, London: Routledge, pp. 1–20.

Young, I.M. (1996) 'Communication and the other: Beyond deliberative democracy', in S. Benhabib (ed.) *Democracy and Difference: Contesting the Boundaries of the Political*, Princeton, NJ: Princeton University Press, pp. 120–35.

2   American Public Journalism Versus Other International Media Models

Angela Romano

The power of journalism to mobilize societies towards action has been recognized for many centuries. It is reflected by Napoléon Bonaparte's famous words, uttered in 1810: 'A journalist is a grumbler, a censurer, a giver of advice, a regent of sovereigns, a tutor of nations. Four hostile newspapers are more to be feared than a thousand bayonets.'

Chapter 1 has discussed how the media does not act in isolation, and instead can be understood as one of many important actors within society that can potentially bring issues to public attention, create public understandings and motivate a response. Nor does journalism work in one homogenous body called the 'community' or 'public'. Any individual journalistic report may be used by overlapping communities and publics that contain many differences within them. Chapter 2 describes a range of journalism models that attempt to encourage and support deliberation among these communities and publics.

PUBLIC JOURNALISM IN AMERICA

Public journalism has been described as a philosophy, set of practices and a movement (Rosen 1995: v) that originated in the United States as an attempt to cultivate deliberative democracy. Concerns about the American media's capacity to contribute to meaningful public debate had been intermittently expressed in academic and professional circles since the 1920s. However, the literature on public journalism commonly points to the US House of Representatives and Senate elections between 1988 and 1992 as low points in the performance of both journalists and politicians, leading to a major rethinking of journalists' role in public life. This was a key impetus that stimulated the development of public journalism—often also called civic journalism or communitarian journalism.

In contrast to Napoleon's depiction of the journalist as 'a tutor of nations', Cole Campbell describes public journalism as 'a technology of community rather than a technology of tutelage'. In other words, journalists—in common with other professionals—need to throw off the concept that they are 'guardians' who can 'guide and direct citizens about what's best for them' (Campbell 2007: 40). Campbell, one of the founding fathers of public journalism, argues that journalists must help to generate what he calls 'public knowledge', a commodity that is continuously used and generated whenever a public exercises its experience and reason to identify and address problems. He advises journalists to consider how their practices can advance or subvert the five categories of activities that produce public knowledge. These are:

- myths and meanings: the myths that citizens and communities generate about themselves and their capacities to act;
- surveillance and assessment: how citizens and communities pay attention to what is happening and conduct their own 'SWOT analysis' of strengths, weaknesses, opportunities and threats in order to respond appropriately;
- public discourse: how communities talk about opportunities, threats, and how to leverage strengths or mitigate weaknesses;
- public judgement: a process (which may take months, years or sometimes generations) of working through the phases of consciousness raising, assessing choices and trade-offs associated with possible courses of action, and reaching resolutions about how to respond;
- public work: individuals and communities translate their judgements into action, including assessments and revision of those actions (Campbell 2007: 43–5).

Campbell echoes the perspectives of other American public journalism proponents, who advocate that journalists move beyond the 'conventional view of press power'. This conventional view is that journalists should bring facts to light, raise consciousness, focus public attention, uncover abuses, recommend action, distribute praise and blame, and 'afflict the comfortable; comfort the afflicted' (Rosen 1997: 9). Advocates of public journalism accept the importance of these traditional roles for the media as disseminators of information or watchdogs of power (e.g., Campbell 2007, Rosen 1997). They do not suggest that journalism conventions be overturned in cases 'when traditional approaches work perfectly well' (Rosen 1999: 8). However, public journalism's promoters maintain that societies need more than conventional journalism, because 'such information—even if it is freely collected and widely consumed—is not sufficient to make a successful democracy. Citizens also must *deliberate* about policy' (Levine 1996: 1). In other words, an *informed* citizen is not necessarily an *active* citizen.

Judith Lichtenberg identifies two attributes that characterize public journalism. The first is that journalists use their values to play a role in helping communities to create a healthy public climate. The second is that journalists rely on citizens to identify issues of importance in the public arena and to help set the agenda for what stories and issues should be covered. They aim to connect with citizens in their communities and not merely provide a one-way flow of information to consumers (Lichtenberg 1999: 341–2). Rather than viewing the public as 'an audience to educate or a problem to manage', public journalism encourages citizens to be thoughtful on complex issues by creating 'a meaningful process that allows them to learn, discuss, and decide' (Remaley 2009: 29).

Public journalism consequently promotes the importance of 'public listening' to identify public perspectives and trends, issues and events occurring within the wider community. Public listening involves far more than shallow market research with polls, phone-ins or off-the-cuff responses from people on the street to ill-conceived questions like 'What do you think about the economy?' Arthur Charity notes that such strategies 'invite narrow-mindedness at least as much as reflection' (1995: 20). The pressure to insert a quote from 'some average Joe' into every news story can also lead to 'tokenism' (Stepp 2000: 28).

If public journalism strategies are to work well, then newsroom staff need to learn how to draw ordinary people into conversations that elicit a real representation of public concerns and how to frame these issues in meaningful stories. While polls, phone-ins and interviews with people on the street are regularly part of public journalism, they should ideally involve or follow lengthy and thoughtful conversations that allow journalists to connect with people on a personal level, to clarify people's position, to both seek and provide information, and to challenge them to examine and change ideas (Charity 1995: 21–2). Techniques that have been used include in-depth interviews with major cross-sections of the population, town hall meetings, focus group-style community conversations, and civic mapping. (For examples of these techniques in practice, see Charity 1995: 20–49; Dzur 2008: 144–9; Harwood and McCrehan 2000; Phillips N.D.)

Such interactions with the community may not provide journalists with an immediate story that can be published or aired that day. To be effective, public engagement can rarely be a 'one and done' activity (Remaley 2009: 30). Editor Jennie Buckner instead notes that such interactions require journalists to think of themselves as part of 'a learning organization' (Sirianni and Friedland 2001: 217). As members of learning organizations, journalists need to develop new skills for gathering and synthesizing the input from numerous sources across different levels of society to provide meaningful observations about public life, and an appreciation of the ways in which communities might understand and respond to the information that the media provides.

The concept and practices of public journalism have attracted considerable criticism and commentary. Questions have been raised about objectivity (see Chapter 17). Critics claim that journalists' independence, balance and effectiveness might be compromised if they collaborate with the public, community organizations and/or governments on identifying and addressing civic problems. Some public journalism projects have been unduly upbeat in their approach, accentuating positive elements, ignoring disagreements, and glossing over the problems and issues at stake in order to create a veneer of consensus or to rally citizens to action (Hoyt 1995: 27; Lichtenberg 1999: 343). In many cases, this has resulted from a poor understanding by journalists about how the media might potentially foster deliberation to fully recognize problems and devise appropriate solutions. This is not necessarily an indictment of public journalism itself.

Another criticism of the public journalism movement is that there has been insufficient thought about when and how to address communities as conversation partners. For example, there are no clear standards that determine what kinds of projects are suitable for the organizational capacity of newsrooms and the role of journalists in a democracy (Dzur 2008: 163). Steve Davis goes so far as to claim that 'public journalism has been proselytized by people who do not understand it in ways that do not make sense' (2000: 687). Many activities that have been labelled 'public journalism' certainly have been sloppily conceived or designed (e.g., see Rosen 1999: 257). Some editors and proprietors have promoted public journalism-style activities that were more aimed at raising circulations or satisfying advertisers than encouraging deliberation (Campbell 1998: 408–10; Hardt 1999; Rosen 1999: 253–61). Many of the critics who identify these faults do not dismiss public journalism overall, but point to the need to better conceptualize its ideals, theory and practice.

Critics furthermore argue that public journalism does not suggest a new way for ensuring journalists' accountability, increasing public participation within news media organizations, or altering the media's reliance on market systems (Schudson 1999: 138). Hanno Hardt, for example, suggests that public journalism:

> remains ideologically committed to journalism as a business that relies on the satisfaction of its particular consumer community, redirects journalistic practices accordingly, and offers a recipe for temporary relief from the symptoms of a deeper social and economic crisis. . . . there is a preoccupation with the surface phenomena of content matter and topical concerns, rather than with structural constraints due to the changing objectives of media enterprises that may have contributed to the demise of newspaper journalism over the past 30 years (Hardt 1997: 94–5).

CITIZEN JOURNALISM

The citizen journalism movement addresses some of these concerns about media ownership, public participation and reform of media traditions. Citizen journalism, sometimes also called participatory journalism, involves citizens using the Internet to play an active role in the process of collecting, reporting, analyzing and disseminating news and information. Media designers and consultants Shayne Bowman and Chris Willis note that: 'The intent of this participation is to provide independent, reliable, accurate, wide-ranging and relevant information that a democracy requires' (2003: 9). The founder of the Center for Citizen Media, Dan Gillmor, furthermore envisages that an evolution 'from journalism as lecture to journalism as a conversation or seminar—will force the various communities of interest to adapt. Everyone, from journalists to the people we cover to our sources and the former audience, must change their ways' (Gillmor 2004: xii).

Many types of citizen journalism do not resemble traditional journalism. Examples are comments or postings in blogs, YouTube, discussion groups, chat rooms and social networking sites like Facebook and Twitter. US research shows that the 'explosive growth' in users of social networking and citizen video sharing platforms has led them to become increasingly important as 'means of distributing news, not just for social interaction and entertainment' (Project for Excellence in Journalism 2009). Lasica argues that when these often haphazard and spontaneous online musings offer 'summary, synthesis, analysis or commentary' then they can be considered 'random acts of journalism' (Lasica 2003).

Among the most prominent actors in the citizen journalism movement are those sites that resemble traditional news media journalism in their news values, formats and aesthetics of presentation, but which allow ordinary citizens to upload news, features, audio, visuals and other content. This includes the collectively run Independent Media Center websites that link to indymedia.org. It also includes sites like DigitalJournal.com, GroundReport.com, NowPublic.com and OhmyNews (*OMN*), which are run by professional editors and journalists, who may contribute a proportion of content in addition to overseeing the contributions of thousands of public contributors worldwide.

When former journalist Oh Yeon-ho set up *OMN* in South Korea in 2000, he established a new model for editing and publishing articles, digital photographs and video feeds from a massive army of citizen journalists. Oh observes that *OMN* is often compared with Web 2.0 in the way that it harnesses and generates 'participation, openness and collective intelligence' (Oh 2007). The organization has more than 50,000 registered citizen reporters, dubbed the 'news guerrillas', who contribute more than 70 per cent of stories.

The significance of *OMN* and similar sites are often measured in terms of their massive scope and influence. *OMN* is one of the most popular news providers in South Korea. A commonly cited example of its public influence is the role it played in Roh Moo-Hyun's victory in the 2002 South Korean presidential elections. Oh also argues that the value of user-generated content lies in its potential 'to generate positive impact on the public spheres' that it works within. Oh says that stories have influence if they:

- are 'worthwhile sharing',
- draw the attention of a critical mass so that public opinion can be built,
- help to resolve issues rather than simply raise matters to public attention or criticise problems, and
- bring about 'repercussions not only in the cyber world but also in real life' (Oh 2007).

Other types of citizen journalism sites, like Digg and Newswire, do not allow users to present much if any original reporting, but do allow them to generate news agendas from existing information. Users share news stories and other content that they have found on the web, and those stories and links attain prominence on the websites according to the number of votes they attract. The opportunity to add comments also provides the potential to extend and deepen the discussion.

The definition of citizen journalism also includes mainstream media websites that provide the public with opportunities to upload comments, images and other information. Among the mainstream media innovators is Al Jazeera, which was believed to be the first media outlet with a Twitter widget on its news page (Verclas 2008). Another of Al Jazeera's noteworthy experiments involves development of a new technological platform, which was set up in 2009 following the ongoing Israeli–Palestinian fighting over the blockade of Gaza. It allows a massive body of both citizens and journalists to reports of attacks, damage and casualties, which are mapped as they unfold.[1] Despite notable initiatives like these, many large mainstream media have witnessed spectacular failures in their citizen journalism projects (Project for Excellence in Journalism 2009; *The Economist* 2006: 9). This has exacerbated a situation in which many mainstream media sites limit citizens to tokenistic inclusion.

Regardless of mainstream media reluctance, technologically savvy news sources are helping to propel a change in media cultures. An example was when the Israeli consulate in New York held a 'citizen press conference' on Twitter, spending more than an hour answering questions and posting longer answers on the consulate's blog, as part of a massive Israeli international public relations campaign during the 2008 Gaza War (Verclas 2008).

Although such a disparate array of activities may not necessarily encourage deliberation, Bowman and Willis argue that they are means for users 'to create, increase or renew their social capital. These communities are not merely trading grounds for information but a powerful extension of our social networks' (Bowman and Willis 2003: 38). Chapter 17 discusses the conditions needed if citizen journalism websites are to provide a setting that encourages an inclusive deliberation rather than distracting chatter or discourses that may be destructive to individual liberties and healthy public life.

If citizen journalism sites are spaces that support deliberative conversation, then their achievements are regularly overrated. In contrast to Axel Bruns' observations that citizen journalism involves an ongoing process of

community discussion, analysis and revision (Bruns 2008: 75), Thomas
Chase notes that for many casual Internet users:

> participation in a continuing process of community critique and evalu-
> ation is an unrealistic expectation. . . . To venerate broad participation
> in news production while neglecting the quality of news output risks
> creating a public sphere dominated by diverse yet devalued political
> communication; what Nicholas Carr has dubbed the 'hegemony of the
> amateur' (Chase 2008: 15).

Citizen journalism is also frequently criticized for being deficient in elements
associated with traditional journalism—objectivity, accuracy and ability
to shape a shared public consciousness. Andrew Keen is one of the high-
profile figures who bemoan the lack of high-quality, reliable material amid
the masses of user-generated content. Keen claims that this undermines the
influence and economic sustainability of professional new sources, which
play an important role in 'the telling of common stories, formation of communal myths, the shared sense of participating in the same daily narrative
of life' (Keen 2007: 80).

COMMUNITY AND ALTERNATIVE MEDIA

Citizen-based media existed long before the advent of the Internet or so-
called citizen journalism, being evident in the long tradition of community
and alternative media. Olga Guedes Bailey and her colleagues note that in
contrast to the mainstream media, the community and alternative media
have at least one of the following characteristics:

- They are small-scale operations that serve disadvantaged groups or
  specific communities, respecting their diversity;
- They are independent of state and market;
- They have horizontal or non-hierarchical structures, which assists
  community access and participation and suits the organizational
  agenda of supporting democratization and multiplicity;
- They offer non-dominant and possibly counter-hegemonic discourses
  and representations, stressing the importance of self-representation
  (Bailey, Cammaerts and Carpentier 2008: 18).

The news created by community and alternative media is generated by
people who rarely perceive themselves as journalists. It is often presented
through community announcements, talk programs, discussion panels and
a myriad of other informational formats rather than formal news stories
or bulletins. These activities sometimes fit within a definition of journalism
because of the nature of their reporting of issues of community significance.

The significance of this news and information can be seen by the response of Australia's Indigenous communities to their community media. Many Aboriginal and Torres Strait Islander people consider the community media to provide an essential service that plays a central role in organizing community life. Indigenous audiences describe their community media as a primary source of news and information that helps to sustain social networks, promote self-esteem, nourish community identities and kinship ties, maintain languages and culture, educate people, and support cross-cultural dialogue (Meadows et al. 2007: 51–68).

The community and alternative media have been subjected to many criticisms or more often, simply ignored, due to perceived inadequacies of their presentation style and the quality, objectivity and originality of their content. At a more fundamental level, Armand Mattelart and Jean-Marie Piemme purport that the community media do not revitalize democracy. They argue that the community media instead replicate the moral, social and economic order, and even successful alternative media are generally linked to social movements whose structure and organization have been established within the existing hierarchy of power (Mattelart and Piemme 1980: 322–6).

The report by the International Commission for the Study of Communication Problems, *Many Voices, One World*, acknowledges that the importance of the alternative media 'is probably exaggerated by its more enthusiastic partisans.'

> Measured quantitatively—by the content and regularity of transmission, or by the audience reached—it cannot compare with the mass media, and, indeed, that is not its purpose. Yet the radical departure from the dominant assumptions of vertical flow and the capacity it provides to develop horizontal networks, the achievement in strengthening self-awareness of coherent groups, give it a significance out of all proportion to its quantitative scale (MacBride et al. 1980: 171).

Nick Couldry goes so far as to describe these media as being 'the weapons of the weak' (Couldry 2002: 27). Bailey and her colleagues argue that: 'Societal groups that are represented one-sidedly, disadvantaged, stigmatized, or even repressed can especially benefit from using the channels of communication opened by alternative media, to strengthen their internal identity, manifest this identity to the outside world, and thus enable social change and/or development' (Bailey, Cammaerts and Carpentier 2008: 14–15).

Much of the importance of community and alternative media stems from the opportunities they create for volunteers to develop interpersonal relationships, learn to speak publicly, gain self-confidence, and learn to manage their own projects (MacBride et al. 1980: 171; Van Vuuren 2008: Ch. 5). These networks and personal attributes are critical characteristics that citizens require if they are to be able to engage effectively in civil society and democratic life.

Most of the projects and activities of community and alternative media cannot be seen as processes that have consciously been planned and neatly coordinated to step progressively towards a common goal. The human ambitions, production activities and media products that can be seen in the community media sphere are often disjointed, muddled and contradictory in their nature (Rennie 2006: 21; Rodríguez 2001: 22). Thus the processes involved in the creation and consumption of citizen-based media resemble those that occur within normal community life, where numerous citizens and collectives are constantly a competing, challenging, collaborating, compromising or negotiating over a myriad of overlapping issues.

DELIBERATIVE DEVELOPMENT JOURNALISM

An editorial printed in an Indonesian newspaper many decades ago summed the broader principles of development journalism as being that 'every bit of printed news . . . is for the sake of national development, or at least won't hamper it' (NZPA-AAP 1986: 8). There are at least five major interpretations of development journalism, due to very different assumptions in developing countries about the journalist's role in supporting socioeconomic and political development, and the news media's correct relationship with governments and the broader populace (Romano 2005: 1–12; Romano 2010: 255–7). This chapter discusses only those forms of development journalism that are interactive, advocative and educational, and that aim to build community self-reliance.

Deliberative development journalism puts communication 'at the service of development to elicit a human, and ultimately, a social response in the people it seeks to serve' (Ponteñila 1990: 27). Examples of international news services that have pursued this journalism style include Inter Press Service (IPS), OneWorld.net, DEPTHnews and the now defunct Gemini News Service, even though they may not necessarily use the terms deliberative or development media to describe what they do. Localized initiatives can be seen in most economically developing countries (e.g., see Chapters 4, 14, 15 and 16).

Eric Loo (1995), Johan Galtung and Richard Vincent (1992), and IPS (Dixit 1994) are among those who have proposed means by which the deliberative ideals of development journalism can be expressed in practice. A common factor is the commitment to explaining government policies, social issues and events from the viewpoint of the individuals and communities they affect. The deliberative development journalism task commences with exploring the concerns of people outside the centres of business, politics and mainstream political power and giving 'a voice to the voiceless', including the marginalized, the minorities and the underprivileged (Dixit 1994: 23–4). Personal interaction with sources is encouraged, and some even suggest that such journalism should be ethnographic, involving participant observation of communities (e.g., Loo 1995). Rather than merely top-down communications, deliberative development journalism also seeks a bottom-up flow and, most importantly, horizontal flows where citizens share information with fellow citizens (Hester 1987: 9).

This does not, however, mean pandering to the shrill majority or even to an anguished minority. Instead, the goal is to use the experiences of the masses to examine both the detail and the 'big picture', while also identifying which stakeholders are involved in the issue and who may potentially take action to address the situation. This form of journalism aims to build a stronger 'sense of community' and 'foster direct democratic participation and cooperation . . . which helps to create new models and visions for the future that may serve as the basis for autonomous critique and transformation' (Shah 1996: 152). IPS, for example, describes itself as 'building an information bridge' that links individuals, civil society organizations, international institutions, policymakers and donors 'to promote an ongoing dialogue about communication and development for a better world' (IPS 2009).

Proponents of development journalism—deliberative or otherwise—place less emphasis on the news 'event' in favour of the news 'process'. Process reporting ignores many of the stipulations of regular deadline reporting, requiring time for journalists to consider the consequences of news events in their wider historical, economic and political frameworks. IPS's Kunda Dixit, for example, urges journalists to not simply report the coups and earthquakes, but to predict them. 'Kneel down to the human level of the tragedies and look at the causes. Be there after the parachute journalists with their satellite dishes have come and gone' (Dixit 1994: 24). Proponents of development journalism also focus on possible solutions to problems and examples of successes, so that audiences can visualize ways that they might potentially contribute to rectifying crises rather than being overcome by despair at seemingly hopeless situations (e.g., Galtung and Vincent 1992: 13). This style of journalism stands in stark contrast to mainstream Western-style reporting (or for that matter, most mainstream reporting in non-Western countries), which has been criticized for its focus on 'spot' news and crisis reporting rather than coverage of changing patterns within developing nations.

Much deliberative development journalism draws from the thinking associated with Freire's ideas of conscientization (see pages 6–7 of this book). Development and community media specialist Alfonso Gumucio Dagron, for example, describes the need for communicators to assist and illuminate the process of change. They can do this by working with rather than for communities, raising consciousness rather than simply informing or persuading an audience, supporting the development of a collective, and recognizing the long-term nature of change (Gumucio Dagron 2001: 26). Hemant Shah goes so far as to describe deliberative development journalism as 'emancipatory journalism', because journalists are 'participants in a process of progressive social change' (Shah 1996: 144). They do this by helping individuals in communities in 'voicing critique and articulating alternative visions of society' and 'challenging and changing oppressive structures' (Shah 1996: 145).

Questions are sometimes posed about whether the development journalists' objectivity is affected by their close association with communities. However, proponents of this form of development journalism often argue that Western standards of objectivity need major renegotiation, as they are 'biased by virtue of being blind to wrong' (Dixit 1994: 22).

Media practitioners and theorists who promote deliberative development journalism do not propose that the news media should be perceived as a government 'mouthpiece'. Nor do they suggest that journalists should necessarily feel a commitment towards governments or their programs. IPS, for example, has consistently proved willing to contest government and business policies (e.g., Romano 2010: 364). IPS advises journalists to discard the notion that development reporting must be positive, and to cover the grime and injustice as well as the success stories (Dixit 1994: 23).

Deliberative development journalism involves a major rethinking of journalistic technique. For example, there would be substantive changes to journalist–source relationships. Issues to be considered include the journalist's preferred sources; the timing, location and contexts of meetings and interactions with sources; the types of questions asked during interviews; standards of proof required before the journalist accepts a source's information at face value; and how the journalist would attempt to sift through the varying experiences and perspectives of their sources to arrive at a 'big picture'. This alone requires a considerable restructuring of the daily routines, practices and patterns of journalistic professionalism, as well as the resources required to support such journalism.

PEACE JOURNALISM

The mass media alone are rarely the prime instigators of peace or violence in their communities, but they can be a powerful force in determining how publics identify and deal with disagreements and tensions. Peace journalism attempts to provide 'a new road map tracing the connections between journalists, their sources, the stories they cover and the consequences of their reporting—the ethics of journalistic intervention' (McGoldrick and Lynch 2000: 5). Ross Howard, who conducts international training programs in what he calls 'conflict sensitive journalism', says journalists should not aim to hide or reduce conflict. Instead, they should 'seek to present accurate and impartial news', as 'it is often through good reporting

that conflict is reduced' (Howard 2003: 2). In this definition, good reporting includes information that 'creates opportunities for society at large to
consider and value non-violent responses to conflict' (Lynch and McGoldrick 2004: 137).

Training courses in peace journalism generally attempt to instil a deeper
understanding among journalists about the nature of both conflict and
conflict resolution. These courses clarify the types of conflict that lead to
violence, the nature of violence (physical, cultural and structural), and the
timing and methods for intervening in a cycle of conflict to prevent violence. Most particularly, such courses aim to develop a perspective that
conflicts are not a zero-sum game where there is inevitably a winner and
a loser, as if they were sporting matches. They explore the conditions that
are required to enable publics to identify, and indeed create, options that
might allow them to develop win-win situations (McGoldrick and Lynch
2000; Howard 2003).

At the simplest level, peace journalism relies on traditions of fact-based
journalism, with close scrutiny of words and images.[2] Journalists must
avoid emotive and imprecise expressions, dichotomies of good versus bad, a
focus on the victimhood and grievances or the abuses and misdemeanours
of one side only, and the use of racial and cultural identities when they are
not necessary. Journalists must attribute unsubstantiated claims to their
sources rather than presenting them as facts, avoid focussing on the victimhood or causes of one party to the exclusion of other, and seek diverse
sources and viewpoints. Such approaches are espoused by traditional journalism, although the conditions in conflict-wracked environments and the
economic imperatives of newsrooms mean that journalists do not always
scrupulously follow these ideals.

Peace journalism also moves beyond an approach of presenting 'just the
facts', due to an awareness of how easily the facts that present themselves
to journalists can be 'manipulated by narrow interests and unchallenged
mythologies, especially from traditional elites' (Howard 2006). Peace journalism involves an active attempt to see beyond the immediate and most
obvious elements of the story. Journalists must therefore attempt to present
conflicts as multifaceted rather than simple Side A versus Side B oppositions
and identify commonalities as well as points of disagreement among dis-
putants. They must trace the links and consequences of conflict to parties
not immediately involved in the dispute, and assess the impact of violent
actions or policies not just in terms of their immediate and visible outcomes
but also for their long-term and indirect consequences. Rather than allowing parties to simply restate familiar demands or positions, peace journalists aim to inquire deeply into the goals. They question how people are
affected by conflict in their everyday lives, what they want changed, and
whether the positions stated by leaders are the only or best ways to achieve
the changes that the public wants.

Peace journalism can thus help to prevent or resolve violence by:

- channelling communication between the different sides of the conflict;
- educating each side on the difficulties experienced by other sides in moving towards reconciliation;
- building confidence and trust by exploring efforts at reconciliation and also digging into hot issues and revealing them, so there are no secrets to fear;
- examining, reporting and correcting each side's misperceptions of each other;
- analysing conflict to enhance public understanding of the situation as well as the dynamics of efforts to manage it;
- making each side 'human' to other sides, by including real people in the stories with names and faces, and describing how the issues affect them;
- identifying the bottom-line interests and motives that underlie the issues;
- providing an emotional outlet that allows parties to express their grievances in non-violent ways;
- framing and defining the conflict and the ways in which it can be managed;
- supporting consensus-building by allowing individuals/groups who are attempting to resolve the conflict to explain their negotiating positions to the public and attempt to build support for those positions;
- promoting solution-building by asking the parties to identify possible resolutions rather than just grievances;
- encouraging a balance of power so that all conflicting groups, regardless of inequalities, believe their concerns will be given attention (Manoff 1998: 15–16).

Some traditional journalists express concern that peace journalism strategies require a suspension of the news media's traditions of objectivity. Most sponsors of peace journalism, however, do not advocate that journalists downplay conflict, exaggerate the possibilities of peace, play favourites, fabricate or embellish facts, or circulate propaganda. Peace journalism is not peace mongering, in opposition to war mongering. If ethnic, religious or other social divisions are not acknowledged, then unresolved issues will simmer and disgruntled parties may express themselves in other ways and channels that intensify the tensions. Instead of playing down conflict, peace journalism 'uses conflict analysis and transformation to update the concept of balance, fairness and accuracy in reporting' (McGoldrick and Lynch 2000: 5).

Chapter 13 presents a study of the circumstances that beset the journalists who covered the bloody conflicts that divided the Indonesian island of Ambon from 1999 to 2002. The chapter illustrates that peace journalism should not be left to individual journalists who take the initiative to act as 'lone rangers' who fight for justice and peace. Instead, the Ambon case indicates that a constellation of non-government and community organizations, government agencies and media groups should ideally collaborate to establish secure channels for accessing sources from all sides of the conflict and to create safe spaces for journalists to operate in.

ISSUES IN DELIBERATIVE JOURNALISM

These types of journalism, if practised well, have great promise to increase citizen participation in political processes by extending people's means of identifying, expressing, understanding and responding to issues affecting their immediate publics and wider communities. However, even professional media people who support deliberative democracy have a limited vision of the best practices that might support deliberation about different issues and in different communities. In citizen journalism and community media, it is often even tendentious to identify what kind of activities can be considered journalism, let alone assume that the media creators have any awareness that the public might use their work for deliberative activity or what strategies might best support this. It should be remembered, however, that even these deliberative forms of journalism may not always result in immediate or obvious acts of deliberation, they form an important part of the root system of what David Mathews has dubbed the wetlands of political life (see Chapter 1).

NOTES

1. The site was set up at http://labs.aljazeera.net/warongaza/ on 3 January 2009.
2. The information in this paragraph and the next one summarize the peace journalism strategies devised by Annabel McGoldrick and Jake Lynch (2000: 30–3) as a practical application and development of principles originated by Johan Galtung.

BIBLIOGRAPHY

Bailey, O. G., Cammaerts, B., and Carpentier, N. (2008) *Understanding Alternative Media*, Berkshire, UK: Open University Press.

Bowman, S. and Willis, C. (2003) *We Media: How Audiences are Shaping the Future of News and Information*, The Media Center at the American Press Institute. Available at http://www.hypergene.net/wemedia/download/we_media.pdf (Accessed 1 September 2009).

Bruns, A. (2008). *Blogs, Wikipedia, Second Life and Beyond: From Production to Produsage*, New York: Peter Lang.

Campbell, C. (2007) 'Journalism and public knowledge', *Kettering Review*, 25(1): 39–49.

Campbell, R. (1998) *Media and Culture: An Introduction to Mass Communication*, New York: St Martin's Press.

Charity, A. (1995) *Doing Public Journalism*, New York: Guildford Press.

Chase, T. (2008) 'How new is online news? Online news services in China and South Korea', *Australian Studies Association of Australia Conference*, Melbourne, 1–3 July.

Couldry, N. (2002) 'Mediation and alternative media, or relocating the centre of media and communication studies', *Media International Australia*, (103): 25–31.

Davis, S. (2000) 'Public journalism: The case against', *Journalism Studies* 1(4): 686–9.

Dixit, K. (1994) 'Global news: A view from the South', in P. O'Donnell and P. Cunningham (eds) *Who's Telling the Story: A Conference on Media and Development in Australia and the Region*, Fitzroy, Melbourne: Community Aid Abroad, pp. 20–5.

Dzur, A.W. (2008) *Democratic Professionalism: Citizen Participation and the Reconstruction of Professional Ethics*, University Park, PA: Pennsylvania State University Press.

The Economist (2006) 'Compose yourself', 22 April: 9.

Galtung, J. and Vincent, R.C. (1992) *Toward a New World Information and Communication Order?*, Cresskill, NJ: Hampton Press.

Gillmor, D. (2004) *We the Media: Grassroots Journalism by the People, for the People*. Sebastopol, CA: O'Reilly Media.

Gumucio Dagron, A. (2001) *Making Waves: Stories of Participatory Communication for Social Change*, New York: Rockerfeller Foundation.

Hardt, H. (1997) 'The quest for public journalism' *Journal of Communication*, 47(3): 94–101.

Hardt, H. (1999) 'Reinventing the press for the age of commercial appeals: Writings on and about public journalism', in T. Glasser (ed.) *The Idea of Public Journalism*, New York: Guildford, pp. 197–209.

Harwood, R.C. and McCrehan, J. (2000) 'Tapping civic life: How to report first, and best, what's happening in your community' *A Pew Center for Civic Journalism Workbook*, 2ⁿᵈ edition. Available at http://www.pewcenter.org/doingcj/pubs/tcl/index.html (Accessed 1 September 2009).

Hester, A.L. (1987) 'The role of the Third World journalist', in A.L. Hester and W.L.J. To (eds) *Handbook for Third World Journalists*, Athens, GA: University of Georgia, pp. 5–12.

Howard, R. (2003) *Conflict Sensitive Journalism*, Denmark: IMS (International Media Support) and IMPACS (Institute for Media, Policy and Civil Society).

Howard, R. (2006) 'The case for conflict sensitive journalism', *Canadian Journalism Project*, 7 November. Available at http://www.jsource.ca/english_new/detail.php?id=292 (Accessed 1 September 2009).

Hoyt, M. (1995) 'Are you now or will you ever be, a civic journalist?' *Columbia Journalism Review*, 34(3): 27–33.

Inter Press Service (2009) 'Inter Press Service: Journalism and communication for global change: Our mission'. Available at http://www.ips.org/institutional/get-to-know-us-2/our-mission/ (Accessed 1 September 2009).

Keen, A. (2007) *The Cult of the Amateur: How Today's Internet is Killing Our Culture*, New York: Doubleday.

Lasica, J.D. (2003) 'Random acts of journalism', *New Media Musings*, 12 March. Available at http://www.jdlasica.com/blog/archives/2003_03_12.html (Accessed 30 September 2009).

Levine, P. (1996) 'Public journalism and deliberation', *Report from the Institute for Philosophy and Public Policy*, 16(1): 1–9.

Lichtenberg, J. (1999) 'Beyond the public journalism controversy', in R.K. Fullinwider (ed.) *Civil Society, Democracy, and Civic Renewal*, Lanham, MD: Rowman and Littlefield, pp. 341–354.

Loo, E. (1995) 'Teaching community service reporting values as an identifiable component of Asian-centred journalism', Asian Values in Journalism conference, Asian Mass Communication Research and Information Centre (AMIC), Kuala Lumpur, 24–25 August.

Lynch, J. and McGoldrick, A. (2004) 'Reporting conflict', in T. Hanitzsch, M. Löffelholz, and R. Mustamu (eds) *Agents of Peace: Public Communication and Conflict Resolution in an Asian Setting*, Ilmenau: Technische Universität Ilmenau and Jakarta: Friedrich-Ebert-Stiftung, pp. 107–48.

MacBride, S. et al. (1980) *Many Voices, One World*, Report by the International Commission for the Study of Communications Problems, Paris: UNESCO and London: Kogan Page.

McGoldrick, A. and Lynch, J. (2000) *Peace Journalism: What is It? How to Do It?* Available at http://www.waccglobal.org/images/stories/website/programme/communication_for_peace/Peace-Journalism.pdf (Accessed 1 September 2009).

Manoff, R. (1998) 'Role plays: Potential media roles in conflict prevention and management', *Track Two*, 7(4): 11–16.

Mattelart, A. and Piemme, J.-M. (1980) 'New means of communication: New questions for the left', *Media, Culture, and Society*, 2(4): 321–38.

Meadows, M., Forde, S., Ewart, J. and Foxwell, K. (2007) *Community Media Matters*, Nathan, Brisbane: Griffith University.

NZPA-AAP (1986) 'Press freedom runs full gamut in Asean nations', *NZ Herald*, 29 December, Section 2, p. 8.

Oh Y.-H. (2007) '10 preconditions for the value of user-generated content', *OhmyNews*, 26 February. Available at http://english.ohmynews.com/articleview/article_view.asp?article_class=8&no=347268&rel_no=1 (Accessed 1 September 2009)

Phillips, M. (N.D.) 'How your newspaper can be a readership success story, too', *Readers First: Readership Case Studies*. Available at http://www.readersfirst.com/virtuals/readersfirst/conclusion.html (Accessed 1 September 2009).

Ponteñila, R. (1990) 'Development communication and total human development', in F. Imperial-Soledad (ed.) *Monograph on Development Communication*, Manila: Communication Foundation for Asia Media Group, pp. 19–33.

Project for Excellence in Journalism (2009) 'Special reports: Citizen media', *The State of the News Media: An Annual Report on American Journalism*, Washington, DC: Project for Excellence in Journalism. Available at http://www.stateofthemedia.org/2009/narrative_special_citzenbasedmedia.php?media=12&cat=0 (Accessed 1 September 2009).

Rennie, E. (2006) *Community Media: A Global Introduction*, Lanham, MD: Rowman and Littlefield.

Remaley, M.H. (2009) 'Fifteen things every journalist should know about public engagement', *Kettering Review*, 27(1): 26–35.

Rodríguez, C. (2001) *Fissures in the Mediascape: An International Study of Citizens' Media*, Cresskill, NJ: Hampton Press.

Romano, A. (2005) 'Introduction: Journalism and the tides of liberalization and technology', in A. Romano and M. Bromley (eds) *Journalism and Democracy in Asia*, London: RoutledgeCurzon, pp. 1–14.

Romano, A. (2010) 'Asia' in P. Norris (ed.) *Public Sentinel: News Media and the Governance Agenda*, Washington, DC: The World Bank, pp. 353–75.

Ronfeldt, D. and Arquilla, J. (2001) 'Networks, netwars and the fight for the future', *First Monday*, 6(10). Available at http://firstmonday.org/htbin/cgiwrap/bin/ojs/index.php/fm/article/view/889/798 (Accessed 1 September 2009)

Rosen, J. (1995) 'Foreward', in A. Charity (ed.) *Doing Public Journalism*, New York: Guildford, pp. v–vi.

Rosen, J. (1997) 'Public journalism as a democratic art', in C. Gibbs (ed.) *Public Journalism Theory and Practice: Lessons from Experience*, Dayton, OH: Kettering Foundation, pp. 3–24.

Rosen, J. (1999) *What are Journalists For?* New Haven, CT: Yale University Press.

Schudson, M. (1999) 'What public journalism knows about journalism but doesn't know about "public"', in T.L. Glasser (ed.) *The Idea of Public Journalism*, New York: Guilford Press, pp. 118–33

Shah, H. (1996) 'Modernization, marginalization and emancipation: Toward a normative model of journalism and national development', *Communication Theory*, 6(2): 143–66.

Sirianni, C. and Friedland, L. (2001) *Civic Innovation in America: Community Empowerment, Public Policy, and the Movement for Civic Renewal*, Berkeley, CA: University of California Press.

Stepp, C.S. (2000) 'Reader friendly', *American Journalism Review*, 22(6): 23–35.

Verclas, K. (2008) 'The conflict in Gaza: The role (or lack thereof) of mobile phones', *MobileActive*, http://mobileactive.org/conflict-gaza-role-or-lack-there-of-mobile-phones (Access 1 September 2009)

Van Vuuren, K. (2008). *Participation in Australian Community Broadcasting: A Comparison of Rural, Regional and Remote Radio*, VDM Verlag Dr Müeller: Sarbrücken.

Part II
Public and Citizen Journalism

3 Public Journalism in South Africa

Experiences and Experiments with Local and Community Media

Brett Davidson

Public journalism, according to Sirianni and Friedland (2001), began as a series of experiments in local newspapers in the United States, and later spread to public and commercial television and public radio in America and further afield:

> [Public journalism] arose in response to a perceived failure of the press to constitute a public sphere in which citizens could understand and engage productively with public problems, rather than simply respond to election soundbites, horserace coverage [of elections] and polarized framing of issues (Sirianni and Friedland 2001: 186).

In essence, the innovations were rooted in the desire to bring about greater citizen involvement in the news media, in order to build a genuinely democratic public sphere (Rosen 1999).

In recent years, the discourse around public journalism seems to have been overtaken and obscured by the idea of citizen journalism—acts of journalism performed by ordinary people, generally with the aid of new media technology—mobile/cellular telephones, digital cameras and the Internet. However, citizen journalism is not necessarily a replacement for public journalism. For all the benefits and challenges posed by citizen journalism, there remains a need and space for good quality professional journalism. Yet professional journalism is under threat, and this chapter supports the contention that it is surely in the ideals and practices of public journalism that the potential lies for journalism as we know it to transform itself to once again become vitally relevant to citizens.

It is not often clear, however, how the ideals of public journalism should be translated into newsroom practices. Indeed, this has probably been part of the reason for the failure of public journalism to take greater hold within the mainstream. It has been left to a few innovative and questing editors, reporters and educators to experiment and explore new ways of doing things. This chapter outlines several such initiatives undertaken by Idasa, a democracy institute based in South Africa, to support the existence of a genuinely democratic public sphere in South Africa. This chapter draws from insights obtained in my position as a manager and trainer for Idasa between 2000 and 2007. I also use research that I conducted for the Kettering Foundation, a United States foundation that works on strategies for developing democracy. I offer some reflections on the lessons learnt from these initiatives, in the hope that this will prove useful to those seeking to promote the practice of public journalism in South Africa and further afield.

SOUTH AFRICAN MEDIA AND PUBLIC JOURNALISM

South Africa's mainstream mass media have barely, if at all, taken note of the ideas of public journalism. One or two initiatives have displayed the principles associated with public journalism, but these have been ad hoc and show no evidence of being part of a coherent vision of a different kind of journalism. Examples are a campaign by *The Sowetan* newspaper in the late 1980s and early 1990s aimed at 'Nation Building' during South Africa's fraught political transition. A more contemporary example is a series run by the *Sunday Times* in 2008–09 featuring personal stories submitted by readers on living with HIV/AIDS.

In contrast to this, in recent times, several news organizations have begun to integrate citizen journalism into their publications. For example, the major media conglomerates have made it possible for readers to blog on their websites, and their associated newspapers have begun to incorporate some of these blogs as columns in the printed product.

As might be expected, it is the media operating at the very local level that have been most open to public journalism-type initiatives, and they offer the most interesting possibilities for implementing the principles of public journalism. These local media mainly comprise community radio stations and small commercial newspapers and magazines.

South Africa is fortunate in that legislation makes provision for a community radio sector—nonprofit radio stations owned and run by members of local communities. Such stations are licensed according to fairly stringent regulations. These include the requirement that community radio stations should broadcast news and current affairs programming which deals with developmental issues, and promotes an environment conducive to democracy (Broadcasting Act No. 4 of 1999). The legal framework identifies community participation as key to community radio's mission and identity, and as one of the elements differentiating it from public and commercial broadcasting.

There is also a vibrant local newspaper sector, which, unlike their radio counterparts, faces no legislated requirements with respect to ownership and content. While some local newspapers are run as small businesses, most local titles are owned by the large national news corporations. Ownership aside, however, because of increasingly stiff competition, all local newspapers have an incentive to report on their communities in a compelling way.

Nevertheless, despite legal and economic incentives to do so, the local media has struggled to find ways to operate in a participatory manner, and to cover local news in a manner that supports local development and the practice of democracy (in the case of radio) or to break away from the expert and authority and conflict-driven model of news reportage that has become the mainstream (in the case of newspapers) (Davidson 2004). This can be explained by a number of factors. In the case of community radio, the principle of community involvement and participation is often compromised because stations are preoccupied with generating income for survival (MISA 2001). Stations also tend to copy the approach and format of their larger, commercial counterparts. Furthermore, community radio staff and volunteers often find it difficult to figure out how to find and gather local news, partly because they tend not to have formal journalism training. Staff in the local press have similarly tended to follow the example of the larger media organizations, adopting a confrontational, conflict-driven approach to coverage of local government. These journalists turn almost exclusively to municipal spokespeople, local police, local government councillors, and other established authorities and 'experts' as sources of quotes and information for news stories.

One organization that is trying to help these local media to resolve such problems is Idasa, an independent nonprofit public interest organization that promotes sustainable democracy based on active citizenship, democratic institutions and social justice. It maintains international links with many similar organizations through the World Movement for Democracy. Several of Idasa's staff members were exposed to the concept of public journalism through their contact with the Ohio-based Kettering Foundation, an organization which has been active in both originating the philosophy of public journalism and promoting it in the United States and further afield. Since 2003, Idasa has instituted a range of initiatives aimed at overcoming these challenges, and incorporating the principles and practices of public journalism into the work of South Africa's local media sector.

COMMUNITY MAPPING

Idasa developed a curriculum for workshops based largely on a set of techniques for 'civic mapping' developed by Harwood and McCrehan (1996) under the auspices of the Pew Center for Civic Journalism. These workshops in 'community mapping' have been presented to journalists and producers since 2003 at a range of community radio stations and local newspapers across South Africa.

At the start of the process, participants are asked to draw maps of their community based on memory alone. Once participants have drawn their maps, these are used as the focus of a discussion on the concept of community, and of the way in which one's perspective influences one's perception of the nature and the boundaries of one's community. The relative sizes and positioning of objects within the map lead to a discussion and questioning of value systems. Likewise, the level of detail of the maps, and parts thereof, make apparent issues of value judgement and perspective, and how these are shaped by everyday experience (Downs and Stea 1977). This leads to a discussion of the way in which participants' perspectives on their community influence and shape their choices in their work.

Following the map drawing exercise, participants are taken through the process of 'community mapping'. This is based largely on Harwood and McCrehan's (1996) work, but adapted for the South African context. The first phase of the process involves making participants aware of various layers and dimensions of community. Examples include the official layer of local office holders and the informal layer of social organizations, networks and gatherings. This includes all places where different types of people meet and discuss issues that affect their lives, such as parent–teacher meetings, hairdressing salons, taxi ranks and public bars. It may also include Internet cafes, clubs and music venues and the like.

In addition to identifying various community layers, Harwood and McCrehan (1996) point out that there are many types of leaders to be found within communities—ordinary people who energize and organize those around them—as well as the leaders with official titles. This breakdown of various types of community leaders is also presented to the participants, and through practical exercises the participants go about applying the concepts to their own community. The point of these exercises is to point out that news, as well as news sources, can be found in all sorts of places within the community—not merely within the official realm, which often tends to be overrepresented in standard coverage.

These initial discussions and exercises are precursors to field excursions during which the participants go out in teams to various areas and neighbourhoods within their coverage footprint to conduct their own research in each area. This research is designed to unearth information about the issues people find important, the places where people gather and where story and program ideas can be found, and the various leaders who can be important contacts for journalists. Following the series of research excursions, the participants organize several community focus groups. They are asked to invite community members to the workshop venue for discussions based around questions designed to lead to further information about the community, possible news and programming contacts, and so forth. Usually a series of separate focus groups are held, each involving members of a specific demographic or interest group such as the elderly, children, people with disabilities, business people, and so forth.

Once the research exercises are complete, the participants go about designing and compiling their community or civic 'map'. This is essentially a file or chart of places, people and issues within various neighbourhoods in the community. This community map is intended to be a reference tool for the radio station or newspaper's personnel, and ideally will help guide them to a wide range of community members, voices and stories for inclusion in their news and programming.

REPORTING ON LOCAL GOVERNMENT

From years of working with the local media, Idasa staff members observed that in community after community there was an unhealthy degree of hostility between the local news media on one side, and municipal representatives and officials on the other. This was eventually confirmed through more structured research, conducted by Idasa's radio manager, Shepi Mati (2005). Mati conducted interviews with journalists, citizens and officials in several municipal areas. On the one hand, it seemed many of the local media were being rather overzealous in trying to hold officials to account. Illustrative are comments by the board member of one community radio station, who says people in leadership positions have repeatedly been 'very, very angry' about 'quite dramatic statements' that the station had aired:

> The station's position on this has tended to be that people need to take criticism from journalists. The council's position has been you don't work with us, this hits us from the side without us having being told about it, and you don't consult with us and so on. So there's a relationship problem there and it's one in which I think there's a need for [the station] to build far better relationships with the people that they cover in their programming (Mati 2005: 9).

A journalism educator furthermore made suggestions about how the station needed to develop itself:

> You know one of the words that I've heard the station use is that [name of program] tends to be hot, they are a hot show. And the idea there is that this is hard hitting journalism. But I think that means that they are borrowing from traditions of journalism which are not necessarily appropriate for community radio. . . . you also have to have journalism that involves ordinary people and give people a chance to speak for themselves rather than just going off half cocked with very little information and pointing fingers at people. And working with people towards solutions. . . . (Mati 2005: 10).

Another problem was a lack of understanding on the part of journalists about how local government works, and how roles and responsibilities are divided up between different spheres of government. This can be seen in the comments from one member of municipal management about a report in a local newspaper that had blamed the local government about dysfunctional water supply in one of the local housing projects:

> You know there were leaking pipes; there was this and that and so on. Now we are not responsible for the supply of water, it's now a district function. Any reporter of note would have been aware of that fact and then reported it correctly. And in that instance also there was no serious effort to get us to comment. We would have given them the correct information (Mati 2005: 38).

On the other hand, many journalists criticized municipalities for their poor communication skills, and lack of understanding of how to deal with the media. This was exemplified by comments from one local newspaper journalist who normally liked to establish a personal relationship with a key person in the municipality:

> But we've been instructed to put all our communications through X, and it's just been a complete failure. They don't respond to faxes, e-mails, phone-calls, everything. You've come at a very apt time because we've been sitting around for three weeks and I finally sent an e-mail and Friday today, I don't even have any hopes and I phone X today I said, I mean I'm keeping it low-key, I said 'hey X' I'm getting cross now, please you know', and he said it's coming, it's coming today (Mati 2005: 32).

The research also provided useful insights into what ordinary citizens felt about, and expected from, the news media. In general, citizens felt the local media were not providing them with enough relevant or useful information about municipal issues. One public meeting participant expressed concern that stories about local government only covered controversial issues, and called for more explanatory and informative reports about what different Acts mean and how the municipality works.

> Otherwise how would you keep your public representatives and your municipality accountable if you do not know how the system works? Why don't we have a section on new by-laws that have been gazetted or local municipality resolutions appearing in our local newspaper so that we can hold them accountable? But now you find that we cannot engage them because we don't know how these things work and are supposed to happen. . . . (Mati 2005: 16).

This research has led to the implementation of a series of training workshops for local journalists in a range of municipal areas. The training covers topics such as how local government works, reporting on municipal budgets, identifying local sources and stories. Workshops are also held with municipal communications officers, in which they are encouraged to understand why it is important for them to speak to the media, and in which they are provided with insight into how the media work.

In addition, a website has been set up, providing ongoing support to the trained journalists, as well as anyone else who wishes to access it. The Word on the Street site (*www.wordonthestreet.org.za*) provides a glossary of terms related to local government, toolkits providing guidance on such topics as 'Reporting on Municipal Budgets' or 'Reporting on Opinion Surveys', a directory of experts and other resources. Most important is a newsletter emailed to subscribers every fortnight. This provides regular updates and explanations of issues related to local government, along with suggestions for following up with stories and reportage.

DISCUSSION ABOUT THE JOURNALIST'S ROLE

In addition to training and support, seminars have been held in a number of municipal districts, where a range of role-players are invited to come together to discuss the role of the news media in their communities. Participants include journalists and editors from local radio stations and newspapers, academics, and municipal officials and politicians.

The nature of such seminars can be shown by considering the processes and outcomes of one day-long meeting between local journalists and municipal role-players, which was organized at the suggestion of community newspapers from a region on South Africa's West Coast. Staff from one community newspaper group told Idasa a familiar tale of extremely hostile relationships between the media and municipalities. They accepted a certain amount of tension as unavoidable and even necessary in the relationship between government and the media, but felt that there should at least be a certain degree of mutual acceptance and understanding—a collegial relationship. After discussions with the newspaper group, a workshop was facilitated between local journalists and municipal role-players. This not only took the form of a discussion of the role of the news media, but also involved a certain amount of conflict resolution.

The meeting was attended by journalists and editors from two local newspapers and a local radio station, municipal managers from two local municipalities, and a handful of police officials with whom the journalists also wished to establish a better working relationship. The meeting was divided into two phases. In the first phase, representatives from each sector had a chance to talk, present their situation, and outline the key issues or areas of conflict as they saw them. After this, the meeting broke up into two smaller groups, based on the participants' municipal area.

Each group contained a mix of journalists, municipal officials and police officers. Each person in the group was asked to explain why they had decided to attend the meeting—and what their personal stake was. Next, participants were asked to share insights about the internal operation of their own organizations. The aim of this was to create better mutual understanding. The journalists would begin to understand the problems the municipalities faced in the area of communications: such as staff shortages, bureaucratic rules and a fear of the media. The municipal officials would in turn gain some understanding of problems and limitations within the media: staff shortages, demanding deadlines, the need to make a profit through improved sales, and so on. Finally, the small groups were asked to discuss ideas for improving the situation and creating more collegial relationships in future.

The discussion was fairly polite and superficial until one of the municipal managers got up and said he was going to speak frankly. He then pointed to specific examples where he felt offended by newspaper articles. The manager's comments took the discussion to a new level, and participants all began to speak more openly. The municipal managers and the editors were able to discuss the articles the managers had found offensive. The editors explained their thinking, and acknowledged that sometimes certain expressions and headlines did not come across as intended. At the same time, the municipal managers acknowledged their municipalities' shortcomings with respect to good communication. By the end of the morning, the atmosphere had completely changed, with the editors and municipal officials expressing willingness to continue a less hostile working arrangement and to acknowledge one another's roles.

TRAINING AND EXPERIMENTATION IN DELIBERATIVE TALK SHOWS

In 2006–07, as a research project for the Kettering Foundation, I worked with the Valley FM community radio station, in the town of Worcester, about a 90 minute drive from Cape Town. The station decided to experiment with a series of call-in talk shows, focusing on key issues in their community. They wanted to explore whether they could adopt an approach that would involve more deliberative talk about difficult local issues, rather than the usual pattern—where callers would call in simply to complain or point fingers of blame. In this case, we can define deliberative talk as a form of talk that 'will construe issues in public terms; will create relationships or rights, obligations and duties between participants; and, will coordinate individuals to reflect on possible forms of collective action' (Ryfe 2002).

After considering various issues in the community, the five-member program production team decided to focus on the topic of education, framing the issue as: Schooling in the Breede Valley—what can we do to improve our children's education? They identified three subtopics under this theme:

- How do we improve parent participation in children's education?
- How do we create a safe learning environment for our children, conducive to learning and teaching?

- How do we support teachers and principals to do a better job of teaching and managing schools, to ensure quality education?

Each subtopic would be tackled in a separate program, and the programs would be aired over the course of several weeks. The approach was fairly experimental. For each program the first stage was to convene a panel of various role-players concerned with the issue. This meeting took place off air, with discussion facilitated by one or more of the radio station's presenters. It was recorded and edited. Panel members included parents of school children, teachers and principals as well as other role-players, such as school bus drivers.

The next step was to air a live call-in program. During the program, education officials and teacher union representatives were guests in the studio. Extracts from the panel discussion were played over the air. The studio guests were invited to respond to and reflect on the forum discussion, and listeners were invited to call in and continue the conversation. In the program's introduction, the presenter made participants aware that the station wanted to encourage a different type of talk, and she continued to remind people of this throughout the program:

> The purpose of tonight's and the previous two programs is to get the community talking together, to look at problems, but also to search for solutions together, and to come with suggestions, so that the department heads, heads of curriculum, the director of EMDC [Education Management and Development Centre], and also our unions, can hear these are the problems but these are also the suggestions that have been made. Tonight, after the teachers have told us this is what gives them sleepless nights or headaches, I'd like to ask you talk with our community a little about what we can do to get involved together, (our community, our children, our parents, and people in management positions), to at the end of the day ensure that we can have quality education.

So what were the results? Whereas many call-in shows on radio tend to be a forum for complaints and fault finding, it does seem that the experiment by Valley FM led to a more deliberative type of conversation, in Ryfe's (2002) terms. The issues were construed in public terms, with a discussion of rights, duties and obligations, and participants did reflect on possible courses of public action.

Comments by studio guests were often focused on trying to make obvious or tease out the different perspectives from which the issue was being discussed. For example, Dr Brian Wilson, head of curriculum at the local Education Management and Development Centre (EMDC), tried to articulate the difference between viewing quality education as the attainment of 'standards', versus seeing it as a holistic process involving diverse outcomes:

'Many people confuse quality education with standards. . . . I always want to know whose standards, which standards?'

Furthermore, some of the conversation was devoted to taking a step back, to attempt to name the very nature and causes of the problem itself. During one of the prerecorded panels, for example, one participant remarked that 'the whole special needs and support system at the moment is not functional and it's failing our learners', thus identifying the problem as being based in how the education system is set up. Another classified it as a problem of insufficient training for teachers, by saying: 'We sit with huge classrooms and nobody is trained in how to manage such huge classes'.

At times, the conversation moved onto the weighing of options, and grappling with tough choices and trade-offs. For example, during one of the panels, teachers grappled with the challenge of how to maintain discipline in the classroom, while ensuring that children are able to explore problems themselves, and discuss issues in small groups:

> a teacher of the old school, who is used to making children keep quiet and lecturing from the front, struggles with the new approach where an 'educational noise' is encouraged as children work in groups to solve problems themselves.

There was also a grappling with, or at least an awareness of, the tensions between trying to implement an ideal, and taking into account the realities on the ground:

> We've got the most wonderful policies on paper, and a lot of the times I think, 'it's supposed to be like this', but it's not working. Let's do regular evaluations, and then also most important, listen to us as teachers. Policies are being made up there. Come back to us more often and listen to what we are saying, and all those wonderful policies that are on paper, it will become a reality soon.

Perhaps even more interesting, was the fact that all participants at times raised possible solutions to problems. In doing this, they made a connection between quality education and the inculcation of democratic values, and in offering solutions, talked about public or communal forms of action, in addition to individual initiatives:

Individual action:

> I think the onus is still on us as teachers, in the way in which we communicate with our learners. We need to develop alternative communication strategies and ways to reach our learners.

> Most of us have to go the extra mile, to be more skilled in how to facilitate your classrooms.

Link between quality education and democracy:

> The curriculum reform aims to put democratic values in place, so that the child can be a democratic citizen of the country.

Public or collective action:

> There must be reading programs at our schools, we need to look at maybe a specific month or day where we have an awareness. As a parent we can be aware, but what are we doing as a school community about that?

> We have to see our schools as community hubs. . . . if we as communities make our schools our own, we're going to achieve so much more.

> It is time that communities take ownership of our schools. In South American countries there are places where the schools don't have fences, and the community comes in and uses the school and I think we need to move in that direction.

Perhaps most exciting of all were the final remarks made by the studio guests when asked for their concluding remarks at the end of the program. It was clear that the participants had noticed the difference between these programs and the usual type of talk that happens on radio discussion programs. An example was the comment of Piet Hermanus, from a teachers' trade union:

> What keeps me up at night, and luckily tonight it didn't happen: tonight we had a conflict-free conversation with the department, and that's because we all came to the table with a positive contribution and it is about the promotion of public education.

These remarks indicate that the program had helped create some common ground, and appreciation for others' perspectives and points of view. In addition to the remarks quoted above, other feedback from the various participants in the Valley FM project indicate that all found the process valuable, and that they did perceive this approach to discussing issues on talk radio as unique and very helpful.

REFLECTIONS

The initiatives and examples described hold several lessons for those seeking to implement public journalism projects in South Africa and elsewhere. In a nutshell, the success or failure of public journalism initiatives often has less to do with the inherent value of this approach to journalism, than with the challenges of implementing it in the real world. If public journalism is to spread and thrive, those seeking to make it work need to pay attention to the internal politics and dynamics of news organizations, as well as to the economics of news production and distribution—particularly in a time when these organizations are facing unprecedented financial pressures.

It is difficult to bring about change in the way that any organization operates—and media organizations are no different. Old habits die hard, and systems and structures take time and effort to change. In addition, there are always complex power relationships at work in organizations, and it is often the case that individuals with vested interests in old ways of doing things resist the new. Perhaps ironically, this is probably even more so in community media organizations, set up to run on democratic lines.

Because there is no owner or an all-powerful manager whose word is law, change is a complex process of negotiation and contestation. In the case of democratically run news media, deliberative politics must be applied at two levels—at the level of the actual work (applying the principles of public journalism), but also at the organizational level (to deliberate on how, and even whether, public journalism should be practised). One of the key lessons gained during these initiatives is that even when work is done mainly with a small team, it is always best to keep the whole organization in the loop—to have managers involved, and to find ways to incorporate learning into broader strategic planning within the organization.

Another key observation is that in trying to implement practices that align with the principles of public journalism, there is often a tension involved between these ideals, the nature of the medium (including the deadlines, and demanding twenty-four-hour schedules), received formats and formulae (often adopted simply because of the assumption that the way that the large mass media do things is how media 'should' be), and audience habits and expectations.

For example, in trying to implement a more deliberative format for a talk show on radio, the team had to grapple with several factors relating to the nature of radio as a medium. The first issue was that of time. The format involved in this experiment, entailing prerecorded panels, editing and preproduction, was time consuming. But program schedules are demanding, and producers are under pressure.

A further question facing broadcasters is how to ensure that the resulting program makes for good listening. One of the objectives of attempting to adopt a deliberative format for talk radio is to move away from the prevalent sensation- and conflict-driven model, in favour of a way of talking that is more considered, more respectful and, well, more deliberative. The people gathered together physically for the prerecorded panel were experiencing all sorts of things—the verbal exchange was only one element of the experience. Body language, gestures and the like played a role and sometimes there were silences as the participants mulled things over. Not all of this necessarily translated very well over the microphone. Thus, the panel discussion had to be cut up into shorter chunks and interspersed with the studio discussion and listeners' calls in order to ensure interesting and captivating listening, without resorting to distortion and false sensationalism.

In the case of news, both on radio and in the local press, papers and stations are competing not only with other local media, but with the wide range of news outlets available—national, regional and international radio, TV, newspapers, satellite TV and the Internet. The pressures to adopt a conflict-driven and sensational approach can be overwhelming.

The adoption of practices aligned to the principles of public journalism takes time and resources, and in the cases described above, the impetus and support had to come from outside in order to create the space and time for the journalists, producers and editors involved to embark upon the process of experimentation and discovery.

Nevertheless, in many cases, once they had been exposed to a new way of doing things, those involved expressed excitement and a new sense of commitment. Often participants would exclaim that this was what they had been looking for, or wanting to do, but did not know how to or where to begin. Despite the pressures of competition too, it soon became clear that the practices described were an asset to these media organizations as they enabled them to carve out a distinctive space—to become vitally relevant to their audiences by dealing with the issues that people were really concerned about, in a way people could relate to.

> [I learnt] that my role as a journalist is not only limited to getting to the truth and reporting about it but that it is also my duty to find problems and offer solutions (Workshop participant, in Mati and Levy 2008).

> I learnt how to negotiate with each other in a different way and to understand someone's opinion . . . I learnt how to listen and how to write (Workshop participant, in Mati and Levy 2008).

> It should be agreed that our coexistence will always be a contentious issue. We need to accept that and try to forge a healthy tension between the two of us [media and municipalities]. Both [must] understand that we have a role to play in the development of our communities (Ranyabu Madimetsa, Editor of *Sekhukhune Mail*, in Mati and Levy 2008).

BIBLIOGRAPHY

Broadcasting Act No. 4 of 1999. (South Africa). Available at http://www.info.gov.za/view/DownloadFileAction?id=70607 (Accessed 1 September 2009)

Davidson, B. (2004) 'Mapping the Radio KC Community', *Ecquid Novi*, 25(1): 43–59.

Downs, R.M. and Stea, D. (1977) *Maps in Minds: Reflections on Cognitive Mapping*, New York: Harper & Row.

Harwood, R. and McCrehan, J. (1996) *Tapping Civic Life*. Baltimore, MD: Pew Center for Civic Journalism. Available at http://www.pewcenter.org/doingcj/pubs/tcl/intro.html (Accessed 1 September 2009).

Mati, S. (2005) *Municipal Journalism and Reporting—Restoring a Sense of Public Responsibility and Mission in the News Media: Training Needs Assessment Report*, Cape Town: Idasa.

Mati, S. and Levy, M. (2008) *Improved Municipal Journalism and Reporting Roll-Out*, Cape Town: Idasa.

MISA (Media Institute of Southern Africa) (2001) *Role of Community Broadcasting*, unpublished background paper on community broadcasting: MISA.

Ryfe, D.M. (2002) *What is Deliberative Talk? A Study of NIF Forums*, unpublished paper: Kettering Foundation.

Rosen, J. (1999) *What Are Journalists For?* New Haven, CT: Yale University Press.

Sirianni, C. and Friedland, L. (2001) *Civic Innovation in America: Community Empowerment, Public Policy, and the Movement for Civic Renewal*, Berkeley, CA: University of California Press.

4 Civic Journalism Initiatives in Nigeria

Tokunbo (Tokz) Awoshakin

Over the years, journalists and journalism have played different roles in Nigeria's democratic journey. These roles changed as the country struggled during colonial rule and evolved after its independence from Britain in 1960. The journalism landscape in Nigeria continued to evolve in response to the oil boom era and the first democratic government of the early 1970s, the series of dictatorial military rulers who led in the 1980s to the late 1990s, and the current struggle to grow Nigeria's nascent democracy. Throughout these periods of change, Nigerian journalists' major preoccupation has been with reporting politics and public life. Although military rule has given way to democracy, Nigerian citizens and journalists often express frustration that there is no place for their initiatives and actions. Politics and public life in Nigeria is often controlled by politicians and policymakers who speak another language, one that citizens describe as the language of avoidance.

For a long time, therefore, there has been the impression that the role of Nigerians as citizens ends on Election Day. There is a feeling of impotence among the Nigerian people. It is not uncommon to hear citizens label some Nigerian journalists as coconspirators in pushing the people further away from engagement in politics and public life. Nigeria in the post-military era is caught in a debate as to the role of the press in strengthening the country's budding democracy and her development needs. Should the press simply report, inform and educate as it used to, or should the press become more involved in civil society initiatives to build a more virile democracy?

This chapter discusses the history and social dynamics under which journalism is practised in Nigeria, and how public journalism-style activities have grown organically in this culture, to a certain extent independently from the US experience. This chapter reviews news reporting trends across a range of media organizations, and highlights attempts by journalists to tear through the dead weight of social inertia and the ineptitude of formal politics by empowering citizens to become participants in community problem-solving processes. The chapter will highlight some significant case contributions of Nigerian journalism to the practice of public journalism, and discuss some challenges and emergent ideas for the practice of public journalism in Nigeria, including how journalists' work may be considered civic leadership.

BACKGROUND

Nigeria has seen dramatic changes in journalism since its first newspaper was published in the city of Abeokuta around 1859. Newspapers evolved from the evangelical (church) journalism of the 1850s to 1920s, as exemplified by Reverend Henry Townsend's *Iwe-Irohinin* in Abeokuta, to the 1960s nationalism journalism of Herbert Macaulay's *Lagos Daily News* and Nnamdi Azikiwe's *West African Pilot*. Journalists were among the professional corps who commenced the journey of reinventing the Nigerian state after the slave trade was abolished in 1936. The news media was also at the forefront of the call to end colonial rule in Nigeria. After Nigeria gained independence in 1960, the media promoted postindependence communication consciousness. From 1958 to 1999, pro-democracy alliance communication flourished, and during this period various forms of what might be described as public or civic journalism also emerged.

Journalism in Nigeria has therefore always been a vehicle for social reengineering and political redirection. Journalism and the way it is practised in Nigeria is influenced by external circumstances, which often compel the profession to assume its duty as the ultimate vehicle for social rehabilitation and citizen engagement (Oyovbaire 2001). The journey has not been free of hitches. Journalism and journalists in Nigeria had to contend with state leverages and gag tactics. This includes the Newspaper Act of 1903, which enabled governmental regulation and regimentation of the press. There was also the 1909 Sedition Law, and the 1940 banning of the fiercely outspoken *West African Pilot*. As recently as 1984, a draconian military gag, Decree Number 4, was introduced to control journalists. Fortunately, in 1985, Decree Number 4 was repealed and victims of the gag law were released from jail.

In contrast to evangelical journalism, which was basically a colonial government-sponsored effort to use the press to further spread the gospel, nationalistic journalism media emerged as a result of resistance to colonial and military rules respectively. Hence, just as agitation against British colonial rule motivated the practice of nationalistic journalism, journalists in Nigeria also assumed the role of defenders of democracy between 1985 to 1999 when Nigerians were suppressed under the military rulership of Ibrahim Babangida and Sani Abacha. This military era witnessed the emergence of what came to be popularly called guerrilla journalism (Dare 2007) and an alliance between pro-democracy activists and like-minded non-government organizations (NGOs). In a curious twist, the military rule in Nigeria not only sharpened the adversarial role of the journalism in the country, but also acted as a catalyst for the practice of various forms of public journalism once democracy returned (this will be discussed next).

The advent of representative democracy has foisted on Nigeria's media, particularly the press, the multidimensional responsibility of acting as a civic forum, a watchdog and a mobilizing agent. All these fit the four basic roles that Pippa Norris (2001: 142) conceives for representative democracy:

- A civic forum that encourages pluralistic debate about public affairs;
- A watchdog against the abuse of power;
- A mobilizing agent for encouraging public learning;
- A mobilizing agent for public participation in the political process.

In the battle to build democracy, Nigerian journalism faces many complexities. Nigerian journalists continue to struggle with censorship and the need to partner with other civil-society institutions in an attempt to play an active civic role in a democratic country. Alade Odunewu of the Nigerian Press Council (Odunewu 1997: 7–16) also points to the challenges of communicating matters of civic importance to a diverse audience:

> Nothing is more important to the media than their ties with their audiences, that is, the society in which they operate. . . . As vehicles of communication journalists cater to a mass audience with divergent backgrounds, taste, views and interest. They are expected to give vent to a free flow of ideas thereby enabling their audiences to make meaning out of the issues of their time.

Since Nigeria elected a democratic government into power in 1999, some of these adversarial roles have waned, but new forms of public journalism that allow for the coverage of issues in ways that reflect the realities faced by citizens have emerged. The new practices (discussed later in this chapter) have attempted to create a civic forum for the participation of Nigerians who have felt disconnected from the actions of their elected representatives.

AMERICAN THEORY, NIGERIAN PRACTICE

Public journalism in Nigeria has also been influenced by US theories and practices (see Chapter 2 for more details). Before discussing how this has been playing out, it might be helpful to emphasize that some media practices, which have subsequently been described as civic or public journalism in the United States, have long been evident in Nigeria. The initial name that Nigerians gave to the kind of journalism that sought to raise the people's consciousness and involve them in public problem solving was guerrilla journalism.

This name emerged because journalists often operated 'underground' for fear of persecution from military or civilian dictators. Journalists from guerrilla news organizations would hold clandestine editorial meetings in restaurants, public libraries and car parks. In their attempt to raise public consciousness and defend the role of citizens in public problem-solving processes, these journalists had to constantly transfer their business from one printing company to another to avoid detection by state security operatives.

In the beginning, this form of journalism was essentially investigative. Several other news organizations soon adopted this practice and it continued even when the military dictators were eventually forced out of government in 1999. After the period of military rule in Nigeria, news organizations that were actively engaged with the people stopped their underground operations, but retained the network they had developed over the years with citizens, NGOs and pro-democracy activists.

Following the end of military rule, reporters cooperated with NGOs more, particularly in the coverage of HIV/AIDS. This helped journalists to move beyond their approach of merely disseminating health and other messages, to improve their training and resources, and to increase the number of issues-oriented reports and field investigations of development projects.

This kind of journalism was comparable in many ways to public journalism. Journalists reported issues in ways that reflect the realities faced by citizens and attempted to create a civic forum. While these practices were dubbed civic or public journalism in the United States, in Nigeria it was called the 'people's journalism'.

PARAMETERS OF PULIC JOURNALISM IN NIGERIA

Journalism as a practice that facilitates citizen participation in a polity is not a Western construct. The practices of such journalism may vary from one news organization to the other, but the underlying philosophy remains the same. It helps to engage citizens in public discourse and connect people with the process of weighing up options, making decisions and solving problems about issues that affect their lives. In other words, public affairs issues are framed in ways that enable people who are directly affected by them to see themselves as active citizens rather than as mere spectators, victims or consumers of information.

The next section of this chapter will use several parameters to study public journalism in Nigeria. It will look for evidence of public journalism in the process of gathering, defining and distributing information about concerns associated with public life. This includes journalistic practices such as special reports on major public concerns, but can also involve forms such as editorials that have been written from multiple perspectives, opinion polls, surveys, and studio forums with audience participation. Practices like radio deliberation with viewer/listener phone-in opportunities may be considered public journalism. Other forms include facilitating interaction among citizens or even providing basic information like official email addresses and telephone numbers.

Another parameter is the media organization's role as an intermediary institution which provides access for citizens to reach government and international institution at local, national and even global levels. This allows civil society organizations to monitor and check the behaviour of political and economic institutions and empowers citizens at the local level to potentially influence decision making.

POVERTY, WOMEN AND HUMAN RIGHTS

Ibiba Don Pedro, a staff reporter for *The Guardian* newspaper and later for *Tell* magazine, has written series of stories that underscore the nature and extent of poverty in Nigeria's oil-rich Niger Delta region. Don Pedro's reports like 'Life on the Harsh Lane', 'The Travails of the Swamp in a Bleak Landscape' and several others engaged citizens first by presenting a different lens to the issue of how poverty in oil-rich communities affects the health and well-being of ordinary women. They publicized the risks of rape and human rights violations faced by women in the Niger Delta, and exposed how women bear the brunt of oil-generated pollution. The stories also reported citizen-generated approaches to tackling these concerns. In doing so, *The Guardian* engaged citizens as potential participants in defining these concerns and empowered local nonprofits to confront the issues through access to relevant civic institutions. In their quest for solutions, Don Pedro's stories often make a connection to the goals for the millennium celebration of Year of Women.

Rather than providing one isolated and thus easily forgettable story, Don Pedro and her newspaper kept a spotlight on these issues and mobilized public opinion and international attention that resulted in a redefinition of the issue. For instance, rather than the usual conflict framing of the issue of how oil exploration and oil spills pollute the streams and farmland and make it difficult for the local people to eke a living, the issue was redefined in the frame of how oil exploration and sundry activities result in poverty and health concerns in local communities. Rather than focus on the problem of youth unemployment as a result of polluted farmlands, Don Pedro's articles redefined the problem as a major health concern for local women. By doing this, the stories got more attention from both local and international agencies, which usually see women as one of the more vulnerable groups in any crisis. Simultaneously, Don Pedro's newspaper published ideas that drew from her continuous engagement with the issues and the women involved, to present possible actions that public organizations and individuals could take.

Don Pedro's reporting may not have looked like American public journalism, but it is a classic example of using journalism to drive change in the society. Don Pedro's reporting did this by broadening readers' horizons, focusing attention and raising aspirations, creating a climate for development, helping to change attitudes or valued practices, feeding into interpersonal channels, and conferring status on the female perception of the problem. This approach is a sharp contrast to the Western perception of the public put forward by early scholars of development, such as Lerner (1958) and Schramm (1964). The models from these two scholars saw the public of developing nations as being deficient in the attributes of Western nations. These Western scholars envisaged a model that saw the poor masses as empty vessels to be filled with knowledge by the more learned teachers, journalists and government people.

OIL AND THE ENVIRONMENT

Journalism that initiates citizen engagement in policymaking or problem solving can play a central function in the pursuit of sustainable development in Nigeria. Nigerian journalists have played an important role in accelerating environmental changes in the oil-rich Niger Delta by convening participatory forums and reporting from them. The media handling of the Ogoniland crisis during the military era, especially between 1993 and 1997, is a good example.

Ogoniland is a region in Rivers State, Nigeria, that occupies an area of 650 km^2. It is home to about 500,000 people, mostly farmers and fishermen. The region is rich in oil and thus attractive as a base for Shell Petroleum Development Company (SPDC), which operates in Nigeria in a joint venture agreement with the Nigerian National Petroleum Corporation (NNPC). Shell's operations soon became a threat to Ogoniland people's agrarian lifestyle. To protest this and the Nigerian government's indifference, the Ogoni people founded the Movement for the Survival of Ogoni People (MOSOP) in 1992 under the leadership of the author, Ken Saro-Wiwa.

Several news organizations were reporting the conflict involving the Ogoni communities on one hand, and Shell, NNPC and Nigeria's military dictators on the other. However, two national newspapers, *Vanguard* and *ThisDay*, started special sections in health and environmental concerns. The processes of news gathering and reporting were radically different from the traditional journalism practice. The *Vanguard* newspaper deployed reporters to the region to survey the problem by engaging Shell, NNPC, the Ogoni community, local institutions, other oil companies in the region and academics. This survey generated several weeks of newspaper stories, citizens' columns and editorials that reported and analyzed the problem in public terms. Meanwhile, *ThisDay* formed an alliance with an NGO, Friends of the Earth Nigeria/Environmental Rights Agenda (ERA), to organize town hall meetings and a stakeholder conference on environmental risks in the region. Journalists then reported the discussions from the meetings. These two types of reporting were able to help all stakeholders in the oil communities to identify a problem as a prelude to action.

The stories published also improved the climate of global discussion on the impact of oil exploration to the ecosystem.

These practices also resembled public journalism in the way that *Vanguard* and *ThisDay*'s reporting framed the issues involved and positioned the audience/citizens as stakeholders in the problem. The issues were defined as public problems involving everyone and not just the oil companies or government. Rather than portray citizens as victims, spectators or audiences to be entertained, the newspapers conveyed to readers their sense of personal stake and responsibility as potential actors. The reporting allowed for a reframing of what these stakes are, how these stakes fit into the people's realities and what citizens, government and institutions might be able to do differently. Essentially these kinds of stories offer citizens a road map for change. It was an attempt to undertake what Charity (1995: 4–8) describes as a critical function for public journalists, which is to make it as easy as possible for citizens to make intelligent decisions about public affairs and to get them carried out.

THE FUTURE OF LOCAL GOVERNMENT

While most traditional Western-style reporting of public affairs merely raises consciousness about the issues, the discussed examples help citizens to consider possibilities for resolution. Such reporting also points out the stakes that citizens and community groups have in the issue, including how these sometimes conflicting stakes may actually work for the common good. Friedland (2003: 3–4) argues that the values and ideas of the common good are essential for the successful practice of public journalism. This becomes obvious in *The Guardian's* coverage of the 2004 local council polls in Nigeria, particularly in the kinds of reporting in the months before the elections.

The year prior to the election was charged with intense debate about what would become of the third tier of governance in Nigeria. The central government had suspended elections into the 774 local councils and appointed local administrators to run county affairs. At the end of the first tenure of the centrally appointed administrators, some state governors quickly appointed fresh administrators. Other governors made preparation to organize elections in the offices.

The Guardian newspaper used the situation for a public journalism experiment. The editors interviewed a wide range of citizens and identified four distinct perceptions about the future of local governance in the country. These are:

- Those who prefer administrators appointed by central government;
- Those who prefer state government to appoint administrators;
- Those who prefer each state to organize local elections on dates separate from other states;

- Those who prefer to have a central government to organize one uniform election into all local government office.

Three *Guardian* reporters were assigned to write about the issue of local government elections from the viewpoint of each group of citizens. Rather than following traditional strategies of simply interviewing members of each group and juxtaposing their views, or using the conflict inherent in the issue to arrive at supposedly 'balanced' stories, these reporters interviewed people representing each group with the idea that each might understand and perhaps appreciate the others' different positions.

The Guardian then produced four different stories, each one designed to synthesize those public views and argue for that group's point of view. These stories were published as special reports on consecutive weekends, each carrying a headline bullet indicating that the story was from the point of view of one group of citizens.

The reporting received public acclaim. There was an influx of letters to the editor and telephone calls to *The Guardian*, and an increase in sales due to community demand for copies of these reports. The reports and the excitement they generated gave Nigerians, who ultimately hold different opinions on the issue, the opportunity to read and consider the arguments and positions of other groups. There were discussions, arising from *The Guardian* reporting in barbershops, beauty salons, bars, marketplaces and other public spaces.

This style of reporting also helped people in the different communities in the country to have a civil dialogue about the various directions that were possible. It was different from traditional journalism which usually allows the competing sides to frame the issue in a vacuum. The reporting was copiously referred to by the state and central parliaments, and the deliberation eventually led to the decision that the federal government would organize a uniform local government poll across Nigeria.

BLOGGING: PARTICIPATORY JOURNALISM

Nigerian journalists are also using digital tools like blogging, wikis and listserv and social media sites like Yahoo! Groups, MySpace and Facebook to circulate stories or comments on issues affecting citizens. These online platforms are also being used by journalists to start conversations and share opinions on issues of corruption, fiscal transparency and accountability in government. Lawmakers in the National Assembly pay attention to these online conversations.

Others in Nigeria's civil society are also taking advantage of the technologies. Blogging has opened up the media landscape, so that ordinary citizens can reach large audiences to express their opinions or provide 'real time' reports on events in their communities. As this form of journalism spreads in Nigeria, nonprofit institutions are also taking advantage of blogging to communicate with journalists and other organizations, and collaborate more effectively. For example, the nonprofit organization *Network for Success* has successfully used these online media tools to connect with journalists on women's right issues. Blogging, as a form of citizens' journalism, has led to the pooling of knowledge and has become a source of empowerment for women who are able to connect with journalists on women's issues. The outcomes that have been achieved provide support for the contention that the content, conventions, structure and practices of 'blogging' often lend themselves to applications of meaningful participatory democracy (Lori Cooke 2004).

COMMUNITY RADIO: SHIFT IN MEDIUM AND LANGUAGE

Nigeria has the highest literacy rate in West Africa, second only to Ghana. Despite this, hardly any newspaper has a circulation beyond 80,000 copies a day even though the country's population exceeds 145 million. Additionally, Nigerian newspapers mainly print in the English language, even though the majority of people are not literate in English. Consequently, radio, especially stations that use local languages, has an increasing influence in Nigeria. For instance, *Radio Nigeria* claims 100 million listeners alone; the *Raypower FM* network claims to reach 23 million listeners.

UNESCO reports that there were 101 radio station operating in Nigeria in 2005, compared to 58 in 2000 (UNESCO 2008). This increase in radio broadcasting and the proliferation of community radio outlets allowed journalists—professional or otherwise—to pay closer attention to community issues, communicate these in the local languages, and engage local communities as participants in the processes of both politics and media making. This is particularly true for the reporting of health concerns like polio, malaria and HIV/AIDS, and for political engagement of people prior to local government elections. Journalists have reported the issues that the local communities were wrestling with, brought local people into the studios to have conversations with politicians, and broadcast these conversations in local languages.

Although military dictatorship has given way to democratic governance, many of these radio stations cannot broadcast anything that is critical of the government or critical of a political leader or a staunch member of the ruling political party for fear of censorship, arrest of for fear of being blacklisted for advertisement opportunities. In just one example, *Rhythm 93.7 FM*, a privately owned radio station in Port Harcourt, Rivers State, was raided in March 2009 by a unit of the State Security Services (SSS). The news editor, Segun Owolabi, was arrested for airing a statement the day before by a consumer association, Claims Directory of Nigeria (CDN), calling for a protest against the regular power outages. *Reporters San*

Frontier reports that the Owolabi was held for 24 hours for trying to 'disturb the peace'. His detention followed several SSS raids on *Rhythm 93.7 FM* because of its attempts to provide a public service.

Widespread poverty, the commercial imperatives of media proprietors, and lack of proper training and expertise are other factors that also limit the full potential of public journalism in the medium of radio. Commercial radio broadcasting stations are still largely owned by wealthy individuals, politicians or the state government, whose vested interests often promote journalism that injures rather than supports public-oriented journalism. Studies have shown that even community radio, like other forms of journalism, is also a business. It requires income, market share, identity and a programming niche (Gillis and Moore 2004).

RESPONDING TO THE GLOBAL FINANCIAL CRISIS

As nations across the globe wrestled with the financial meltdown that commenced in 2008, *ThisDay* newspaper convened a public event where stakeholders in the Nigerian financial industry engaged both global players and citizens. The town hall event, held on 3 October 2008 in the nation's capital, Abuja, was a partnership between the media organization and a series of public and private partners and helped take the practice of journalism to another level in Nigeria. The town hall forum had the following goals:

- To dig deep into the challenges of Nigeria's policy and market environment,
- To appraise global market conditions,
- To explore options and proffer solutions to Nigeria as one of the fastest growing markets in the world determined to be a leading global economy by 2020.

ThisDay's editors worked for months on the project. They met with financial players in the different sectors and developed a list of areas that may be affected by the financial crisis, including banking, insurance, manufacturing, oil and gas, and the stock exchange, among others. Four reporting teams were then constituted, each charged with the task of talking to ordinary citizens about their fears, to conduct research and gather information. The results of these activities helped to determine which stakeholders were invited as participants. At the heart of this process was learning new ways of listening, which also led to the two major discussion themes for the town hall meeting. These were:

- When and How Should Governments Intervene in Markets?
- Nigeria's Markets and the Global Financial Crisis.

Participants at the town hall were told that the event was an opportunity for deliberation, not speechmaking. The organizers agreed that the global economic problem required the kind of reasoning and talking that allows for weighing of possible actions carefully by examining what is most valuable to Nigerians. This reflects the definition of deliberation outlined by scholars like David Mathews (2002). The deliberative process at the town hall was expected to enlighten citizens about their own and other people's needs and experiences, helping them to be more engaged in shaping a healthier civic life. Twelve reporters were assigned to listen to and report on the six-hour-long deliberations, but with the framing of public problem solving.

COMMON LINKS

Most of the activities discussed in these case studies fit into the range of public journalism as defined by Jay Rosen, one of the originators of America's public journalism movement. According to Rosen, the media is supposed to:

1. Address people as potential participants in public life,
2. Help communities act upon their problems,
3. Improve the climate of public discussion, and
4. Speak honestly about civic values and take on the role as a civic actor (Rosen 1999: 44).

Public journalism as portrayed in these Nigerian exemplars is considered effective for three main reasons:

- The reporting sparks public deliberation, which gives meaning to democracy.
- The reporting encourages citizen participation and this contributes normatively to the legitimization of policy development and implementation.
- The reporting enlarges the domain of public discourse, thereby leading to professional inquiry and new knowledge.

PUBLIC JOURNALISM AS CIVIC LEADERSHIP

Public journalism is a leadership phenomenon. Some historical perspective will be useful here. It was Joseph Pulitzer who first had the idea in the United States of people-oriented journalism. His was a form whereby writing was done in accessible English, so that new immigrants to the United States could learn the language, enter into conversation and not feel excluded.

Pulitzer therefore brought a sense of 'public-ness' to journalism. In a way, he was advocating that journalism was a public trust which needed to serve public interests and engage citizens with the public interest.

Journalism's role is to help people rule themselves. This is a leadership role. James MacGregor Burns defines leadership as 'leaders inducing followers to act for certain goals that represent the values and motivations—the wants and needs, the aspirations, and the expectations—of both the leaders and citizens' (Burns 1978: 429) According to Burns, leadership is both a transactional and transforming phenomenon of influencing citizens to participate in public life. This type of leadership is transforming in the sense that one or more people engage with others in such a way that leaders and followers raise one another to higher levels of motivation and morality.

Similarly, Howard Gardner speaks of 'ordinary and innovative leadership'. While ordinary leadership reinforces familiar values that support the status quo and continue doing things as they have been done in the past, innovative leaders imply change in a practice, if not values (Gardner 1993: 223).

Public journalism requires making innovative changes. 'Innovative leadership calls for significant change-action to increase the amount and to improve the forms of investments that we make to the social goods of a community' (Couto and Eken 2002: 13). Sustaining the young democracy in Nigeria depends on citizens' participation, and journalism has the potential to play a civic leadership role in helping society to work towards democracy and better public life without sacrificing its cherished values and traditions. To add democratic value and use their craft to influence citizens to participate in public life, journalists in Nigeria might need to do the following:

• Identify new partners;
• Use internet tools and platforms;
• Change reporting to meet the emerging needs of their community; and
• Become more closely connected to the community they serve.

CONCLUSION

This chapter has highlighted some significant features of Nigerian journalism that may potentially enhance understandings of international public journalism. The chapter has discussed the historical and social dynamics around which public journalism evolved in Nigeria. The struggle against colonial rule and military dictatorship are two landmark periods that acted as catalysts for the media to address not only the fight for democratic rule but also the need for development in Nigerian communities and citizen engagement in public life.

The case studies illustrate ways in which journalism in Nigeria, a country with limited press freedom, has been able to negotiate institutional and environmental disadvantages to engage with audiences. The case studies show that even in a developing country, it is possible for journalism to alter the perception that the public is a mere audience, an electorate to be 'won' by politicians, or a victim of the misdeeds of the powerful. Nigerian journalists have attempted to change the mind-set of citizens so that they can shift from being mere receivers of news and information to the realization that they can also be a powerful part of making change in their communities.

This attempt to change how Nigerians see themselves is intricately connected to the journalists' commitment to changing the processes by which communities and a fledgling democracy should work. Nigerian journalists have varying perspectives about the willingness and ability of citizens to contribute to public life. Some journalists think that Nigerians simply want to receive accurate information or, in other words, to be told what is going on, and hence it is the job of journalists to objectively report news and issues. Many other Nigerian journalists are often frustrated by the difficulty of conveying the complexity of issues to the public. Despite this, Nigerian journalists have shown consistent attempts to look for more effective ways to engage the public, even though the task is fraught with occupational hazards that usually characterize societies with limited press freedom. For example, as representative democracy takes root in Nigeria and civil society becomes stronger, journalists have been exploring alliances with NGOs as one way of building some roles for Nigerians as active participants by providing a platform for citizens' voices. They also aim to create opportunities for members of the public to come aboard and shoulder some stake in a participatory democracy.

BIBLIOGRAPHY

Burns, J.M. (1978) *Leadership*, New York: Harper and Row.

Charity, A. (1995) *Doing Public Journalism*, New York: Guildford Press.

Couto, R.A. and Eken, S.C. (2002) *To Give their Gifts: Health, Community, and Democracy*, Nashville, TN: Vanderbilt University Press.

Dare, S. (2007) *Guerrilla Journalism: Dispatches from the Underground*, Philadelphia, PA: Xlibris Corporation

Don Pedro, I. (2003) 'Life on the harsh lane' *The Guardian* (Nigeria), 3 July: A4–A6.

Friedland, L.A. (2003) *Public Journalism: Past and Future*, Dayton, OH: Kettering Foundation.

Gardner, H. (1993) *Creating Minds: An Anatomy of Creativity Seen through the Lives of Freud, Einstein, Picasso, Stravinsky, Eliot, Graham, and Gandhi*, New York: Basic Books.

Gillis, T. and Moore, R. (2004) 'Engaging journalism: Community journalism and its effects on social interaction and citizen empowerment in sub-Saharan Africa', Paper presented at the *Global Fusion Convention*, St. Louis, Missouri, October.

Lerner, D. (1958) *The Passing of Traditional Society*, New York: Free Press.

Lori Cooke, S. (2004) 'Deliberative communities online: Towards a model of public journalism based on the blog', Paper submitted to Association of Educators in Journalism and Mass Communication annual convention, Toronto, 30 June–4 August.

Mathews, D. (2002) *For Communities to Work*, Dayton, OH: Kettering Foundation.

Norris, P. (2001) *Digital divide: Civic Engagement, Information Poverty, and the Internet Worldwide*, Cambridge, UK: Cambridge University Press.

Odunewu, A. (1997) 'Media, civil society and democracy', *Media Rights Monitor*, 2(2): 7–16

Oyovbaire, S. (2001) 'The media and democratic process in Nigeria', lecture at the National Institute for Policy and Strategic Studies, Kuru, 7 August.

Rosen, J. (1999) 'The action of the idea: Public journalism in built form', in T. Glasser (ed.) *The Idea of Public Journalism*, New York: Guildford Press, pp. 21–48.

Schramm, W. (1964) *Mass Media and National Development*, Palo Alto, CA: Stanford University Press.

UNESCO (2008) *Beyond 20/20: Broadcast: Institutions and Public channel*, Available at http://stats.uis.unesco.org/unesco/TableViewer/tableView.aspx?ReportId=857 (Accessed 1 September 2009).

5 Sustaining Public Journalism Practices
The Australian Experience

Angela Romano

An ongoing challenge for journalists with an interest in public journalism or other deliberative journalism is how to embed and sustain the ideas and practices within newsrooms. The issues that Australian journalists face are similar to those that have been observed among their counterparts in the United States. One challenge for many public journalism exponents lies in how to develop a set of news-gathering, reporting and editing practices that place journalists in the best position to support deliberation. Another is how to ensure that these practices and ideas are maintained after the projects have finished or the newsroom leaders who have instigated such activities move to new positions.

Many of the strategies associated with public journalism are often well outside journalists' traditional experiences, such as organizing forums and other public meetings, or facilitating community conversations. Public journalism also requires a refinement of the art of listening, so that the journalist is seeking not just facts and story 'angles', but is also attuned to themes and trends (see page 18 of this book). This may lead to a slowing of the news gathering processes. Given the deadline-driven nature of journalistic work, many journalists may find that the art of listening to public conversation contradicts their most deeply ingrained customs, habits and reflexes. Furthermore, stories must be told to provide an overview not just of problems, but of their roots, their potential trajectory in the future, and the implications of these. Max Frankel, former managing editor of the *New York Times*, is among those who suggest that such demands overstretch journalists' capacities. 'The elemental tasks of describing events and discerning their causes are already beyond the skills and budgets of many newsrooms,' he says (Frankel 1995: 28).

The experiences of newsrooms in America and other countries indicate that innovation with public journalism concepts and practices often depends on the will of the editor and other senior staff; public journalism activities thus often slow or stop with the departure of those newsroom leaders (Sirianni and Friedland 2001: 196; also Chapter 6 of this book). One idealistic reporter might produce individual stories by using civic mapping or other public journalism strategies, regardless of the overall professional culture of his or her newsroom. However, it is doubtful whether one lone ranger can either lead a substantive project or transform the internal dynamics of newsrooms in the absence of other significant pressures for change. Even attempts by newsroom leaders to instigate a shift to public journalism-style approaches have resulted in mixed success. This is evident in the newsrooms led by Cole Campbell, an American public journalism pioneer. When Campbell left the Norfolk *Virginian-Pilot* in 1995, after setting up a 'public life' team and other initiatives in community conversation, the newspaper staff continued to sustain public journalism practices and experiment with new strategies. By contrast, when Campbell left the *St Louis Post Dispatch* in 2000, after five years as editor, the remaining staff indicated ambivalence about public journalism and its future at the newspaper (Sirianni and Friedland 2001: 203; Gade and Perry 2003).

The longevity of public journalism practices can be affected by practical issues of resource allocations that ultimately support or smother such projects. As a tool for face-to-face meetings with representative groups of citizens, public journalism projects are generally expensive, time consuming and episodic in nature (Witt 2004: 3; Meyer 1998; Potter and Kurpius 2000). Mainstream newspapers rely on wire services, syndicated copy, and bread-and-butter reporting via 'rounds' or 'beat' reporting or following up media releases. Public journalism projects regularly involve expensive strategies such as town hall meetings, surveys, focus groups or massive numbers of interviews. Many journalists also find that it can take much time to find appropriate citizen sources and prepare for a conversation, if it is to have any consequence (Yancey 2000). Sirianni and Friedland calculate that there can be four hours of preparation to every hour of conversation (2001: 202). Projects are also often accompanied by special design features to make them stand out from regular reporting. In newsrooms as far afield as the United States and New Zealand, there may be hostility and resentment among journalists who believe that the designated teams who run labour- and resource-intensive public journalism projects effectively relegate all of the organization's 'bread and butter' reporting and editorial work to the rest of their colleagues (e.g., see McGregor, Comrie and Campbell 1998: 12, 14; Waddell 1997: 94–5).

This chapter describes the experiences of significant public journalism-style projects by national, statewide and local Australian newsrooms, describing the organizational and environmental factors that drove decisions about whether and how they ran. The chapter traces some of the factors that have led to newsrooms adopting public journalism-style projects as an ongoing venture, while in other newsrooms the planned initiatives have been stillborn or were destined to a very limited life span. While some of these projects have been dubbed 'public journalism' by their initiators, many have not. Most Australian editors are familiar with the concepts of public journalism, but the philosophy was never popularized in the country as it was in the United States.

CROSSED PATHS, DIFFERENT DESTINATIONS

The following section will summarize the nature and outcomes of some of Australia's best-known public journalism-style projects. The aim is to identify similarities and differences in the motives, goals, resources and activities of these projects, and the degree to which the projects have gained momentum due to key players crossing paths.

Australian Broadcasting Corporation Forums (1997)

Popular radio presenter Anna Reynolds was led into an extended engagement and series of progressive learning experiences with public journalism-style projects by an ostensibly one-off project by the national broadcasting service, the Australian Broadcasting Corporation (ABC), in the state of Queensland in 1997. Reynolds says the ABC decided to conduct the project in order to 'revive a slow downward trend in ratings, and to get the public more involved with the radio station by physically being among their communities, touching their lives in a constructive way, and hopefully convincing them to become regular listeners' (Reynolds 1998a).To that end, the ABC gathered information through field research and community consultation. It also commissioned a survey that questioned residents about local issues including crime, politics, race, and the availability of government services in the state's southeast. Armed with this data, the ABC invited the public to two forums in the state capital, Brisbane, and nearby Ipswich, to discuss town planning and social issues affecting the two cities. The Brisbane forum was broadcast live on the ABC's local radio station and followed by a lively talkback program, while the Ipswich event was edited into a half-hour program for ABC TV.

The Public Journalism Project (1998)

This experience soon became useful to Reynolds when a few months later she moved to *The Courier-Mail*, Queensland's statewide daily newspaper. *The Courier-Mail* had partnered with Cratis Hippocrates, a Queensland University of Technology (QUT) academic, in a successful application for federal government funding for an applied research project. The Public Journalism Project was inspired by American public journalism, most particularly the *Akron Beacon Journal*'s 1994 'A Question of Color' series. The project's first two phases were broken into the themes of 'Immigration: Beyond 2000' and 'Reconciliation: Local Solutions'. The Ethnic Communities Council and Australians for Reconciliation Project became community partners. Reynolds became the newspaper's Project Coordinator, was the most prolific writer of reports for the series and was the project's public face. She liaised with community partners and also compèred and moderated two public forums, one at the end of the

'Immigration' project phase and the other at the completion of the 'Reconciliation' project phase.

The Public Journalism Project had some noteworthy achievements (see Romano 2001), but problems in conceptualization started to emerge during the early phases, suggesting that the project would not be sustainable. Apart from Reynolds and one other reporter, Debra Aldred, no other journalists were drawn out of their daily routines to become involved in the project or substantially altered their patterns of professional activity (Romano 2001: 52–5). Many of those who contributed stories admitted that that they had little or no concept of what public journalism was or what the project was meant to achieve. A considerable number of the project's stories had arisen from regular reporting routines or media releases, and were included under the project logo because they coincidentally fitted the race relations themes. Subeditors were not trained in public journalism, and community members who had provided extensive input were sometimes dismayed by the way in which their stories were edited or dropped altogether rather than reworked to make the contents more appealing or newsworthy. *The Courier-Mail* also faced commercial pressures to find well-known figures and 'big names' to talk about issues of national or state significance, rather than to represent the initiatives of small people operating at a local level.

The Courier-Mail published an eight-page lift-out supplement following both the "Immigration' and 'Reconciliation' forum. Although the two lift-outs provided a focussed understanding of the issues and potential responses to them, the reporting did not reflect the community input into the actual forums. The newspaper's printing deadlines meant that the lift-outs' content was written *before* the forums took place, using the prewritten text of the official speeches and other input. Each phase of the project effectively ended with the forums, meaning that the input of the forums—the major face-to-face gatherings in which citizens chewed over the issues—were not directly included in the newspaper's reports.

Planning and moderating forums was not part of the newspaper's usual business, and simple organizational issues disrupted the nature and quality of deliberation. Among these were a gender imbalance among official speakers at the first forum; a physical and psychological division that was created by having official speakers on a stage and citizens as the audience, which was contrary to the principle of equal discussion; insufficient time to discuss issues fully or concentrate on local issues; and polarizing debate, particularly at the 'Immigration' forum.

Another issue arose from the project's dependence on an unequally structured partnership. QUT provided the expertise and obtained an Australian Research Council grant to fund research, town hall meetings and other community listening activities. The community organizations provided grassroots contacts and rich insights about community experiences, values and opinions. The newspaper attempted to knit this wealth of information into coherent stories with an overarching narrative.

However, the partnership was reliant on key personalities, most particularly on Hippocrates, whose zest drove the project, and *The Courier-Mail* editor, Chris Mitchell, who had overarching responsibility and power to approve or veto project ideas. Hippocrates left QUT to take up a position at the *Sydney Morning Herald*, run by the rival Fairfax Media, and the Public Journalism Project skidded to a rapid halt. A mooted third phase of the project was promptly terminated, and no further public journalism-style projects were run under Mitchell's leadership.

If public journalism requires journalists to think of themselves as part of 'a learning organization' (see page 18 of this book), then this was one of the project's most problematic elements. Public journalism requires a substantive change of mindset and practices, as Reynolds candidly acknowledged at the beginning of the Public Journalism Project's second phase. Reynolds' previous background as a popular ABC radio talk show host, as well as her experience in the ABC project, meant that she had strong community networks, good communications skills and a better-than-average understanding of the processes of public discussion. However, she recognized that her outlook was limited when a fellow journalist 'laughed uproariously' at Reynolds' query as to whether the colleague had any story ideas for the project's second phase. 'You shouldn't be asking me,' the colleague replied. 'You should be out there in the true spirit of Public Journalism asking the community what they think the issues are' (Reynolds 1998b: 19).

Aldred similarly describes a learning experience, particularly from simple experiences such as staying for the post-forum refreshments. This provided a comfortable environment for people to engage in friendly but spirited banter over tea and sandwiches, without the fear of the point scoring or scorn that is often associated with debates in more formal settings. She gained many contacts and insights from these kinds of interactions, which continued to enrich her reportage for years after the project's completion (Romano 2001: 57–8).

Such projects thus involve a learning curve about the subjects that are being reported on, the ways in which the public have coalesced around an issue, as well as the actual techniques of deliberative journalism. However, with the learning confined to a relatively small number of staff, the institutional knowledge and understanding can easily be lost completely with a few movements of staff into new positions or organizations.

Victorian Local Government Association Projects (1998–99)

During the period in which he was leading the Public Journalism Project, Hippocrates delivered a presentation about public journalism to a conference attended by a number of municipal government bodies in the state of Victoria. This introduced a number of people to the concepts, which stimulated a further wave of attempts at public journalism. At the time, the Victorian Local Governance Association (VLGA) and the philanthropic

Stegley Foundation were providing grants and other support for municipal councils seeking to undertake community development programs. Four
regional councils expressed interest in including the media in these development initiatives, although ultimately only one development program in the
Latrobe Valley progressed into a public journalism project.

The Latrobe Valley project commenced in March 1998 when the Latrobe
City Council invited community participants and staff from local media
organizations to a meeting that had no set agenda except to identify a topic
that the community would want to discuss and become involved in. The
then editor of the *Latrobe Valley Express*, Lynne Smith, admits that the
group had no clear vision or role model for how to set and achieve goals.
Thus 'it took a little time to get down to the nitty gritty' and to some participants, the process appeared to be 'a bit of shemozzle' (Smith 2002: pers.
comm.). After several meetings, the topic of transport for young people was
selected. By that stage, most of the media representatives had opted out of
the public journalism team, although many continued to support the development program by resuming normal journalistic coverage of the issues.

This left the *Express*, a newspaper that publishes twice a week, and the
Gippsland FM community radio station as the chief media protagonists.
Express journalists sought out venues where young people and other stakeholders meet, in order to identify the topics and stories that would appear
in every edition of the newspaper for eight weeks. Gippsland FM also dedicated a thirty-minute program every Saturday over the same period to the
council's community consultation and listener input. The coverage peaked
in May 1999 with a Council-organized Community Transport Summit.
The development program took five years to reach fruition, and both media
organizations have provided ongoing coverage of the proposed solutions
and their implementation (Romano 2006: 176). As a learning experience,
the public journalism project shaped journalists' understanding of the significance and nature of the issue of transport disadvantage.

The grant funding and Latrobe City Council involvement meant that the
media organizations bore no cost apart from the labour of their staff and
the page space or airtime. Since the *Express* is a free newspaper, the editorial space is determined by how many pages are left after advertisements
have been purchased. While news print is an expensive commodity, Smith
dedicated one to two pages of each issue in the lead-up to the Summit. She
took the view that the time spent on the project should be 'absorbed' as part
of the normal duties involved in compiling the newspaper and not regarded
as an additional expense (Smith 2002: pers. comm.).

Smith says that the project was worth the considerable extra time and
effort involved, and the strategies could work again if a sufficiently important issue was identified (Smith 2002: pers. comm.). However, Smith did not
conduct further public journalism-style projects in the years that followed.
Given the budgets of regional newsrooms, such commitments of funds are
rare, leaving organizations like the *Express* dependent on external financial

support for such activities. With the closure of the Stegley Foundation, and few other options, such activities thus remain improbable.

In contrast to the Latrobe Valley project, the three other VLGA community development projects did not move beyond traditional relations between the community, councils and the media. In Moreland, the City Council's efforts to build a power-sharing arrangement with young people left little time to work with the media on a strategy for a public journalism approach. Thus, plans to try to work with journalists to increase the youth voice in the media were not progressed. In Cardinia and Buloke Shires, the councils and community members were happy with the contribution of traditional media reporting in raising issues to public awareness. In Cardinia, the community was negotiating with both the Shire Council and the state government to provide assistance in building housing for families with special needs. The groups involved realized that many levels of the negotiations were best conducted without the pressure of media scrutiny. The experiences suggested that the public's energy may often be better directed towards community-based activities rather than engagement with the media. These three cases also support the dictum that there is no need to overturn journalism conventions when traditional approaches are proving sufficient for community needs (see page 17 of this book).

The Australian Newspaper's 'Specials' (1999 Onwards)

The national quality broadsheet, *The Australian*, also began experimenting with public journalism-style activities under the initiative of then editor-in-chief David Armstrong in 1999. Armstrong claimed to not have been affected by the American debate on public journalism. He felt that public journalism could lock media organizations into 'some kind of agenda which is determined by a market research model' (Armstrong 2002: pers. comm.). He was, however, concerned by perceived gaps in public debate, claiming that under the federal government of the time the political processes were not 'forward looking' and government leaders saw 'the vision thing' as 'something to be frowned upon' (Armstrong 2002: pers. comm.). His aim was to use the newspaper's resources to generate original stories about the state of the nation and where it was heading.

The Australian's staff attempted to meet these goals through various means, particularly through in-depth 'specials'. Each 'special' comprised a focused series of news and/or feature stories based on intensive research and analysis, which were usually printed over a period of days or weeks. The first 'special' probed the Constitutional debate that preceded the 1999 referendum, which was conducted to determine whether Australia should become a republic or remain a constitutional monarchy. In the following three years, *The Australian* ran numerous specials about economic and social issues. These specials investigated issues affecting Australia's future and the shifts that were occurring in the daily, lived experiences of the general population (e.g. the 'Work and Family', 'Advance Australia Where?' and 'The Cultural Divide' series) and targeted groupings (e.g. the 'Mabo: Land is Not Enough' series on the needs of Indigenous Australians).

The Australian's strategies for these specials were at the upper end of the budgetary scale for most Australian newsrooms. For example, the special on the Constitutional debate set up a model of sending staff around Australia to locations that would not usually be considered as throbbing pulse points of news. *The Australian* hosted a series of innovative and carefully balanced town hall meetings across the country, and used these as opportunities to probe the nature and depth of issues affecting different communities. Armstrong took a laid-back approach to the travel costs for the 'specials'. He noted that because *The Australian* was a national quality newspaper, this necessitated constant travel for its reporters. Armstrong described the travel costs for the newspaper's mainstream journalism as 'mind boggling'. He casually dismissed the bills for the 'specials' as being the same as for normal stories, except that they were 'just more concentrated' (Armstrong 2002: pers. comm.).

The time that reporters spent in community hubs, and not just the distance of various destinations, was a further expense. An example is 'The Cultural Divide' series, which involved an almost ethnographic technique, rather than the more common journalistic technique of 'interview Side A and then get a quote from Side B'. Some reporters spent days or even weeks within particular communities to identify what were significant issues from those communities' viewpoints. 'The brief was that we would send reporters where there were concentrations of ethnic groups or ethnic diversity, and talk with people and observe with their own eyes what was going on rather than going to things with preconceptions either way,' Armstrong said (2002: pers. comm.). Armstrong was again relaxed about the expense. He justified it by defining the staffing costs as a general newspaper expense rather than a figure that he budgeted against any particular project.

The newspaper also commissioned research to identify issues and trends, often using the information as a basis for community consultations. For example, the 'Advance Australia Where' special series, which took approximately six months in planning, used commissioned research from the National Centre for Social and Economic Modelling (NATSEM), which provided the team with a map of the increasing gap in the fortunes of the nation's citizens. Australian news organizations can anticipate that research by these types of specialist consultants will commonly cost US$5,000 to US$15,000—the equivalent of six to twenty week's salary for a middle-ranking journalist at the organization—with the bill usually at the upper end of that scale.

Queensland Infrastructure and Social Issues Series (2003 Onwards)

David Fagan was working at *The Australian* when Armstrong instituted the specials. When Mitchell replaced Armstrong as editor-in-chief at *The*

Australian in mid-2002, Fagan returned to his home state of Queensland to take over the helm at *The Courier-Mail.* Ironically, although Fagan was never associated with the Public Journalism Project, it was he rather than Mitchell who revived public journalism-style projects and instituted them as a regular feature of the newspaper. Fagan is a close friend of Hippocrates and was familiar with the public journalism concept. However, he cites Armstrong as the inspiration for his public journalism-style projects and the source of the approach that he takes (2009: pers. comm.). A little of the institutional learning has remained from the Public Journalism Project, with a small number of staff remembering the experience. In particular, Reynolds, who is now managing editor, has used her previously honed skills to conduct and moderate the dozens of public forums that have formed part of Fagan's projects.

While the Queensland government proudly touted the state's growth and attractiveness as a place to live, with 1,000 new residents arriving each week, Fagan was concerned that the political sector seemed to have few plans for the implications of this expansion. Fagan initiated a series of 'specials'-styled projects in 2003. They commenced with themes relating to infrastructure and the physical environment, starting with a 'green-space' series, and followed by projects about roads, water and the health system. Following the success of these infrastructure/environment projects, Fagan set up an investigative team of four journalists in 2008 to study social issues. The first outcomes were seen in 2009 with a major series on drugs and smaller series on other issues like homelessness and alcohol-fuelled violence.

The Courier-Mail's projects are similarly resource intensive to those led by Armstrong. The infrastructure/environment projects each commenced with major commissioned reports by specialists. The 'Drug Scourge' series broke with the pattern and instead devoted one key journalist to a three-month investigation period prior to the series being published. In addition to dedicating staff to the investigative unit and other project activities, *The Courier-Mail* has also conducted at least four forums per year across Queensland. Fagan takes a similar approach to Armstrong, and considers these costs as part of the newspaper's ongoing expenses rather than viewing them as the budgets for specific projects. In terms of staffing, he saw this as prioritization, reorganizing numbers in different newsroom departments to find the staff to pull into his investigative unit (Fagan 2009: pers. comm.).

COSTS AND REWARDS

The simplest lesson that can be drawn from these case studies is that regardless of whatever zeal journalists may feel towards public journalism strategies, traditional 'disengaged' journalism still serves a socially useful purpose in many circumstances. From the three planned Latrobe Valley projects that ultimately did not run, the message is that it is not sufficient to simply replicate public journalism strategies with any story or issue that arises. Journalists need to be sophisticated enough to identify what type of community agendas require the intensive exploration associated with public journalism and what forms of engagement are appropriate. (As Chapter 6 suggests, this has been a fault with some public journalism activities in New Zealand.)

The contrasting experiences of the *Latrobe Valley Express* and *Courier-Mail* indicate the challenges that journalists face in conceptualizing how to apply broader concepts of community inclusion and engagement into newsroom routines. The *Express* started its project with the advantage of strong identification with a geographically delimited target community and well-established networks within the region. The project's topic had an easy-to-see, direct, practical impact on many community members' lives. However, the *Express* journalists and their partners in the City Council and community had no role models or experience of how to use community input to set goals or set up processes for achieving their objectives. By contrast, *The Courier-Mail* was receiving advice from QUT about established strategies for the Public Journalism Project and had clear, predesignated topics and goals. However, when I interviewed *The Courier-Mail* reporters who had contributed stories to the project, several expressed confusion about how to serve an identifiable 'community' through civic journalism while working for a publication that served many disparate communities across the state.

A study of the specials run by *The Australian* under Armstrong and *The Courier-Mail* under Fagan suggest that lack of clarity about both the nature of the target communities and appropriate reporting strategies can be overcome by dedicating a pre-project period to defining and researching the topic. For projects like 'Advance Australia Where?', Armstrong gathered a team of about twenty senior staff to talk about the project aims and its implementation (2002: pers. comm.). This meant that the design phase directly engaged *The Australian*'s most experienced journalists, giving these newsroom leaders a stake in ensuring the project ran well. It combined their skills and inspiration to seed and fertilize the overall concept and the reporting activities that would follow. *The Australian* successfully managed to capture the flavour and character of local issues while remaining grounded in a perspective of national relevance. The early investment of time and creative/intellectual energies paid off later with greater capacity and confidence to conduct projects that were coherently and competently conceived and executed.

Resourcing is another common problem. As this chapter has explained, public journalism projects generally involve time-consuming reporting activities, commissioning of expert reports or lengthy community consultations, additional travel costs, and facilities for forums and other special activities. Given these factors, it is unsurprising that even notable public journalism adopters have tended to run projects intermittently at best. If newsrooms continue to run well-designed public journalism projects with clearly articulated outcomes, then the increasing exposure to the approach must logically increase journalists' confidence, skills, strategies and proficiency in undertaking project-related tasks. This should in turn increase the speed and cost efficiency of reporting activities.

While the cases above indicate that journalists can and do progressively learn much from public journalism-style projects, a key problem with one-off or intermittent projects is that newsrooms are less able to become 'learning organizations'. The importance of learning is evident in the extent to which many public journalism-style activities have been inspired or sustained from the crossing of paths or collaboration of people with common interests and insights in deliberative democracy, allowing mentorship and building of capacities and competencies.

Australian newsrooms have been facing major staff cuts in 2008–09 in the face of the global economic downturn, which must exacerbate pressures to avoid time- and cost-intensive projects. However, Fagan indicates that creative editors can still show support for public journalism-style projects and similar approaches in the face of such belt-tightening. Fagan says he could not let *The Courier-Mail* 'just be whittled away and become an anodyne brand newspaper. What would make us stand out is that if we did things that boldly stood up for our community.' While *The Courier-Mail* has looked for efficiencies and scrutinized staff numbers, Fagan has taken the approach that it would be best to reduce the resources that the newspaper dedicates to covering certain basic stories if they might be covered effectively via wire or syndicated copy. This would allow staff to concentrate their energies on 'something really special' and produce stories that would distinguish *The Courier-Mail* from rival information sources. *The Courier-Mail*'s first 'special' led by Fagan, the 'Our Future, Your Say: Greenspace' series, was indeed so unique that it won the Planning Institute of Australia's highest state award for best planning initiative of 2003. This itself was a special or at least unusual type of award for a news organization to win. It should be remembered, however, that with more than 200 full-time staff members, *The Courier-Mail* is one of Australia's largest news organizations, and it is imminently easier to shuffle staff between departments at large newsrooms than at smaller ones.

It is hard to prove whether or not these Australian attempts at large-scale, civic journalism-style activities have been productive for the newspapers themselves or the communities that they serve. As Arthur Charity (1995: 156) has noted, public journalism provides no easy solution to problems of declining print media circulations or radio/television rating figures. Armstrong joked that if increasing circulations was his goal, it would have been more productive for him to run comics on the front page than to do such in-depth, focused reporting.

In considering the motivation to conduct such projects, Armstrong described *The Australian*'s 'specials' as an avenue for providing information that could not have been obtained by other means and for developing 'the respect and the relationship between the newspaper and its audience' (Armstrong 2002: pers. comm.). Fagan furthermore added that the most valuable outcome a media organization can achieve is not circulations, exposing a scandal or forcing a government to act differently, but in helping people to focus on an issue, educating them and helping them to talk about it (2009: pers comm.). Thus the rewards that encourage journalists to continue public journalism-style projects may not be tangible, but lie in the ways in which media leaders perceive the media's place in society.

BIBLIOGRAPHY

Charity, A. (1995) *Doing Public Journalism*, New York: Guildford Press.

Frankel, M. (1995) 'Fix-it journalism', *New York Times Magazine*, 21 May: 28.

Gade, P.J. and Perry, E.L. (2003) 'Changing the newsroom culture: A four-year case study of organizational development at the *St Louis Post-Dispatch*', *Journalism and Mass Communication Quarterly*, 80(2): 327–47.

McGregor, J., Comrie, M. and Campbell, J. (1998) 'Public journalism and proportional representation: The New Zealand experiment, *Australian Journalism Review*, 20(1): 1–22.

Meyer, P. (1998) 'If it works well, how will we know?' in E. Lambeth, P. Meyer and E. Thorson (eds) *Assessing Public Journalism*, Columbia, MO: University of Missouri Press, pp. 251–83.

Potter, D. and Kurpius, D. (2000) 'Public journalism and television news', in A.J. Eksterowicz and R.N. Roberts (eds), *Public Journalism and Political Knowledge*, Lanham, MD: Rowman and Littlefield, pp. 77–90.

Reynolds, A. (1998a) 'Between the theory and the reality: A practical assessment of public journalism', *Journalism Education Association Conference*, Capricorn International Resort, Yeppoon, Queensland, 1–4 December.

Reynolds, A. (1998b). 'Public voice vital in immigration reporting', *The Courier-Mail*, 5 September: 19.

Romano, A. (2001) 'Inculcating public journalism philosophies into newsroom culture', *Australian Journalism Review*, 32(2): 43–62.

Romano, A. (2006) 'Public journalism and the "frugal correspondent" in multicultural societies', *Australian Studies in Journalism*, (6): 169–88.

Sirianni, C. and Friedland, L. (2001) *Civic Innovation in America: Community Empowerment, Public Policy, and the Movement for Civic Renewal*, Berkeley, CA: University of California Press.

Waddell, L. (1997) 'Voices: In the beginning there was Columbus', in J. Black (ed.) *Mixed News: The Public/Civic/Communitarian Journalism Debate*, Mahwah, NJ: L. Erlbaum Associates, pp. 94–5.

Witt, L. (2004) 'Is public journalism morphing into the public's journalism?', *AEJMC (Association for Education in Journalism and Mass Communication) Winter Meeting*, Rutgers University, New Brunswick, New Jersey, 28 February.

Yancey, D. (2000) 'Is anybody out there?', in A.J. Eksterowicz and R.N. Roberts (eds) *Public Journalism and Political Knowledge*, Lanham, MD: Rowman and Littlefield, pp. 61–76.

6 Public Journalism, Kiwi Style

Lingering Echoes of a Big Bang

Margie Comrie and David Venables

Public journalism has made only sporadic appearances in New Zealand and it is a safe bet that few Kiwi journalists know it exists. Despite a promising beginning, involving three major newspapers in 1996, public journalism never caught on, surviving today as a series of routine practices in local body election coverage and sporadic newspaper 'campaigns'. In this chapter we trace the history of public journalism in New Zealand, covering perspectives of pioneers and assessing the impact on election coverage.

In contrast to well-publicized, theorized and often well-funded projects in the United States, New Zealand's public journalism experiments have been low-key, even though they happened in newspapers of national importance. The burst of initial enthusiasm from editors concerned about scant public knowledge of a new electoral system in 1996 quickly faded. Projects moved from national politics to a series of local issues in a number of one-off advocacy campaigns. The 1999 general election saw a more limited revival of public journalism initiatives, but by 2001 three newspapers were trying these techniques in local body election coverage. As editors moved and managers totted up the costs and benefits, newspapers dropped the approach during national elections. However, the public journalism style gradually became embedded in coverage of local elections across New Zealand.

Despite its isolation and small population of 4.2 million, New Zealand has a highly competitive, commercially driven mediascape dominated by overseas companies. The community focus of public journalism makes it unattractive for radio (nationally centralized and minimally resourced at local level) and television (almost entirely national in output and focus). Public journalism, therefore, has remained almost entirely the province of newspapers in New Zealand.

THE FIRST BIG EXPLOSION

As in the United States, New Zealand public journalism sprang from dissatisfaction with traditional political reportage. From the late 1980s, a growing number of local media commentators focused particularly on television's poor performance, pointing to shrinking political coverage, dominated by conflict and packaged by celebrity correspondents who left little room for sound bites from the real newsmakers.

Meanwhile, public dissatisfaction with politics found expression in New Zealand, not in low voter turnout, but in a 1993 referendum vote to dump the traditional First Past the Post election system. Its replacement, Mixed Member Proportional (MMP) representation, designed to reflect more closely different shades of political opinion, meant that citizens voted both for an electorate representative and a party. Editors, political scientists and politicians voiced fears that the news media were ill-equipped either to provide citizens with information they needed to vote or to report the new style of politics and policy development (e.g., Palmer 1996: 27–8; Morrison 1996: 35–9).

In this atmosphere, three Independent News Limited (INL) newspapers—the metropolitan daily, *The Press*; New Zealand's largest provincial newspaper, the *Waikato Times*; and the smaller *Evening Standard*—took up the challenge of public journalism. The *Waikato Times* had already used public journalism techniques in the 1995 local body elections, while the *Evening Standard* had run a public journalism-style environmental campaign. The editors were influenced by INL training manager Warren Page's booklet of election coverage ideas based on the *Charlotte Observer*'s US Senate election coverage of 1992. The *Observer* had polled 1,000 citizens on issues and put questions from a citizens' panel to candidates, then reporters covered topics that their panel considered relevant (Levine 1996: 8–11). Page's booklet also covered techniques used in other public journalism projects, such as public meetings. However, he avoided the term public journalism as 'off-putting' (Page 2002: pers. comm.).

All three newspapers commissioned telephone opinion polls from university researchers asking readers what they believed were the campaign issues. These polls set the agenda for coverage, breaking with traditional horse race-style polling conducted by private companies (McGregor et al. 1998: 11). Readers' panels commenting on political performance, household forums and newspaper-initiated public meetings were part of the project. Public journalism coverage featured in special pages and the newspapers also relied on conventional campaign coverage.

The *Evening Standard*'s then editor John Harvey said his journalists responded enthusiastically, analyzing political statements from the viewpoint of the issues-poll findings rather than simply writing electoral profiles: 'They saw themselves as genuinely educating the public' (McGregor et al. 1998: 13). David Wilson, *The Press* editor at the time, said politicians were unhappy. The National Party, at that stage in power, at first refused to respond to the newspaper's request. But, in an echo of the *Charlotte Observer*'s experience, Wilson said, leaving a white space and the words 'NO RESPONSE' below a candidate's photo soon changed the

Party's mind. Politicians were also unhappy with a fifty-word response limit at the *Waikato Times*. However, editor Tim Pankhurst said, at its heart, the experiment was more about giving local people a greater say than about the media taking back control of coverage from politicians: 'instead of journalists setting the agenda and deciding what should be covered, we went out and consulted with our readers a hell of a lot more' (2003: pers. comm.).

The 1996 campaign was a special project staffed at each newspaper by a team of four. The process involved educating staff, politicians and readers in the approach, Harvey said. Because the newspapers were proud of the experiment, the dedicated public journalism team had a certain cachet and, at *The Press* at least, other journalists became jealous of those on the team (McGregor et al. 1998: 14).

A study of the 1996 stories has helped quantify and describe a substantive difference in the campaign coverage. A content analysis compared stories in *The Press, Waikato Times* and *Evening Standard* (which mixed public journalism and traditional approaches) with four metropolitan newspapers (using only traditional election-reporting strategies) during the month-long campaign to see if there were differences between public journalism stories and conventional coverage (McGregor et al. 1999).

Table 6.1   Issues Most Referred To: Comparison Between 1996 Conventional Coverage and Public Journalism

Rank	Conventional coverage	%	Public journalism	%
1	Candidates	11.6	Health	15.0
2	Coalition	10.1	Education	9.6
3	Economic policy	9.2	Economic policy	9.2
4	Polls	7.6	Coalition	6.5
5	Health	6.4	Social welfare	6.2
6	Leadership	4.9	Candidates	5.8
7	Advertising and publicity	4.2	Unemployment	5.4
8	Roadshow	3.9	Proportional representation	5.0
9	Political debates	3.6	Style	3.8
10	Style	3.3	Environment (tie)	3.5
			Taxes (tie)	3.5

As can be seen in Table 6.1, the top three topics of stories classified as public journalism (a third of all public journalism stories) all related to policy—health, education and economic policy. Conventional coverage was more focussed on the game of politics—personalities, coalition politicking, polls and similar themes—than issues. In a related finding, public journalism stories were less likely to use a 'horse race' frame (4 per cent) compared to conventional stories (17 per cent), and more public journalism stories were neutral in tone and fewer were negative than conventional stories.

The researchers also used categories developed by Edelstein and colleagues (1989) to examine how issues were framed. The researchers identified up to five campaign issues in each story (out of a list of forty-six). The issues were then examined to see if they had been framed problematically or not problematically according to Edelstein's eight conditions of discrepancy.

As Table 6.2 shows, the four most common problematic situations that stories overall presented were 'loss of value' (defined as where an individual or society perceives something once possessed has been lost), 'conflict' (where problems are represented as disagreements or clashes between individuals, groups, institutions, etc.), 'steps to solutions' (when issues or situations are constructed in terms of solutions proposed for problems), and 'need for value' (when a problem is framed in terms of an individual or societal need that must be satisfied to end a discrepancy). Overall a greater percentage of public journalism stories constructed campaign issues in terms of a problematic situation, demonstrating an interpretive role (McGregor et al. 1999: 73). Across all coverage, 'loss of value' and 'conflict' were the most frequently used problematic frames,

Table 6.2 Problematic Situations for Conventional and Public Journalism Coverage

Problematic situation	Overall percentage	Conventional journalism (%)	Public journalism (%)
Loss of value	26.8	27.7	21.2
Conflict	26.0	29.3	5.8
Steps to solution	18.2	15.6	34.0
Need for value	17.3	14.8	32.0
Consequences	6.0	6.5	3.5
Denial of a problem	3.1	3.3	1.9
Indeterminate situation	2.3	2.4	1.6
Blocking	0.3	0.4	—

and proportionately more campaign issues in conventional news stories featured 'conflict' and 'loss of value'. Public journalism stories, in contrast, featured 'steps to solutions' and 'need for value' as the most frequently occurring problematic situations.

In short, the study shows that public journalism offered quite different analysis of campaign issues to conventional campaign coverage. The study results also 'provided empirical support for those arguing that public journalism provides a different, more constructive framing of the news' (McGregor et al. 1999: 73–4).

SHRINKING GALAXIES? ELECTION 1999 AND BEYOND

By the time of the next national elections in 1999, the political landscape had changed. MMP was now established and the result expected to be clearer. It is likely that this—and a change in editorship at the *Evening Standard*—contributed to the sparse use of public journalism in 1999. Although the *Evening Standard* abandoned public journalism strategies in 1999 following editor John Harvey's retirement, *The Press* and *Waikato Times* continued to embrace elements of the approach. In the capital, Wellington, a small community newspaper and the metropolitan *Evening Post* also adopted public journalism techniques.

The Press promised voter-oriented coverage in which the newspaper would allow voters rather than politicians to set the news agenda, express families' concerns to politicians, submit readers' questions to candidates and stage a leaders' debate. *The Press*'s editors claimed their aim was to 'avoid being hijacked by political stunts, photo opportunities, spin doctors, scare tactics, and manufactured issues' (*The Press* 1999a: 4). But by November, *The Press* was lamenting having to cancel its leaders' debate after the Prime Minister and the New Zealand First leader refused to take part (*The Press* 1999b: 8).

Other newspapers were less vocal. The *Waikato Times*, which in 1996 had embraced public journalism with the logo 'Operation Democracy', took a more subdued approach in 1999. It focused on the two city electorates, sponsoring two electorate meetings, regularly following up the concerns of several 'undecided' voters, and undertaking local polling. The *Evening Post*'s coverage was perhaps more 'enterprise journalism' than public journalism. New Zealand's only remaining metropolitan evening newspaper, the *Post*, struggling against declining sales, had already publicly committed to a more community-oriented, advocacy-based approach to city issues to distinguish itself from morning rival, the *Dominion*. During the campaign, its political reporters visited regional electorates asking voters for their issues, wrote to all candidates asking for their views on the placement of the new city hospital, and interviewed voters on issues, such as genetically engineered food, which they presented in articles along with parties' policies on the topic. The other major daily newspapers—the *New Zealand Herald*, the *Dominion* and the *Otago Daily Times*—did not try public journalism techniques, although the *Herald* did keep in regular contact with a group of voters living in a representative city street.

However, one small community newspaper in Wellington wholeheart-edly embraced the challenge of public journalism election coverage. When Simon Collins, editor of Wellington's *City Voice*, polled voters, it was no one-off dabble in public journalism. *City Voice* was, from its launch in 1993, committed to facilitating a public role for all citizens. The giveaway newspaper's charter affirmed it would 'provide a vehicle for all members of the Wellington community to communicate news and opinions to one another'. It would also ensure concerns of 'the relatively poor and power-less' were fairly represented. The newspaper was characterized by regu-lar sections compiled by members of the city's ethnic and special interest communities.

City Voice interviewed 276 local people, asking them to rate a group of issues. The top polling issues became the topics of a series of five public meetings with candidates in September and October 1999, leading up to the November election. Each meeting was preceded by a news story in *City Voice* and followed by a detailed report.

A survey of participants at the meetings shows attendees were in no way representative even of the well-to-do Wellington Central electorate: 82 per cent had a degree or better in terms of education; 60 per cent were forty years old or older; more than half had voted in all of the previous six elec-tions; and nearly 80 per cent were left or centre-left voters (Venables 2001: 30). Eighty-five per cent of the respondents were in favour of attending similar meetings in the future. But, while the editor had wanted to attract undecided voters to help them decide, it was not clear he had achieved this aim. Just over half those surveyed said the meetings were 'useful' or better in helping them vote, but about a third said they were 'no help at all' (Ven-ables 2001: 30–5).

However, the 1999 election was probably the peak for Kiwi-style pub-lic journalism experiments at general election time. Pankhurst claimed a 'nightmare experience', when *The Press* failed in its main goal of putting party leaders in front of local voters, had convinced him not to attempt it again. In fact, public journalism-influenced general election coverage has now disappeared almost entirely from New Zealand, partly because it was too dependent on the enthusiasm of individual editors. As well as Pankhurst giving up, the *Manawatu Evening Standard*'s John Harvey had already moved on before the 1999 election and Venetia Sherson, who succeeded Tim Pankhurst at the *Waikato Times*, kept up some elements of the approach in 2002, but left the newspaper in 2003.

This outcome exposed the fragile foundations on which the experiments had been built. Pioneering editors who had driven the projects had not

really spread the word to their wider staff. Not only were the philosophical roots of public journalism under-explored—they were actively ignored.
INL training manager Warren Page latched onto individual techniques of
public journalism, but his assumption that even the term could alienate
journalists is indicative of the New Zealand media's aversion to academia
(see Phelan 2008). It is an antagonism that served public journalism badly
in this case.

LOCAL EXPANSION

By contrast, the limited practice model initiated by the first INL editors
has spread in local body election coverage, becoming institutionalized.
The *Waikato Times* had initiated New Zealand's first public journalism
trial in Hamilton's local elections in 1995. Then, when *Times* editor Tim
Pankhurst moved to *The Press* in Christchurch, he used its greater resources
and established the 'Your Voice, Your Vote' slogan to promote the importance of the 1998 local elections.

Pankhurst, disillusioned with public journalism for national elections, believes it is 'a very, very, effective process for local body elections'
(2003: pers. comm.). While there was no attempt to measure the impact
of the 1998 coverage, Pankhurst expressed some satisfaction that the
low turnout level was at least 'turned around as we poured our resources
into it'.

Polling readers to identify issues was a major investment and the guide
to coverage. With some expectation that rates (property taxes) and law
and order would be the major issues, Pankhurst was surprised by 1998
issues polling of the Christchurch public. 'They came back and told us
that winter smog and the associated open fire ban was far and away the
most pressing issue, then safety and crime, the economy, traffic, council spending, health planning, rates—well down—bus services and road
maintenance. So we took those 10 issues, we covered them in huge depth'
(2003: pers. comm.). This 'top ten' issue approach, which systematized
much coverage, taking it out of the reactive mode, became the model for
other newspapers in subsequent years.

Three years later, during the 2001 local body elections, with
Pankhurst now editing Wellington's *Evening Post*, three newspapers
used well-tested public journalism techniques—the *Evening Post*, *The
Press* and *Waikato Times*. An extensive content analysis by Venables
of the 2001 local body election coverage attempted to identify whether
newspapers professing to uphold public journalism ideals differed from
other newspapers. He studied the three newspapers that used public
journalism strategies plus three other metropolitan newspapers offering
more conventional journalism, Auckland's *New Zealand Herald*, Dune-
din's *Otago Daily Times* and *The Dominion*.

Venables coded every local body story from 1 August to 12 October, when postal voting closed. The 11 September terrorist attacks on US soil had a major affect on coverage, particularly at the *Dominion* and *New Zealand Herald,* which viewed themselves as national newspapers. Furthermore, about 100 of the *Herald*'s 120 journalists were on strike for half the campaign, reducing *Herald* coverage.

The findings—reported in full in Venables (2008)—showed a number of differences between the *Evening Post, Waikato Times* and *The Press* (where editors consciously used public journalism techniques or followed precedents set by the newspaper), and the *Dominion* and the *New Zealand Herald* (without such models). However, the independently owned *Otago Daily Times,* with its strong regional and local focus, was much nearer in practice to the 'public journalism newspapers', although its editorial staff believed they were merely practising good 'old fashioned journalism'.

Table 6.3   Aspects of 2001 Local Government Election Coverage

	Public journalism newspapers			Conventional newspapers		
	Evening Post	Waikato Times	The Press	Dominion	NZ Herald	Otago Daily Times
Total coverage: stories	368	158	269	73	100	270
Total coverage: cm²	94,191	45,825	69,376	22,102	45,306	56,598
Stories with mobilizing information	69	36	40	5	13	59
Stories discussing public priority issues	42	5	12	0	1	21
Stories with 'steps to solution' framing	12	0	10	1	3	11
Stories on how councillors have voted	23	0	1	0	9	1
Stories of councillors' views in own words	52	0	0	0	0	15
Stories with views of citizens	50	26	7	3	7	5
% of nonelite sources	11%	13%	13%	6%	4%	5%
% female sources	31%	13%	21%	27%	20%	24%

As Table 6.3 shows, the *Evening Post* was clearly most committed to 2001 election coverage in terms of the quantity of stories. *The Press* followed (with about three quarters the amount of coverage). The *Otago Daily Times* was well ahead of the public journalism-oriented *Waikato Times*. In terms of evidence of public journalism principles, we again see a patchy performance by newspapers espousing such ideals. The *Otago Daily Times* performed at least as well as two public journalism newspapers in providing mobilizing information and discussing issues based on public polling priorities. Also, the *Waikato Times* featured no 'steps to solution' framed coverage nor did it provide candidate information. Meanwhile, the *Otago Daily Times* scored well on 'steps to solution' stories and stories with space for councillor's own words, although editor Robin Charteris said the newspaper used the short biographies in the local authority booklet because it 'saved the newspaper trouble' (Charteris 2002: pers. comm.). The clearest difference between public journalism newspapers and conventional newspapers was in use of nonelite sources. However, all newspapers relied overwhelmingly on elite sources, particularly incumbent candidates. Furthermore, most nonelite sources were casually accessed vox pop-style sources rather than members of community organizations or lobby groups. In terms of gender, the *Evening Post* did relatively well, but the comparatively strong performance of the other Wellington daily indicates this may be related to the candidate mix in the city.

When Venables looked at the balance of his findings, the *Evening Post* stood out, offering more coverage and the best service to readers as citizens. However, it was also clear that the *Otago Daily Times*, with its heavy commitment to local, rather than national or international news, performed at least as well as the *Waikato Times* and *The Press*, despite the conscious attempt by these newspapers to follow what they regarded as public journalism practices.

Venables interviewed editors, chief reporters and local government reporters on all six newspapers finding that, while they all recognized a public duty to cover local government elections, the prominence given to election stories was still largely determined by standard news values. For instance, *Waikato Times* local government reporter Geoff Taylor said the election was moved to the front page by 'a hell of a big story' suggesting that the mayor misused his status to pursue a personal dispute over a marina in Auckland (Venables 2008: 121). This echoes Romano's (2001: 58) finding on a large Brisbane newspaper, where despite an extended public journalism project, participating journalists did not fully understand the public journalism philosophy and 'continued to run by the same routines that suit big-city newspaper production'.

Of all the newspapers, the *Post* placed the most election stories on the front page, but it was content to restrict many to front page 'teaser' status. While proud of his newspaper's effort, calling it 'the epitome' of public journalism, closely modelled on the *Charlotte Observer*, Pankhurst retrospectively described the amount of coverage as 'excessive'. As with the coverage he oversaw at *The Press* in 1998, he had instructed the *Evening Post* to give equal space to all mayoral candidates but believed that this resulted in equal space for 'loonies, the bewildered and the deranged'. The newspaper he said had, to some extent, abrogated its news sense and been unfair to serious contenders (Venables 2008: 142).

This misguided, mechanistic assumption that public journalism requires 'equal space' loses sight of an underpinning aim to reflect diverse opinions in order to allow readers to assess their merits (Romano 2001: 44). Dzur (2008: 160) argues that while public journalists create space for citizens, 'Professional skills are not abdicated in these open spaces, they are reoriented, redirected and critiqued'. The consequences of such mistaken abdication of journalistic judgement are reflected in comments from *The Press*, where editor Paul Thompson and deputy chief reporter Colin Espiner were clearly disillusioned with the value of public input. Thompson said public journalism as they practised it tended to become turgid, while Espiner believed their 'poll-and public-driven approach' during the 1998 local body elections had not really improved the quality of coverage: 'While it won us a journalism award at the time for an innovative approach, I don't think our readers learnt anything, because all they were getting back was what "Disgruntled of Aranui" thought' (Venables 2008: 150).

At the *Waikato Times*, however, editor Venetia Sherson, who had read extensively on public journalism, continued to champion the approach. Although voter turnout dropped during the 2001 elections, public journalism could help people reengage, she said. The *Waikato Times* had packed the halls in three public meetings: 'Barnstorming meetings they were— wonderful meetings' (Venables 2008: 148).

Sherson suggested that public journalism strategies might need rejuvenating. Among the interviewees she was a lone voice in recognizing that New Zealand newspapers had adopted particular aspects of public journalism, but had not really engaged with its philosophy or tried to make it work:

> One of the things which we don't have in New Zealand is that intellectual discussion of such subjects. If editors could get together and discuss public journalism and its benefits and its disadvantages and the way forward, I think we might come up with a good model. (Venables 2008: 149)

The response of public journalism newspapers to the results of their limited practice was thus not to explore further ways to engage voters and stimulate debate, but instead to maintain their restricted public journalism approaches while reducing coverage and trimming resources.

Sherson left the *Waikato Times* in 2003 and other changes in New Zealand's small media industry have continued to impact on public journalism practices. The *Evening Post* closed in mid 2002, folding into the *Dominion* to be recast as the *Dominion Post*. Inaugural *Dominion Post* editor Tim Pankhurst brought public journalism-style techniques across from the *Evening Post* to the new newspaper's coverage of the 2004 local elections. In 2004, the *Dominion Post* commissioned a survey of 1,050 voters, running a series of articles on the issues identified, with mayoral candidates from the region's five district and city councils invited to write a fifty-word piece on each issue.

To update data on local body election coverage, a limited overview of the 2007 elections was conducted, examining the more 'substantive' articles, editorials and visuals from the *New Zealand Herald, Dominion Post, The Press, Otago Daily Times, Waikato Times* and *Manawatu Standard* from 1 August to 12 October. This revealed both losses and gains from 2001. On the negative side, although comparisons to 2001 were difficult because not every local body story from 2007 was counted, there was a considerable drop in the number of stories as shown in Table 6.4.

Table 6.4   Aspects of 2007 Local Government Election Coverage

	The Press	*Waikato Times*	*Dominion Post*	*Manawatu Standard*	*New Zealand Herald*	*Otago Daily Times*
Articles	64	69	62	76	60	103
Polling	Mayor/ poll on selected issues	Mayor/ top ten issues	Mayor/ top ten issues	Mayor and 'straw' poll	Mayor/ poll on selected issues	Mayor only
Features on public issues	Limited to selected issues	In-depth coverage of top ten issues	In-depth coverage of top ten issues	Issues stories selected by newspaper	Issues stories, some poll-based, plus candidates	Candidate views and newspaper selected
Coverage of region	Widespread, not always consistent	Limited, but attempted	In regional editions	Limited, reflects small region	Widespread and consistent	Widespread, in-depth, and consistent
Hosting public meetings	Yes, fully reported	Yes, token reporting	No	No	No	Yes (6)
Editorials	5	3	5	3	5	6
Election pages/ logos	Yes	Yes	Yes	Yes	Yes	Yes

This reduction reflects shrinking local news content across all newspapers (except the *Otago Daily Times*) as it gives way to larger visuals, more syndicated articles and lifestyle supplements, and the creeping incursion of advertising. On the positive side, some public journalism-style techniques have spread, despite Venables' interviews showing scant knowledge of public journalism. The current approach to local election coverage by New Zealand's larger dailies has apparently spread by imitation.

However limited the techniques might be, the model has arguably rescued coverage of local body elections that suffered from both dwindling resourcing and switches in editorial direction (McGregor et al. 2002: 112). Compared with 2001, all newspapers in the sample made a concerted, planned and consistent attempt to cover local elections. Further, they made campaign coverage a feature, with regular full or near full pages distinguished by various election logos. Logos also drew attention to isolated articles on other pages. All newspapers conducted polls for city mayoral contests. Most attempted issue polls, with the *Dominion Post* and *Waikato Times* following through with a series of in-depth features. All newspapers also tried, with varying success, to cover their wider regions. All urged readers to vote, stressing the democratic importance of the elections, and ran election-focused editorials during the election campaign.

The *Otago Daily Times* led the pack with the amount of coverage, the geographical spread and the detail. For instance, it listed all regional nominations as they were received and published a seven-page lift-out covering key candidates and issues for each city and district council, where all candidates responded to two set questions. The *Dominion Post* and *Waikato Times* used similar techniques of issues polling and related features, while the *Waikato Times* and *The Press* hosted and promoted mayoral debates. Of all the newspapers the *Waikato Times* tried most assiduously to inject excitement with punchy headlines, a humorous 'campaign hound' column and plenty of exhortation to vote. A week before postal voting polls closed, this gave way to disillusionment: 'We were wrong' bemoaned an editorial calling the turnout 'a shocking figure' (*Waikato Times* 2007: 4). On 9 October, Warwick Rasmussen's article opened: 'Hamilton, you should be ashamed' (2007: 3).

Arguably, *New Zealand Herald* readers benefited the most. Compared with 2001, coverage no longer centred solely on Auckland's mayoral race, but was systematic across the region, regular, and often issues-focused. New Zealand's major newspapers have now found a way to do greater justice to coverage of local election politics. While this approach had its original inspiration in early US public journalism experiments, it has a tenuous connection to public journalism in its fuller sense. A similar assessment can be made of newspaper campaigns over the last decade.

DARK ENERGY: CAMPAIGNS, COMMUNITY AND COMMERCIALISM

Away from election time, the public journalism model is all but dormant apart from occasional outbreaks of campaign journalism. Some positive campaigns are little more than boosterism, like the *Wanganui Chronicle*'s 2002 attempt to build local pride with a series featuring locals saying why they loved the city. In a more 'solutions journalism' approach, the *Southland Times* has thrown itself behind an ongoing, successful city-wide campaign to promote local tourism and population growth (Venables 2008: 85).

Usually, though, campaigns tackle a local problem identified by newspapers. For example, both Wellington newspapers lobbied for safety improvements on a dangerous stretch of coastal highway over a number of years, and the *Dominion Post* continues this campaign. In 2005, the *Dominion Post*'s weekly series 'In the Neighbourhood' featured complaints about poor or dilatory council workmanship, with prominent pictures of potholed roads and dangerous footpaths and responses from relevant councils. Such local minutiae are at odds with standard *Dominion Post* news values and generally nationally focused coverage.

Such community-focused journalism is naturally not entirely selfless. While public journalism was a response to the excesses of market-driven journalism, the movement has always recognized the link between civic engagement and media prosperity; 'fewer people read newspapers when they are uninterested in public affairs' (Dzur 2008: 130). Former *Waikato Times* editor Venetia Sherson doubted their local election coverage helped sell more newspapers, but saw no conflict between public journalism and commercial goals (Venables 2008: 148–9). In the days of falling readership, becoming a community champion can be a branding initiative, or in the case of the now closed *Evening Post*, a point of difference from its competitor.

While Compton (2000: 460–1) argues that the 'goals of public journalism are presented *as if* they are compatible with the market. *That is the problem of public journalism*' [italics in original], the practice would not be sustainable or indeed fulfil the purpose of engaging the public if it caused readership losses. Campaign issues matching news values are attractive commercially.

One example was *The Press*'s 'Eye on Crime' series in June 2008, which followed a spate of stories about street crime and binge-drinking youngsters. Its weekend Mainlander feature section promised 'a week-long *Press* investigation into the city's crime'. In the three-page launch, the newspaper published a survey on people's opinions of crime and action needed. Police crime statistics were combined with material from nearly 400 members of *The Press*'s readership panel. During the week, the 'Eye on Crime' logo accompanied stories, such as Monday's front page, 'Carnage on city streets', and a series of in-depth features on youth crime, imprisonment, causes of crime, the legal system, the impact on victims and the court process. Articles were accompanied by a section for reader opinions. The following weekend, in a wrap-up, the Mainlander devoted two pages to solutions, talking to a number of experts. Here, though, *The Press* left the issue, not even picking it up during the national election campaign three months later. Such sporadic campaigning, regardless of its call for input, cannot really be termed public journalism, despite using techniques made popular by the civic journalism movement.

THE BIG CRUNCH

Friedland and Nichols (2002: 3–4) estimate that at least a fifth of American newspapers have practised public journalism. They also identified a pattern of development beginning with election coverage in 1988, moving onto large civic projects addressing specific issues and then to 'mapping communities to understand their diversity and integrating new technologies to expand community connection'. In comparison, New Zealand's public journalism experiment, despite its promising beginning, seems still-born.

This partly reflects the country's small size. The original experiments were nationally significant, but driven by just three editors in the country's tiny industry. Experiments relied on personal commitment and had no dedicated funding. When key editors moved on, zest waned and the practice died. The flip side to this reliance on personal enthusiasm is how one editor, Tim Pankhurst, transferred techniques as he took the helm in three major newspapers. At time of writing, Pankhurst was leaving the *Dominion Post* to head the Newspaper Publishers' Association. The newspaper's general manager said Pankhurst's legacy was 'strong journalism and deep community relationships' (*Dominion Post* 2009: A4). It seems likely that the newspaper's public journalism practices will further calcify as a result of the editorial change.

The fate of Kiwi-style public journalism also reflects the anti-intellectual bias of New Zealand journalism. Traditionally, few journalists analyze their craft, or read widely about journalism practice. Research on journalism training in New Zealand suggests that its emphasis on 'learning by doing' excludes both theory and the ability to think critically (Thomas 2009). This chapter makes clear that Kiwi practitioners had little understanding of public journalism's philosophical and theoretical foundations, and the intellectual climate did not encourage them to proselytize.

Regarding public journalism merely as a set of practices, rather than in Rosen's (1999: 23) words as 'an *adventure*, an open-ended and experimental quest for another kind of press', resulted in a defeatist approach. If public journalism had been viewed more clearly as part of a deliberative democracy model, experimenters might have been less swift to abandon the laboratory. The response of disappointed practitioners also indicates what Dzur (2008: 165–66) calls media naiveté and 'delusions of civic grandeur'. He argues: 'Public journalists underestimate how difficult it is to foster the rigorous and representative deliberation that would offer a clear view of community interests' (2008: 165).

Crucially, public journalism has never really had the blessing of management. In a climate of economic constraint, the high profile and ongoing costs of full-blown public journalism make the model both risky and financially unattractive. There is a gulf between pragmatic management goals and ideals of systematic public journalism practice. Moreover, despite gradual readership decline, the continuing strength and general lack of competition among New Zealand dailies means the 'community link' aspect of public journalism has little appeal. Paradoxically, growing understanding about the diversity of communities has led to more conservative, risk-averse coverage, rather than robust efforts of community engagement.

The future for public journalism in New Zealand looks bleak. However, the country has been left with a deeper and more systematic coverage of issues in local election coverage at all its major newspapers, an enduring legacy of the 1990's 'big bang' of experimentation.

BIBLIOGRAPHY

Compton, J. (2000) 'Communicative Politics and Public Journalism', *Journalism Studies,* 1(3): 449–67.

Dominion Post (2009) 'DomPost editor takes on new role', 26 February: A4.

Dzur, A.W. (2008) *Democratic Professionalism: Citizen Participation and the Reconstruction of Professional Ethics, Identity, and Practice,* University Park, PA: Pennsylvania University Press.

Edelstein, A.S., Ito, Y. and Kepplinger, H.M. (1989) *Communication and Culture: A Comparative Approach,* New York: Longman.

Friedland, L.A. and Nichols, S. (2002) *Measuring Civic Journalism's Progress: A Report Across a Decade of Activity.* Available at http://www.pewcenter.org/ doingcj/research/r_measuringcj.html (Accessed 1 September 2009).

Levine, P. (1996) *Public Journalism and Deliberation, Report from the Institute for Philosophy and Public Policy,* 16(1): 1–9.

McGregor, J., Comrie, M. and Campbell, J. (1998) 'Public journalism and proportional representation: The New Zealand experiment, *Australian Journalism Review,* 20(1): 1–22.

McGregor, J., Comrie, M. and Fountaine, S. (1999) 'Beyond the feel-good factor: Measuring public journalism in the 1996 New Zealand election campaign', *Harvard International Journal of Press and Politics,* 4(1): 66–77.

McGregor, J., O'Leary, E., Fountaine, S. and Comrie, M. (2002) 'Local government and news', in J. Drage (ed.) *Empowering Communities: Representation and Participation in New Zealand's Local Government,* Wellington, New Zealand: Victoria University Press.

Morrison, A. (1996) 'The challenge of MMP (Or will Journalism be caught with its pants down?)', in J. McGregor (ed.) *Dangerous Democracy? News Media Politics in New Zealand,* Palmerston North: Dunmore Press: 30–44.

Palmer, G. (1996) 'Towards a constitutional theory for the media in the MMP era', in J. McGregor (ed.) *Dangerous Democracy? News Media Politics in New Zealand*, Palmerston North, New Zealand: Dunmore Press, pp. 17–29.

Phelan, S. (2008) 'Democracy, the academic field and the (New Zealand) journalistic habitus', *Studies in Language & Capitalism*, 3(4): 161–80.

The Press (1999a) 'Power to the people', 21 September: 4.

The Press (1999b) 'Debating politics', 17 November: 8.

Rasmussen, W. (2007) 'City's voter turnout poorest of the country's main centres', *Waikato Times*, 9 October: 3.

Romano, A. (2001) 'Inculcating public journalism philosophies into newsroom culture', *Australian Journalism Review*, 24(2): 43–62.

Rosen, J. (1999) 'The action and the idea: Public journalism in built form', in T.L. Glasser (ed.) *The Idea of Public Journalism*, New York: Guilford Press, pp. 21–48.

Thomas, R. (2009) *The Making of a Journalist the New Zealand Way*, unpublished PhD thesis, AUT University, Auckland.

Venables, D. (2001) 'City Voice: A Community Newspaper Does Public Journalism', *Australian Journalism Review*, 23(2): 21–41.

Venables, D. (2008) *Making Politics Go Well Down Under: Public Journalism in New Zealand Daily Newspapers,* unpublished Master of Management thesis, Massey University, Wellington.

Waikato Times (2007) 'Apathy set to win the day', 6 October: 4.

7   Public Journalism in Japan
Experiments by a National Paper

Yohtaro Hamada

Public journalism was launched in Japan by *Asahi Shimbun*, the world's second largest newspaper (WAN 2005), with a circulation of 11.5 million copies daily of its morning and afternoon editions (Japan Audit Bureau of Circulation 2008). The newspaper established a *Kurashi* or 'Section for Civic Welfare' in April 2000, with a team of about forty reporters and editors who adopted the idea of public journalism and practised it on a daily basis. As a founding member of the *Kurashi*, I will analyze how public journalism was introduced into this huge national newspaper, the nature of the team's reporting, and the dilution of public journalism due to organizational changes within *Asahi*. From this, I will explore how Japanese journalists have adapted and interpreted an American concept, and future possibilities for public journalism in the country.[1]

INTRODUCTION OF PUBLIC JOURNALISM TO JAPAN

The first Japanese journalist to take a notable interest in public journalism was Shin-ichi Yoshida, when he was the *Asahi*'s Washington correspondent in 1994. While he was there, he wrote a series of stories about the relationship between American politics and the media, including one story about public journalism (Yoshida 1994: 25). When Yoshida returned to Japan to take a position as a political news editor, he launched the 'Focus on Shizuoka' project in an attempt to take the roots of the American public journalism concept and put them into practice (Yoshida 1995). Yoshida contended that Japanese political coverage focused on conveying and analyzing the messages from the politicians to the voters, but with Japan's political system facing fundamental change, the media needed to assume a new role to establish interactive relationships between politicians and voters. Yoshida indicated that Japan's problems paralleled those in the United States.

> There has been a growing criticism against media in the U.S. that political reporting relies too heavily on viewpoint of Washington insiders,

which has increased the level of distrust among citizens toward politics. In its efforts to answer this criticism, public journalists have been trying to observe and report politics and government from where ordinary citizens stand (Yoshida 1995).

Yoshida's project team of thirteen reporters tracked how politics was viewed by voters in Shizuoka, a prefecture considered to represent a 'typical' segment of Japanese life. The team conducted an opinion poll with 2,000 citizens, followed by six polls with 1,000 voters, and one-on-one interviews with 350 people to provide a deep understanding of their expectations and dissatisfactions with politics. The resulting stories won a Japan Newspaper Publishers and Editors' Association Award (*Nihon Shimbun Kyokai Shou*), Japan's equivalent of the Pulitzer Prize.

Just as public journalism arose as 'an American expression of a certain anxiety about the public mission of the press' (Rosen 2001), Japanese public journalism arose in the wake of similar expressions of concern. In 1999, *Asahi*'s then editor in chief, Akihiko Miura, wrote an essay in the newspaper's staff magazine arguing that Japan had lost its confidence as an economic power. He asserted that economic growth, the nationally agreed goal of postwar Japan, was no longer the driving value. People were preoccupied with security and safety, and this was expressed through public anxieties about what would happen with Japan's consumption (sales) tax, interest rates, the social security system, health insurance, and air and water quality (Miura 1999).

Miura claimed that reporters had not covered these issues to the satisfaction of readers. For example, reporters had written numerous stories about how political turmoil had distorted the social security system, but they failed to show the readers how the system could be improved. Miura advised that issues needed to be presented from the perspectives of ordinary citizens, not politicians and bureaucrats. He also warned that the consequence of journalists submerging themselves in the midst of bureaucracy and political punditry was that they thought like bureaucrats and politicians, resulting in a growing distance between reporters and readers.

Miura's philosophy took shape later that year in the form of a fifteen-member team called *Kurashi No Ashita* (Our Life Tomorrow) to report on the government's introduction of a new pension scheme and nursing care insurance. Both policies were aimed at meeting the challenges of an aging society and could have tremendous impact on people's sense of security and safety. A key element of the two-page section that the team produced each week were stories that were garnered by soliciting questions from readers based on their experiences of the health care, long-term care and social security systems. Reporters would invite the person who had sent the most intriguing question to help them interview public officials or other figures who might be able to answer the question or resolve the issue. The readers often asked insightful questions based on their personal experience, and this reader-tag-along model of reporting became the basis of *Kurashi* journalism.

After ten months of this endeavour, Miura more than doubled the number of *Kurashi* reporters and editors, and appointed Yoshida to head the team. Yoshida announced at the outset that the team would embrace public journalism. Along with covering the activities of major institutions such as the Ministry of Health, Labor and Welfare, the Social Security Agency, and the Ministry of Environment, the team was responsible for producing a front-page feature story for each Sunday paper plus a full-page *Kurashi* (*Life*) section four days each week on themes like environment and safety, the job and pension plan, and health care.

DOING JOURNALISM DIFFERENTLY

A resolve among journalists to listen to the voices of citizens was (and arguably still is) quite revolutionary in Japan, where information and facts from the government bureaucracy dominate the news. Journalists' focus on government arises because of the presumed role of the government, especially the central bureaucracies, in bringing about Japan's twentieth-century modernization and so-called 'economic miracles' in the wake of World War II. Paradoxically, the image of the bureaucracy as the source of all wisdom has resulted in a disconnection between the government and people, who expect that the responsibility for solving every public problem rests solely on bureaucrats' shoulders. Reporters are spoon-fed 'the news' by officials, but are also are eager to devour news of any mistakes or malfunctions of policies, without looking at citizen's responsibilities. A framework in which people are victims of government failures is discernible in many news stories. There is no space for citizens' involvement in setting the news agenda or taking accountability for society's problems. The *Kurashi* team's efforts to connect with readers opened a new frontier of issues that we had not previously noticed. 'We hit the treasure island,' some members said.

In response to these initiatives, the *Kurashi* received up to 1,000 communications via letters, emails and text messages each month. One staff member was hired to work full time on compiling a database of the input and writing a one-page newsletter that provided reporters with a daily summary about new letters and trends in the content.

Journalists actively solicited such input by devoting about one-third of the *Kurashi* pages to the 'Want to Say, Want to Hear' column, which usually invited questions from readers or attempted to facilitate discussions among readers about complex topics, such as workplace discrimination against women or the treatment of chronic illness. The section served as an antenna that 'picks up' issues on people's minds and deliberately lowered the bar for readers who wanted to contact the paper, but who would not normally write a traditional letter to the editor.

Kurashi reporters developed a number of strategies of listening to what their readers say and building stories from there. The rest of this section will present examples of different strategies that *Kurashi* reporters used to solicit content, develop story ideas, dig deep in search of answers to community queries and use the information so that people's voices can make a difference.

At the simplest level, the letters and comments allowed journalists to discover new issues. For example, *Asahi* journalists had little idea of the high public dissatisfaction with medical professionals until more than 2,000 comments flooded the newsroom after the *Kurashi* team ran a story on doctors who ill-treat patients. The team interviewed people who sent in comments and ran a series called 'Distrust of Doctors', which prompted responses from doctors and nurses. The conversation on this theme continued for many weeks.

Sometimes *Kurashi* journalists identified an issue and then sought comments from the key stakeholders to establish a 'public space' in which they helped set the agenda. For example, one *Kurashi* journalist, Keiko Ihara, sought stories from about fifty college students to help provide ideas for a series of stories about the highly competitive, stressful and lengthy job-hunting process that most college graduates face. Ihara wrote a long-running, popular column describing the often outrageous and even comical strategies that major companies would use in selecting recruits from large pools of eager candidates. Previously, reporters who wrote stories about the job market for soon-to-graduate college students would write stories based on comments from experts in the Ministry of Labour or college employment advisors. A legacy of Ihara's efforts is that today reporters feel obliged to speak with students themselves.

Other stories aimed to help citizens identify ways that they could participate in problem solving. This sometimes occurred at simple levels. One example was a story about a container filled with earthworms who consume leftover food, thereby creating natural fertiliser and reducing the amount of garbage and carbon dioxide emitted from household wastes (Ito 2000: 21). When the reporter, Keiko Ito, proposed this story, the reception was lukewarm. Other journalists considered it simply as a new product announcement with little news value. However, when the newspaper ran the story, more than 100 people immediately responded with enthusiasm. One letter writer thanked the reporter, saying: 'I have felt guilty about disposing a lot of garbage, but didn't know what to do with it. I would love to use this "worm" container.' The story struck a chord with many readers because typical environmental stories painted pictures of crisis or failures in government's policies for dealing with environmental problems, but this one provided readers with an entry point for problem solving.

Much of *Kurashi*'s work involved 'breaking the mould' of stories about the government and bureaucrat's agendas and perspectives. For example, stories about tax usually cover the angles promoted by the Ministry of Finance and National Tax Agency, such as revisions to tax policies or major cases of tax evasion. Instead, prior to the deadline for filing tax returns, the *Kurashi* team reported on the rising number of people claiming tax refunds. (Most Japanese are not obliged to lodge an income tax return.) The stories provoked reader feedback that led to further stories about problems and issues in the tax system and the fairness of changes to tax codes.

Some of the *Kurashi*'s stories acted as a channel enabling citizens to achieve change in government policies or actions. One example was a story that I wrote about how social security benefits might be greatly reduced for some recipients due to a seemingly minute procedural omission. Nearly 200 people wrote to tell me that they had experienced similar problems. Some readers said that regional government offices had helped them by bending the rules about social security benefits, and I was able to write a series of stories about the unequal treatment of people affected by the problem. The stories prompted two legislators in the Diet to ask questions in committee hearings, which eventually forced the Ministry of Health, Labor and Welfare to promise to rectify the problem. This seven-month campaign would never have been possible without consistent support from readers who kept feeding us new information that helped to substantiate my stories, which argued that government mismanagement was at the root of the problem.

EXPLORING JAPAN'S CHALLENGES

The *Kurashi* reporters also tried to step back from how problems affect people at an individual level to look at issues through a macro lens. Financing the cost of the rapidly aging population had already emerged as the most serious challenge for Japan in the twenty-first century. With this in mind, I worked with a colleague, Satomi Sugihara, to conduct a project on this intergenerational issue with the goal of allowing high school students speak out. We identified high school students as the biggest stakeholders because the population changes mean that in a few decades time there will be fewer workers paying the taxes and premiums needed to support a larger aging community. Those school children will be working adults, probably with families to rear, in 2025. According to government estimates for 2025, the social-security-related tax burden they will face will be nearly three times heavier than what their parents bore.

The four-part 'High School Students Reporting' series was written by students themselves with assistance from professional reporters.[2] It presented their perspective of what Japan's rapidly aging society would look like and how the increasing cost of sustaining an aging population would affect the workers in 2025. The newspaper had previously published numerous stories about the social security 'crisis' and grim forecasts of future fiscal deficits. These stories, written from policymakers' perspectives, rarely resonated with readers because they failed to show how average citizens could be affected by or respond to these large national problems whose ramifications will be spread across many generations. As in any society, people in Japan strongly oppose both raising tax and reducing benefits. There is a strong tendency to procrastinate instead of initiating reforms of social security and entitlement programs. However, could voters maintain these attitudes if they knew doing so would jeopardize the future of their children?

This series carried a label of NIE (Newspaper in Education) because funding came through the program. However, we intended to stand out from the conventional NIE stories in Japan, which are often 'dumbed down' versions of normal news articles. To do this, we ran the project in four phases.

The first phase involved identifying two schools, located in medium-sized cities in the prefectures of Hokkaido (in Japan's northern tip) and Shiga (near Kyoto and Osaka), where students had often won high school newspaper competitions. Since both were public schools, we expected to see students with various family backgrounds.

The second phase involved the ten participating students conducting interviews with their own family members, friends and relatives on this issue. One student talked to her mother who had been looking after her frail grandmother and learned how the recently introduced government-run nursing (long-term) care insurance really works. A friend of one participant lived in an apartment which houses both high school students and elderly folks who need somebody to help them eat and go to the bathroom. They also visited a nursing home and learned about the long waiting lists. While sharing lunch with the elderly residents, the students saw what the entitlement program means to the lives of older generations. Among a wide range of other interviews, the students talked with college students about the social security system and were appalled to find out that most young adults believed the social security system would go bankrupt soon. *Asahi Shimbun* also provided the students with literature about social security and nursing care, to help them put their experience in context and to deliberate on the problems they identified.

In the third phase, *Asahi Shimbun* paid for students to visit Kasumigaseki, Tokyo, where the central offices of national ministries are located. *Kurashi* reporters used their newspaper's connections and influence so that students could meet high-ranking officials in the Ministry of Health, Labor and Welfare and Ministry of Finance, and a university professor who is renowned for his study on the impact of aging populations. Armed with the first-hand experience from their communities, the students asked sharp questions and developed an understanding of the complexity of the problem. They observed the many gaps between what the government advertised and the realities, and the competing interests that needed to be balanced.

The last and possibly most daunting part was organizing the masses of information into coherent stories. The *Kurashi* team coached the students with a few ideas based on the information the students had, but did not want to push their own ideas onto students. They wanted fresh insights to flow from minds that were untainted by newsroom conventions.

While the students were in the process of interviewing people both in their own communities and in Tokyo, we asked them to take detailed notes, type them up with their own reflections attached and come up with the new or unanswered questions. It was very important that they would freely jot down their honest reflections in their own words, because this would allow us to grasp the deliberative process that the students were going through. Anything that had bothered the students could become the focus of the story. We tried to find the tips among those reflections and encourage the students to develop them. The coaches and students threw ideas back and forth via email. Then the reporters and the students spent a weekend together, discussing, writing and editing the stories.

The students developed a range of stories that put forward a variety of perspectives, potential solutions, and pros and cons to each solution. The series stimulated a strong response from readers. Tsutomu Hotta (2001), a famous former prosecutor and now a head of a nonprofit organization, praised the series as 'outstanding' work that 'showed that high school students are capable of pointing out real issues and also proposing serious solutions to the problems.' The Ministry of Health, Labor and Welfare organized a symposium in a hometown of one of the high schools involved and invited the student reporters to be speakers in the panel discussion.

DEFINING PUBLIC JOURNALISM IN JAPAN

In adopting public journalism-style philosophies and practices, Japanese journalists need to consider a number of issues. The first is how to define what they are doing and explain it to their newsroom colleagues.

In the United States, public journalism has become an ambivalent term. *American Journalism Review*'s senior editor Carl Session Stepp notes that when he raises the issue of public journalism in his country 'editors and reporters typically say they don't understand it or dismiss it outright—even at papers, like the [Orange County] Register, where civic-journalism-like projects flourish' (Stepp 2000: 28). Day after day in his visits to newsrooms, Stepp 'saw the footprints of public journalism', but journalists would not call it that or admit to engaging in it (Stepp 2000: 24). Robert Steel, Senior Faculty and Ethics Group Leader at the Poynter Institute, attributes this disaffection with the term 'public journalism' to the background of the philosophy's two founders, Buzz Merritt and Jay Rosen. Neither worked for the largest, most prestigious American media organizations. 'Merritt was an editor of a fairly small newspaper in the Midwest. Jay Rosen was viewed as an academic from the Ivory Tower by many working journalists,' Steel says (2002: pers. comm.).

This was not a problem in Japan, where the organization that first embraced public journalism, *Asahi Shimbun*, is one of the influential 'Big Four' establishment newspapers. It is 'generally considered the paper of record, widely read by almost all political elites' (Krauss and Lambert 2002: 60). Within the newspaper itself, a leading proponent and adopter of the idea, Shin-ichi Yoshida, commands respect from his colleagues and is a rare two-time winner of the Japan Newspaper Publishers and Editors Association Award. Yoshida depicts *Kurashi* reporting as 'actively using the tools of public journalism', which he describes as being 'perfect for reporting from a perspective of people who live everyday lives' (Yoshida 2001: 31).

By 1999, other Japanese news organizations had established new teams similar to *Kurashi*. *Yomiuri Shimbun*, Japan's largest newspaper, set up the Social Security (Safety Net) Department. *Mainichi Shimbun*, Japan's third largest paper, started the 'Where Life Goes' team. *Kyodo News Agency* established a 'Design of Life' team. This indicates heightened interest within the mainstream news media about reporting on civic life.

Yoshida's interpretation and practice of pubic journalism may potentially define and even limit how Japanese journalists perceive the idea. Yoshida promotes a form of reporting that may be called interactive journalism. It generally involves the newspaper printing a small story about the experiences of a few readers and invites other readers to share their stories on the subject, with the responses being used for new stories. The process is repeated, creating a snowball effect of increasing reader responses that help reporters to identify the nature, layers and depth of the problem. Finally, journalists connect what initially looked like isolated episodes to expose a bigger story, such as a master narrative that reveals subtle but important shifts in our society or fundamental flaws of systems that are supposed to protect our lives. These stories sometime run as a front-page scoop.

Yoshida arguably restricts his interpretation and explanation of public journalism to terms of 'public listening'. However, in the United States public journalism has extended beyond simply listening and into the realms of convening citizens and facilitating democracy. Chris Conte notes that: 'If public journalism were simply about paying more attention to citizens, it probably wouldn't have stirred much controversy. But it goes further. Public journalists believe they have a responsibility to make sure, as Davis 'Buzz' Merritt puts it, that "public life goes well"' (Conte 1996: 824). Merritt furthermore notes that public journalism involves a mental shift, moving from a position of 'detachment to being a fair-minded participant in public life' (Merritt 1998: 139). Rosen adds that the aim of public journalism is 'not just to do good journalism but to improve democracy *with* journalism' (Rosen 1999: 178).

Japan's newspapers often sponsor events that 'convene' public life, such as special exhibits of art and craft and seminars on health care. However, these are not planned and conducted by journalists but by employees in a separate division from the newsroom. Even the *Kurashi* team has never physically convened people to deliberate, in the way that American public journalists sometime have. Instead, the *Kurashi* created a forum for citizens to discuss issues within news stories. It built a culture of facilitating citizen conversations by listening carefully to their voices, encouraging them to share their experiences, enriching the conversation by timely input of expert voices and information, and giving them a sense of power when their experiences compel the lawmakers and the government to take actions.

While the *Kurashi* existed, Japanese public journalism had been integrated into a distinctive 'news beat', in contrast to the United States, where public journalism commonly involves large-scale, high-profile projects that run for certain period of time. A project setting has been useful for American reporters, because it allows them to break out of the routines, deadlines and writing formulas associated with beat reporting and provides them with breathing room to think and experiment with new ideas, topics and approaches to journalism. This 'insulation' also limits dissemination and penetration of the idea in a newsroom. Richard Harwood (1991, 1993) has reflected that: 'Most papers got stuck in the project mode. Projects have beginning, middle and end. They really don't affect journalism per se if you don't convert them into new sensibilities and new practices that run throughout the newspaper. If not, they don't have a long term effect' (2002: pers. comm.).

In Japan, the *Kurashi* was formed as a permanent team whose primary purpose was to practise journalism every day, and as not a temporary patchwork group that only existed for the duration of its project. Given the rigidity of the *Asahi*'s organizational structure, this was a significant change. The newspaper was (and still is) dominated by three departments in terms of public affairs reporting: the political news, economic news and city news departments. The last time a team with a unique daily beat was established in the *Asahi* was in 1960.

Yoshida intended to overturn newsroom conventions and change how the newspaper reported news. To Yoshida, the *Asahi*'s compartmentalization into departments with their own coverage areas or beats led to reporting which failed to draw coherent pictures of the issues that impact on people's everyday lives. One of Yoshida's favourite examples was the compartmentalization of reporting on health care and social security. If two reporters who belong to different departments cover health insurance and medical care separately, and are not talking to each other, how can they possibly produce a complete picture of the health care system? To avoid this kind of fragmentation in the news, Yoshida set a goal for *Kurashi* reporters to communicate with each other so that as a team they could synthesize their expertise and produce stories that have what he called 'a new totality'.

Despite this vision, the *Kurashi* faced many challenges within the newsroom. Editorial decision makers outside the *Kurashi* often chopped the team's stories to fit among stories about breaking news events that were more sensational and attention grabbing or that *had to run* on that day if they were to have currency. *Kurashi* stories sometimes became so short that they shed off critical details needed to convey the richness of people's experience.

CHALLENGES IN JAPANESE PUBLIC JOURNALISM

Major changes occurred in 2004, when the *Kurashi* merged with the *Kateimen* (Family Affairs) section to become a new section, called *Seikatsu*. In 2006, teams of reporters who were assigned to focus on labour and health care issues have been separated and become the fourteen-member *Roudou* (Labour) Group and twenty-two-member *Iryo* (Healthcare) Group. As of 2009, these two groups, although directed by different editors, are still allied closely with the *Seikatsu*. The thirty-nine *Seikatsu* reporters and editors continue to cover topics such as the social safety net (pensions, long-term care insurance, etc.), the environment and consumer issues while writing more articles about practical lifestyle issues, such as cooking, pets, gardening and childcare.

This kind of organizational change often takes place in *the Asahi*'s newsroom at the change of leadership and it is usually explained as an attempt to strengthen the newsroom's capacity. In this particular case, the change was top-down and many of the front-line reporters in *Kurashi* never clearly understood its intent, which disappointed and discouraged some of its original members.

When the *Kurashi* was first organized, Yoshida gave it a second name in English, 'Section for Civic Welfare'. By contrast, the *Seikatsu*'s English name is the 'Life Style and Social Security News Section'. Both *Seikatsu* and *Kurashi*, if translated literally in general Japanese terms, mean 'life'. However, disappearance of 'civic' in the English name may reflect changes that have occurred since most of the *Kurashi*'s founding members have been moved back to their original departments. Succeeding editors do not have such a firm grasp of public journalism as Yoshida. Although the enthusiasm for public journalism-style activities has faded, *Seikatsu* reporters do use tools that were developed by the *Kurashi* and clearly make more efforts to connect with readers than journalists in political news or economic news departments, whose sources are usually those in power.

It is too early to judge how deep-seated are the changes that five years of *Kurashi* experiment in Asahi brought to its newsroom culture. To some, including myself, the change seems to be too small and too slow to come.

Yoshida has become a top editor in 2009 and is in charge of restructuring and reorganizing a nationwide network of reporters in *Asahi*. What he has learned from the *Kurashi* project may prove useful. However, the newspaper business in Japan—as in many other countries—is rapidly losing its readership and advertising revenue, so those seeking to change the industry will need to race against time.

NURTURING PUBLIC JOURNALISM

Public journalism is, in part, a critique of conventional journalism. One of its basic tenets is that journalism is in trouble. However, public journalism still develops from conventional journalism and operates beside it. Speaking from the American perspective, Chris Peck, former editor of the *Spokesman-Review* (Washington), observes that:

> Tools of public journalism never replace investigative reporting, beat reporting, issue reporting. It is a tool. You don't throw away the rest. It is a tremendous way to get information from the public. It forces you to listen. It opens you up to the whole range of people you have never dealt with (2000: pers. comm.).

By the same token, talking to citizens does not occur naturally to *Asahi* reporters. In May 2002, it ran a story that reflected on why the change of government in 1993 did not materialize in a 'Citizens' Revolution' (*Asahi Shimbun* 2002: 6). The story quoted only three people directly: a former finance minister, a former official of Ministry of International Trade and Industry (MITI), and a former minister of health and welfare. There was a brief comment ('isn't it necessary to change politics?') from one college student who attended a lecture by the former finance minister. Here, politics is portrayed as an arena where 'insiders' perform. A citizen has no role to play.

Furthermore, journalists who hold a narrow definition that successful journalism involves 'being first' or having a scoop or *tokudane* (exclusive story) are likely to be suspicious of public journalism because it contests their notions of 'success'. In conventional Japanese journalism, a scoop usually originates from official government sources whose status and jurisdiction provides the story with its significance and newsworthiness. This gives reporters more incentive to cultivate ties with officials in order to be better able to gain critical information from bureaucracies at critical times. For conventional journalists, the story is considered more worthy if competitors pick up the idea and follow up with further stories on the topic. This peer review is regarded as a seal of approval on the story.

Pack mentality is exacerbated by the *Kisha Kurabu* or 'Press Club' system in Japan. Almost every national or local government office, political party, quasi-official and industry organization has its own 'club' for reporters to use as a working room. This generates intense conformity among journalists, who largely act as conduits by which bureaucracies disseminate information. Since many reporters spend most of their time in these 'clubs', it is inevitable that they start to think like bureaucrats and assume the truthfulness of bureaucratically supplied information. The club culture is so ingrained that foreign journalists often deride the Japanese press for being spoon-fed their news by bureaucrats (Foreign Press Center 1994: 31).

Given these factors, the challenge exists in how to make the mental leap towards looking at citizens as legitimate, authoritative sources of news and public life. Yoshida calls this 'democratising our perspective'. The problem of how to make this leap is not unique to Japan. When Jeremy Iggers of America's *Star Tribune* introduced a public journalism project to his staff, the typical response in the newsroom was: 'The public is ignorant. They would express uninformed opinions. Why send a reporter for that? It's a waste of time' (2002: pers. comm.).

Prior to the melding of the *Kurashi* into the *Seikatsu*, Yoshida joked that he had designed his team to 'infect' the *Asahi*'s reporters with '*Kurashi* bacteria'. To spread the understanding of public journalism, reporters were rotated between the *Kurashi* and other newsroom departments every few years. The team's reporters experimented with new ideas, and bring these insights and skills back to their old nests. However, since the *Asahi*'s reorganization in 2004, rotations of journalists between the *Seikatsu* and other news departments have been less frequent.

DEVELOPING A JAPANESE MODEL OF PUBLIC JOURNALISM

The journey to developing public journalism starts with public frustration at the way the press portrays political and public life. San-Jyun Kan from Tokyo University noted the problem after Koichi Kato, a young star of the Liberal Democratic Party at the time, attempted a coup against unpopular Prime Minister Yoshiro Mori, then backed off at the last moment. 'Many people should have felt apathetic to see this slapstick comedy of politics,' Kan said. 'Reporters framed it simply as a "split of sworn friends" or "fateful collision"' (Kan 2000: 10). Here politics is portrayed only as a human drama about entangled relationships among politicians. 'The price of this over-dramatization would be deep distrust of politics and a sense of hopelessness among voters. It could well lead from collapse of one political party to collapse of entire politics,' he warned. Kan's call for journalists to rethink their reporting style, methods and perspectives was reflected in readers' letters to *Asahi*'s editor. Some of these argued that rather than bashing Kato for flinching, it would be more important to appreciate his courage to stand up, and encourage politicians in general to explain their positions on real issues.

Conventional Japanese journalism defines news as something extraordinary, different, or a deviation from normal state of things. The news media will always compete for this kind of story. But Yoshida argues that Japan's news media needs to establish a new field in which journalists will compete to help readers to envision what kind of society we should create in the future. This would broaden the meaning of politics beyond something that is just a struggle for power and the domain of politicians only. It would reflect Harry Boyte and Nancy Kari's understanding of politics as including the everyday processes of deliberating, negotiating and making decisions (e.g., Boyte and Kari 1996)—a process in which all Japanese citizens can play a role.

US journalists have developed a number of ways of understanding public journalism, but the vocabularies that they use to describe their purpose and activities are distinctively American. Words associated with public journalism, such as public, citizen, community and deliberation, do not convey the same nuances nor carry the same meaning when they are translated into Japanese. Japanese supporters of public journalism face the challenge of harmonizing the concept with the local conditions and cultures. As Rosen notes, 'every nation engaged in this subject has to do so in their own ways' (2001: pers. comm.).

NOTES

1. The views expressed in this chapter are strictly those of the author and do not necessarily reflect those of *Asahi Shimbun*.
2. The stories were written by eight students from Hikone Higashi High School and Obihiro Hakuyo High School, and edited by Yohtaro Hamada and Satomi Sugihara. They appeared under the title 'Koukousei Ga Syuzai Shita' in the *Asahi Shimbun*'s *Kurashi* Section on 14, 15, 16 and 20 August 2001. Hamada and Sugihara also wrote one column in this series.

BIBLIOGRAPHY

Asahi Shimbun (2002) 'Datsu sengo system no zasetsu', 19 May: 6.

Boyte, H.C. and Kari, N.N. (1996) *Building America: The Democratic Promise of Public Work*, Philadelphia, PA: Temple University Press.

Conte, C. (1996) 'Civic Journalism: Can press reforms revitalize democracy?' *CQ Researcher*, 20 September: 817–40.

Krauss, E. and Lambert, P. (2002) 'The Press and Reform in Japan', *Harvard International Journal of Press/Politics*, 7(1): 57–78.

Foreign Press Center (1994) *Japan's Mass Media*. 'About Japan', Series 7, Tokyo: Foreign Press Center.

Harwood, R. (1991) *Citizens and Politics: A View from Main Street America*, Dayton, OH: Kettering Foundation.

Harwood, R. (1993) *Meaningful Chaos: How People Form Relationships with Public Concerns*, Dayton, OH: Kettering Foundation.

Hotta, T. (2001) 'Wakamono Ni Oshierareta Nenkin Kaikaku', *Asahi Shimbun*, 8 September: 15.

Ito, K. (2000) 'Mimizu ga musha musha, Namagomi ga tsuchi ni natta', *Asahi Shimbun*, 24 April: 21.

Japan Audit Bureau of Circulation (ABC) (2008) Available at http://www.asahi.com/shimbun/honsya/j/sales.html (Accessed 1 September 2009).

Kan, S.-J. (2000) 'Seiji no drama zitate saikou wo', *Asahi Shimbun*, 24 November: 10.

Merritt, D. (1998) *Public Journalism and Pubic Life*, 2nd edn, Mahwah, NJ: Lawrence Erlbaum Associates.

Miura, A. (1999) 'Kouzou kaikakuki shimbun no deban' (The era of restructuring: It's time for the newspaper to step forward), *Enpitsu*, January: 2–5.

Rosen, J. (1999) *What Are Journalists For*, New Haven, CT: Yale University Press.

Rosen, J. (2001) 'Public Journalism and the Anxiety of the American Press', Public address to journalists in Zwolle, The Netherlands, 7 June.

Stepp, C.S. (2000) 'Reader friendly', *American Journalism Review*, July–August: 23–35.

Yoshida, S. (1994) 'Zyumin Mitsuchaku', *Asahi Shimbun*, final edition, 4 August: 25.

Yoshida, S. (1995) Application letter to the chairman of Nihon Shimbun Kyokai for an editorial division award, 13 July.

Yoshida, S. (2001) 'Souhoukou journalism de houdou no shin-chouryu wo tsu-kuru' (Creating a new trend through interactive journalism—A year of *Kurashi* reporting), *Shimbun Kenkyu*, May (598): 28–31.

World Association of Newspapers (WAN) (2005) 'World's 100 Largest Newspapers'. Available at http://www.wan-press.org/article2825.html (accessed 1 September 2009).

8 Civic and Citizen Journalism in Germany

Klaus Forster

This chapter represents the continuation of a research project that was inspired in part by a question that Robert L. Stevenson asked in the late 1990s when he was a guest professor at the University of Munich. Stevenson asked whether public or civic journalism was 'a bad idea', 'a good idea that doesn't work', or 'an innovation that might work in the United States but not in Germany.' These overarching research questions were difficult to solve both theoretically and empirically because the 'idea of public journalism'—to borrow Glasser's term (1999)—was almost unknown in Germany in those days.

More than ten years after I began this research, civic journalism is still an obscure concept to most German journalists as well as to scholars of journalism and mass communication. In this chapter, possible reasons for this long-time disregard of civic journalism in Germany are discussed and German perspectives on citizen-oriented news coverage are outlined. In the closing chapter of the research report (Forster 2006: 382) it was presumed tacitly that civic journalism might finally come to Germany through the back door of what Dan Gillmor calls 'journalism by the people, for the people' (Gillmor 2006). Indeed the citizen journalism hype hit Germany exactly that year. Following Witt's (2004) assumption that public journalism would transform into citizen journalism, I have tried to answer the question of how civic the citizen journalism that is practised in Germany really is.

THE 'FAILURE' OF CIVIC JOURNALISM IN GERMANY

Civic journalism has never been a serious topic in academic or professional debates about 'where journalism should be going'. Accordingly, it could not establish 'a set of practices' for better reporting 'that have been tried in real life settings' and it did definitely not turn into 'a movement of people and institutions concerned about the possibilities for reform' in journalism (Rosen 1995: v). This nearly complete disregard of an influential—though minority—perspective on how to improve news coverage and build citizen engagement in politics seems a little odd for a country with a press system that was reintroduced, shaped, and largely influenced by the American occupation authorities after World War II, particularly during the period of compulsory press licensing from 1945 to 1949 (Humphreys 1994: 24–38). With this historical background one might have assumed that civic journalism should have become an issue in Germany in the same way as is it has in other nations with presumably less American influence on their press systems—like Northern European countries such as Finland, Sweden or Denmark (Haas 2007: 122, 127–135) or Latin American countries such as Mexico (Hughes 2006).

There are several possible reasons for the nonproliferation of the idea of civic-minded news coverage in Germany. A first plausible reason for the failure of civic journalism might be its economical ineffectiveness. Both proponents and critics of civic journalism have often pointed out that this reform of news making has been conceived—not primarily but to a certain extent—to reverse the long-time downturn trend of newspaper circulation in the United States (e.g. Rosen 1996; Frank 2001). From this perspective, civic journalism could be seen as an outright failure, perhaps illustrated best through the fact that the second largest US newspaper chain, Knight Ridder, which was most engaged in the distribution and application of the concept of a civic-minded news coverage from the beginning (e.g. Merritt 1998), ceased to exist in 2006 because of 'pressure from shareholders who were unhappy with performance of its stock' (Seelye and Sorkin 2006). So there was simply no reason for German news organizations to adopt a costly reform concept when there was no proof that it might work for them. But this explanation has to be based on the assumption that German publishers and editors have been at least aware of the existence of civic journalism, which is quite doubtful.

There are other more likely causes why civic-minded news coverage has not caught on in Germany. Civic journalism has been a joint project of professional journalists and scholars in the wider field of communication studies, political science, and political philosophy from its very beginning. Such an extensive collaboration between academic theory and journalistic practice was and still is hardly conceivable in Germany, mainly because of a traditional deep rooted and quite strict distinction between the academic and the practical education of German journalists, where the former is done in the universities and the latter in internships and (nonacademic) journalism schools (Weischenberg, Malik and Scholl 2006: 65–9).

Although there is certain common ground between the civic journalism debate and academic and professional debates about topics such as news quality in Germany (Arnold 2008: 501), a concept like civic journalism was likely to be regarded as theoretically underdeveloped and therefore unattractive for German scholars (e.g. Lünenborg 2005: 152). Vice versa, for the professional journalists in Germany, civic journalism could have been easily seen as too academic to play any useful role in everyday news reporting or the training of it. While civic journalism has been integrated at least partially in some journalism textbooks and the curricula of US journalism training programs, although 'not widely or deeply' (Rauch, Trager and Kim 2003: 175), civic journalism made it neither into the German journalism classrooms nor into the practical training in any significant proportions. A few German textbooks mention civic journalism but not in much depth (e.g. Kunczik and Zipfel 2001: 163–4).

Another reason for the still widespread disregard of civic journalism in Germany, especially in the academic field, may be due to the gaining popularity of system-theoretical perspectives in the tradition of Luhmann (e.g. 1996) on political communication in general and on journalism studies in particular. This corresponds with a reduced influence of normative approaches, namely that of Habermas (e.g. 1997a; 1997b; 1999), which has strongly guided American founders and proponents of civic journalism. While Habermas himself never explicitly referred to civic or public journalism, even where it would have been highly appropriate (e.g. Habermas 2006), his considerable influence on the intellectual grounding and the conception of civic journalism becomes obvious in the various references to his works in the literature on civic journalism (e.g. Rosen 1999: 75; Glasser 1999: 14; Christians 1999: 68). Habermas has even been dubbed public journalism's 'philosophical patron saint' (Lambeth 1998: 21) and one of its 'intellectual heroes' (Meyer 1998: 257). The strong reluctance to even take notice of the concept of a citizen-oriented approach to political news coverage might therefore originate in part from the growing importance of system theory in German journalism and communication studies (e.g. Scholl and Weischenberg 1998: 47–51).

Admittedly, Scholl (2007: 461) observes that systemic conceptions of journalism, politics and mass communication do not necessarily preclude analysis and research of a citizen-oriented news coverage—and this area could even benefit highly from these perspectives. Nevertheless, it still can be assumed that the different theoretical positions adopted by American advocates of civic journalism compared to a growing number of scholars in German journalism research could at least have been contributing to the failure of civic journalism to be of any significant influence on the academic debate or the press itself in Germany. Accordingly, Habermas' views on the public sphere, communicative action and deliberative democracy are discussed extensively in the United States but not in Germany. Despite being an honoured and respected philosopher and commentator on contemporary politics, Habermas's influence on German scholars in communication studies is limited these days.

Notwithstanding the influence of American concepts on the press after World War II, one final reason for disregarding civic journalism in Germany could be seen in a journalistic tradition which was never as committed to the paradigm of objectivity as in the United States (e.g. Weischenberg 1995: 163). If this is the case, German journalists could be considerably less detached from the citizenry—a major point of critique of US mainstream journalism by civic journalists and their advocates (e.g. Rosen 1996: 79–81)—and therefore more civic than traditional journalists in the United States. This contention will be explored in the next two sections.

USING CONTENT ANALYSIS TO IDENTIFY CIVIC JOURNALISM

This research commenced with a content analysis to explore whether and how civic journalism might be practised in Germany. The analysis was based on an operational definition of citizen-oriented news coverage that draws from the basic literature on public or civic journalism from key sources such as Charity (1995), Merritt (1998) and Rosen (1999): Public or civic journalism requires journalists to be fair-minded participants in the discourses of a democratic community. It aims to provide citizens with resources so that they can devise or support democratic solutions for problems without advocating one-sided positions. Civic journalists are deemed to have some responsibility for the consequences of their news coverage (Forster 2006: 194).

There are numerous content analyses on civic journalism's news coverage (Haas 2007: 53–4). Based on the literature and some of these studies (e.g. Meyer and Potter 2000; Kennamer and South 2001)—mostly concerned with particular aspects of civic journalism—a comprehensive coding instrument for the measurement of civic journalism's content was developed and tested with two American newspapers. The newspapers were the *Richmond Times-Dispatch*, a typical example for the 'traditional' approach to news reporting, and the *Virginian Pilot* as its civic-minded counterpart (Kennamer and South 2001: 11). The idea was to check whether the adoption of civic journalism produces any measurable differences at all, then to identify what differences exist and finally compare the findings with a German newspaper to test the civic-mindedness of journalism in Germany (Forster 2006: 244–291). The characteristics of civic journalism that the analysis compared were issue-centred or mobilizing versus a non-issue-centred news coverage (see Table 8.1 for a more detailed breakdown of these categories)[1] and the number of ordinary citizens as sources versus political actors and experts.

The first test was conducted with one constructed week 'representing a six month 'population' of editions for a daily newspaper' (Lacy et al.

Table 8.1   Aspects of Political News Coverage

General issue-centred- news coverage	*General non-issue-centred news coverage*	*General mobilizing news coverage*
Political positions incomparison	Strategic and tactical coverage of politics	Information for political participation
Discussion of gains, costs and consequences	Political logistics	Presentation of active citizens
Issue-centred surveys	Horse race polling	Appeal to political participation
Addressing of core values	Politics as entertainment	Journalist as activist

2001: 837) of each publication's political coverage at two different points in time: 1988 and 1996, both years with presidential campaigns.[2] The *Pilot* started experimenting with 'the idea of public journalism and moved it several stages ahead' (Rosen 1999: 128) in 1994. If the commitment of the *Virginian Pilot* to public journalism had an impact on its news coverage, its content in 1996 would differ to that in 1988, when civic journalism did not formally exist. For the *Times-Dispatch*, which never adopted public journalism, coverage should be almost the same in both years.

The content analysis showed that the political content of the *Virginian Pilot* in 1996 did indeed differ considerably from the *Richmond Times-Dispatch*'s coverage of politics in the same year as well as from its own coverage eight years prior. Accordingly, there were only slight changes in the content of the *Times* from 1988 to 1996. Though not all variables produced the same strong evidence for the differences between traditional and civic-minded news coverage, the overall tendencies are pointing clearly in the hypothesized direction. It can be concluded that the adoption of public journalism's philosophy by the *Virginian Pilot* altered its news coverage to a measurable extent (Forster 2006: 246–80).

One possible reason for the disregard of civic journalism in Germany could be possibly found in a press which is traditionally less objective and detached and therefore more civic-minded than journalism in the United States, so there is simply less impetus for a civic reshaping of its coverage. To test this assumption, a German newspaper—comparable with the analyzed American papers—was tested with the introduced content analytical tool. For several reasons the *Münchner Merkur* (*Munich Mercury*) was chosen. Similar to the two American newspapers, the *Merkur* is not a leading national newspaper but a big-city based, regional daily with a diverse local coverage in its region of circulation. It is not a tabloid but a paper of record, predominantly subscribed by its readers and is therefore a quite good example for the vast majority of the over 130 editorial independent daily newspapers in Germany (Schütz 2007).[3]

There is indeed some evidence that German journalism might tend to an intermediary position between the traditional news reporting in the United States, exemplified by the *Richmond Times-Dispatch*, and the civic journalism of newspapers like the *Virginian Pilot*. A look at the three main categories of the content analysis (see Table 8.1) and the sourcing suggests this conclusion (Forster 2006: 283–91).

Issue-centred News Coverage

In its general orientation towards issues, the *Merkur* clearly follows the pattern of 'traditional' news coverage. Political positions were seldom compared seldom as costs and consequences were infrequently spelled out. In this main category the German daily can hardly be seen as civic-minded.

Non-Issue-Centred News Coverage

The *Merkur* approaches the public journalism standards set by the *Virginian Pilot* quite closely in its campaign coverage when non-issue-centred news comes into focus. News of the whereabouts of the campaign trail (political logistics) or strategies and tactics of the political contenders played a considerably smaller role than in the coverage of the *Times Dispatch*.

Mobilizing News Coverage

News that is committed to mobilizing citizens for political participation is not a big part of everyday reporting, even in a civic-minded newspaper as the *Virginian Pilot*. But the intermediary position of the German newspaper is quite clear in this part of the analysis. Nearly 25 per cent of the articles in the *Pilot* contained mobilizing information, as do nearly 20 per cent in the *Merkur*, whereas only 8 per cent of the articles in the *Times-Dispatch* were at least a little mobilizing.

Ordinary Citizens as Sources

The *Merkur* was again located between traditional and public journalism when the sourcing of the three publications was compared. While in the *Virginian Pilot* of 1996 ordinary citizens were cited in nearly 18 per cent of all articles, this was the case only in 5.5 per cent of the articles in the *Richmond Times-Dispatch*. The *Merkur* took an intermediary position with nearly 8 per cent of the articles citing normal members of the citizenry in 2002, though tending here to the mainstream coverage (see Table 8.2).

Table 8.2   Percentage of Articles with Sources of Direct and Indirect Citations[1]

The Virginian-Pilot			Richmond Times-Dispatch			Münchner Merkur		
Citizens	Politicians	Experts	Citizens	Politicians	Experts	Citizens	Politicians	Experts
17.9%	68.9%	15.1%	5.5%	68.0%	17.7%	7.9%	60.0%	16.3%

Note: [1] Percentages do not add up to 100 because of possible multiple coding.

CIVIC JOURNALISM IN THE JUDGEMENT OF JOURNALISTS AND READERS

To back this first impression of the German press being located somehow between traditional American news reporting and civic journalism, a survey of 208 journalists was conducted in order to explore German journalists' attitudes towards civic journalism.[4] German journalists see themselves first and foremost as neutral communicators of factual information. A more idealistic perception of their role—compatible with the idea of a civic-minded journalism—is not rejected outright but it is not central to German journalists' self-perception and communicative intentions. German journalists are aware of their social and societal responsibilities as well as being sensitive to the often delicate relationship between journalism and politics, but this does not amount to the civic orientation of public journalism. They are issue and audience oriented and therefore quite sympathetic with less controversial practices of civic journalism (e.g. an issue-centred campaign coverage). However, they strongly reject a more activist role for journalists. These trends were largely reproduced in a study of journalism students (Forster 2006: 303–341).

The audience also came into focus, with the results of a study of 192 readers tending to back the proponents of civic journalism to a certain degree. The readers were asked to evaluate four different versions of two articles concerned with campaign coverage and the issue of immigration. All in all, the respondents showed preferences for the civic-minded deliberative and citizen-oriented versions of the articles when asked to judge the relevance of and the interest in an issue. The deliberative versions were estimated as of a higher quality, especially when it comes to the controversial issue of immigration. Furthermore, there were no significant differences between the deliberative and the citizen-oriented versions on one hand and the strategic as well as the neutral, information centred versions on the other, when the readers rated the objectivity of an article (Forster 2006: 348–67).

HOW CIVIC IS GERMAN CITIZEN JOURNALISM?

In August 2005, a monthly magazine published by the largest association of Germany's professional news makers, stated—or warned—that 'the laymen are coming'. The story in *journalist* magazine discussed the chances and risks of the emerging citizen journalism in Germany and even the link between citizen and public journalism (Stegers 2005: 12). Only one year after Dan Gillmor (2006) published the citizen journalism 'bible', *We the Media*, the 'grassroots journalism by the people for the people' had arrived in Central Europe. At this time, some experiments with user-generated content were successfully initiated by German media companies (e.g. www.jetzt.de; www.opinio.de) and the German blogosphere was evolving quickly.

Drawing from Witt's (2004) notion of a 'public journalism morphing into the public's journalism', it might have been expected that civic journalism's agenda could be raised in Germany. At one major media business event, the 'Medientage München' (Media Days Munich) in 2006, one could observe what Cammaerts (2008: 361) calls the first threat to the participatory potential of the blogosphere—what Habermas (1999) would call 'colonization by the market'. What Rosen dubs 'the people formerly known as the audience' (Rosen 2006)—or in other words, ordinary citizens—did not attend the event. Instead some people formerly known as bloggers started their professional careers.

The same year, an ambitious project was kicked off: the *Readers Edition* (www.readers-edition.de). This online platform for citizen journalism was an offspring of the *Netzeitung* (Netnewspaper), the self-designated first German newspaper published exclusively in the Web (www.netzeitung.de). However, the *Readers Edition* soon found a new home with the *Netzeitung*'s founder and editor in chief, Michael Maier, who left the online newspaper and took the *Readers Edition* with him to his new company, the 'Blogform Group' (www.blogformgroup.com).

The content of the *Readers Edition* can be seen as one indicator for the state of German citizen journalism. Therefore, a slightly modified version of the content analysis methodology was used to analyze archived *Readers Edition* articles from two constructed weeks out of the twelve months in 2008.[5] In this sample of fourteen days, only 140 articles were published in the *Readers Edition*, which seems to be a quite small number compared to a mainstream organization like the *Merkur*, which published 190 articles on political news alone in one constructed week.

One potential participatory feature of online journalism is the possibility for the public to comment on the article immediately. The number of comments can also serve as an indicator—admittedly crude—for the relevance of an article to readers. In this investigation, nearly 40 per cent of all sampled articles had no comments. Few attracted more than ten comments although one article triggered 344 comments (see Table 8.3). Although a content analysis cannot estimate the numbers of readers of an article nor its exact relevance for them, the research suggests that most of the news coverage in the *Readers Edition* does not spark much discussion.

Table 8.3 Formal Variables in Readers Edition

Number of comments

	0	1–2	3–9	10–34	344
Frequency	55	37	36	11	1
Per cent	39.3 %	26.5 %	25.6 %	7.7 %	0.7 %

Authorship

	Staff Member	Professional Journalist	Citizen Journalist
Frequency	7	51	82
Per cent	5.0 %	36.4 %	58.5 %

Types of coverage

	Brief notice	Report	Feature	Interview	Essay	Opinion	Other
Frequency	4	71	6	11	9	37	2
Per cent	2.9 %	50.7 %	4.3 %	7.9 %	6.4	26.5 %	1.4 %

Topics

	Politics	Culture	Sports	Science	Service	Econ.	Crime	Other
Frequency	64	42	12	8	4	4	3	3
Per cent	45.7 %	30.0 %	8.6 %	5.7 %	2.9 %	2.9 %	2.1 %	2.1 %

Geographical reference

	International	National	Federal states	Local/regional
Frequency	66	60	4	10
Per cent	47.1 %	42.9 %	2.9 %	7.1 %

Almost 60 per cent of the stories originated from bloggers, citizen journalists, or experts in the covered issue, meaning that despite the dedication of the platform to citizen journalism, the rate of input from the organization's own reporters and editors and other professional journalists remains high at just over 40 per cent (see Table 8.3). Obviously the *Readers Edition* serves not only as a platform for citizens but also for (1) established journalists to disseminate content that they cannot or do not want to publish in the traditional news media and (2) journalistic beginners as a training ground to exercise their skills. This can be a valuable asset to readers and writers alike, but it is not exactly the goal of citizen journalism.

The articles were categorized according to the standard forms seen in German journalism. Notices and reports are generally objective and neutral in style and content. Feature stories or reportages, interviews and scholarly essays are usually slightly more subjective. The most subjective tend to be the 'opinion forms', such as editorials, commentaries and reviews. According to the literature (e.g. Gillmor 2006: 194) and empirical research (Carpenter 2008: 539), articles with opinion forms should be far more frequent in citizen media than in traditional news media. In fact there was considerably more opinion based news coverage in the *Readers Edition* than in the three newspapers discussed earlier. Altogether, opinion forms (26.5 per cent), essays (6.4 per cent), feature stories (4.3 per cent) and interviews (7.9 per cent) constituted more than 45 per cent of the *Readers Edition*'s content in the two sample weeks. But still more than 50 per cent of the articles were written in the classical report style. With the few brief statements, the traditional 'just the facts' style of reporting was still very present in a majority of articles.

Politics was the single largest topic of the articles comprising 45 per cent of the content. Given that there were no national elections and few state elections of national significance, only five stories discussed campaign issues.

Most of the articles were concerned with international events (47.1 per cent) reflecting the interest of Germans in international affairs. Nearly 43 per cent of the coverage focused on issues of nationwide significance and only 2.9 per cent on state and only 7.1 per cent on local/regional affairs.

It can be concluded that a project like the *Readers Edition* is hardly focused on regional or local news, which runs counter to the assumption that citizen journalism usually starts (e.g. Gillmor 2005: 12) and works best (if not only) in local or regional settings (e.g. Stegers 2005). Therefore, citizen journalism in the *Readers Edition* is definitely not just old-fashioned community journalism. This again leaves the question: How civic is it?

The sixty-four articles on politics contained a substantial amount of information needed to engage in the deliberation or evaluation of potential solutions to societal problems. This includes comparing political positions and outlining gains, costs and consequences of political measures. Issue-centred surveys played nearly no role in the reporting but core values were present in the articles to a notably higher extent than in the newspapers discussed earlier (see Figure 8.1).

Because there was little election and campaign coverage, indicators for non-issue-centred coverage were rare as well. But as Figure 8.2 shows, even in the general political news some of the most criticized characteristics of mainstream journalism by advocates of a civic-minded reporting found their way into the news of the *Readers Edition*. On the other hand, citizen reporters are definitely not presenting politics as entertainment by jumping on the 'politainment' bandwagon.

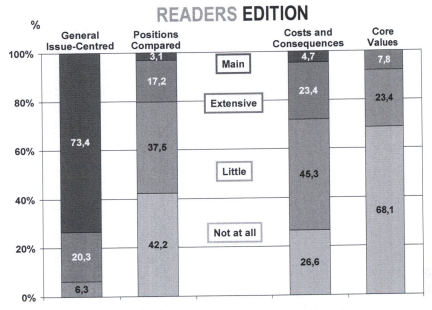

Figure 8.1 Issue-centred news coverage, percentage of given codes.

Note: If you were to look at the 'Positions Compared' column as an example, then only 3.1 per cent of the articles were mainly about comparing political positions. In 17.2 per cent, comparing positions was an extensive part of the articles, 37.5 per cent compared positions only a little, and 42.2 per cent contained no comparisons at all.

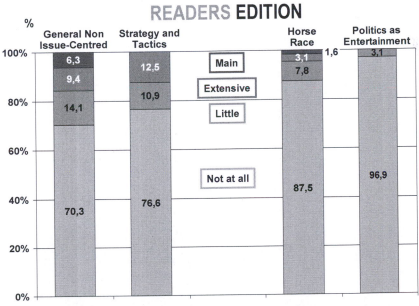

Figure 8.2 Non-issue-centred news coverage, percentage of given codes.

This obviously traditional approach to political news coverage becomes more evident when the mobilizing potentials of the articles are investigated. Mobilizing news was quite rare in the sample, similar to the results in the previous studies discussed. Citizen journalists did not even present active citizens in a significant proportion (see Figure 8.3). Accordingly, *Readers Edition* played almost no function as an activist. In many ways the coverage of this particular platform for citizen journalists resembles the traditional news reporting of German newspapers.

Ordinary citizens had been quoted in only 14 per cent of the political articles in the *Readers Edition*. In nearly 60 per cent, political actors served as sources and in more than 26 per cent independent experts were quoted (see Table 8.4). This sourcing pattern looks similar to the newspapers discussed above, with a little more weight on experts (see Tables 8.2 and 8.4).

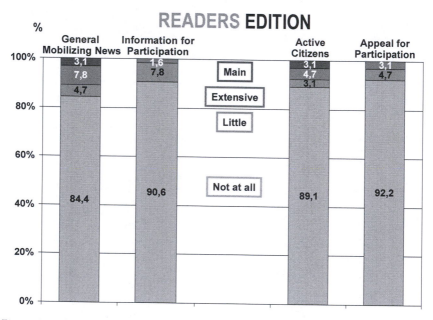

Figure 8.3   Mobilizing news coverage, percentage of given codes.

Table 8.4   Percentage of Articles with Sources of Direct and Indirect Citations[1]

			Sources			
	Citizens	*Politics*	*Experts*	*Blogs*	*Media*	*Grassroots*
Frequency	9	38	17	27	37	5
Per cent	14.1 %	59.4 %	26.6 %	42.2 %	57.8 %	7.8 %

Note: [1] Percentages do not add up to 100 because of possible multiple coding.

Blogs and other citizen media were cited directly or indirectly in over 42 per cent of the stories. Therefore, the cross-referential nature of blogging is visible in the *Readers Edition* although not as clearly as one might have expected. Haas (2006: 148) notes that in blogs, many keywords for the coverage come from the traditional news media publications. Nearly 58 per cent of the articles quoted mainstream news media, whereas not even 8 per cent of the coverage referred to independent grassroots movements or organizations (see Table 8.4). Additionally, we found only a few stories that had not been already channelled through traditional news media.

These findings should not be overestimated, but there are relatively few indicators that news coverage on this particular platform for online citizen journalism is more civic than Germany's mainstream journalism. If that is the case for other citizen media projects as well, there might be little added value for citizen journalism's readers.

CONCLUSION

Despite the advent of citizen journalism in Germany, the citizen media movement here seems to be heading in a different direction than public or civic journalism would. Undoubtedly, blogs and other citizen media can be valuable sources of information, especially in counterbalancing the traditional media's chronically underfinanced local and regional news coverage. But in the case of the *Readers Edition,* citizen journalism in the wider field of political communication mostly just duplicates mainstream media content and adds some opinion. This raises the question of whether this kind of news is—as Wilm Herlyn, editor in chief of the *German Press-Agency (Deutsche Presse-Agentur,* dpa) noted—no journalism at all (Keil and Kilz 2009: 15). Civic journalism was mainly about a different style of reporting the news and there are few indications that it will be adopted from citizen media projects in Germany. This should not be surprising, since citizen journalists can not be expected to embrace something they have—if at all—hardly heard of.

NOTES

1. The unit of analysis was a single article. Each article had to be coded whether categories and subcategories could be found in the text to their proportions. Coding used a quasi-metrical scale with 1 (Not at all), 2 (Little), 3 (Extensive), and 4 (Main).
2. A six-month sampling period in the first half of the respective years was chosen, with 604 articles analysed.
3. A six-month sampling period was chosen again in 2002 before that year's national elections. Altogether 190 *Münchner Merkur* articles were analysed.
4. To assure the sample's representativeness, the population-defining characteristics of German journalists were cross-checked with two representative

studies (Raabe 2005, Scholl and Weischenberg 1998). The questionnaire was based mainly on modified parts of the measurement instruments of Meyer and Potter (2000) and Scholl and Weischenberg (1998).

5. Coding was performed by the author and a colleague. Intercoder reliability ranged from 0.67 to 1.0 with an arithmetic mean of 0.88 over all variables.

BIBLIOGRAPHY

Arnold, K. (2008) 'Qualität im Journalismus—ein integratives Konzept' (Quality in journalism—an integrative concept), *Publizistik,* 53(4): 488–508.
Cammaerts, B. (2008) 'Critiques on the participatory potentials of web 2.0', *Communication, Culture and Critique* 1(4): 358–77.
Carpenter; S. (2008) 'How online citizen journalism publications and online newspapers utilize the objectivity standard and rely on external sources', *Journalism and Mass Communication Quarterly* 85(3): 531–48.
Charity, A. (1995) *Doing Public Journalism.* New York: Guilford Press.
Christians, C. (1999) 'The common good as first principle', in T. Glasser (ed.) *The Idea of Public Journalism,* (pp. 67–84). New York: Guilford Press.
Forster, K. (2006) *Journalismus im Spannungsfeld zwischen Freiheit und Verantwortung: Das Konzept des ‚Public Journalism' und seine empirische Relevanz* (*Journalism in the Area of Conflict between Freedom and Responsibility: The Concept of 'Public Journalism' and its Empirical Relevance*), Cologne: Herbert von Halem.
Frank, T. (2001) *One Market under God: Extreme Capitalism, Market Populism, and the End of Economic Democracy,* New York: Anchor Books.
Gillmor, D. (2005) 'Where citizens and journalists intersect', *Nieman Reports* 59(4): 11–13.
Gillmor, D. (2006) *We the Media: Grassroots Journalism by the People, for the People,* Sebastopol: O'Reilly.
Glasser, T. (ed.) (1999) 'The idea of public journalism', in *The Idea of Public Journalism,* New York: Guilford Press: 3–18.
Haas, T. (2007) *The Pursuit of Public Journalism: Theory, Practice, and Criticism,* New York: Routledge.
Habermas, J. (1997a) *Theorie des kommunikativen Handelns. Band 1: Handlungsrationalität und gesellschaftliche Rationalisierung* (*The Theory of Communicative Action, Vol. 1. Reason and the Rationalization of Society*), 2nd edn. Frankfurt/M.: Suhrkamp.
Habermas, J. (1997b) *Theorie des kommunikativen Handelns. Band 2: Zur Kritik der funktionalistischen Vernunft* (*The Theory of Communicative Action, Vol. 2. Lifeworld and System: A Critique of Functionalist Reason*), 2nd edn, Frankfurt/M.: Suhrkamp.
Habermas, J. (1999) *Strukturwandel der Öffentlichkeit: Untersuchungen zu einer Kategorie der bürgerlichen Gesellschaft. Neuauflage 1990 [The Structural Transformation of the Public Sphere: An Inquiry into a Category of Bourgois Society. Reprint 1990]*, 6th edn. Frankfurt/M.: Suhrkamp.
Habermas, J. (2006) 'Political communication in media society: Does democracy still enjoy an epistemic dimension? The impact of normative theory on empirical research', *Communication Theory* 16(4): 411–426.
Hughes, S. (2006) *Newsrooms in Conflict: Journalism and the Democratization of Mexico,* Pittsburgh, PA: University of Pittsburgh Press.
Humphreys, P. (1994) *Media and Media Policy in Germany: The Press and Broadcasting Since 1945,* 2nd edn. Oxford: Berg.

Keil, C. and Kilz, H. (2009) 'Es gibt Sumpfblüten, die schnell wieder verschwinden (There are swamp blossoms, which will disappear quickly)', *Süddeutsche Zeitung*, February 11: 15.

Kennamer, D. and South, J. (2001) 'Civic journalism in the 2000 U.S. Senate Race in Virginia', Paper presented to the Civic Journalism Interest Group at the Annual Convention of the AEJMC in Washington, 5–8 August.

Kunczik, M. and Zipfel, A. (2001) *Publizistik: Ein Studienhandbuch* (Journalism: A Study Guide), Köln: Böhlau.

Lacy, S., Riffe, D., Stoddard, S., Martin, H. and Chang, K. (2001) 'Sample size for newspaper content analysis in multi-year studies', *Journalism and Mass Communication Quarterly*, 78(4): 836–45.

Lambeth, E. (1998) 'Public journalism as a democratic practice', in E. Lambeth, P. Meyer and E. Thorson (eds.) *Assessing Public Journalism*, Columbia, MO: University of Missouri Press, pp. 15–35.

Luhmann, N. (1996) *Die Realität der Massenmedien* (*The Reality of the Mass Media*), 2nd edn. Opladen: Westdeutscher Verlag.

Lünenborg, M. (2005) 'Public journalism: Konzept–Entstehung–Gesellschaftliche relevanz' (Public journalism: Concept–Development–Social relevance), in M. Behmer, B. Blöbaum, A. Scholl and R. Stöber (eds.) *Journalismus im Wandel: Analysedimensionen, Konzepte, Fallstudien [Journalism in Transformation: Dimensions of Analysis, Concepts, Case Studies]*. Wiesbaden: VS Verlag: 143–159.

Merritt, D. (1998) *Public Journalism and Public Life: Why Telling the News is Not Enough*, Mahwah, NJ: Lawrence Erlbaum.

Meyer, P. (1998) 'If it works, how will we know?', in E. Lambeth, P Meyer and E. Thorson (eds.) *Assessing Public Journalism*, Columbia, MO: University of Missouri Press, pp. 251–73.

Meyer, P. and Potter, D. (2000) 'Hidden value: polls and public journalism', in P. Lavrakas and M. Traugott (eds.) *Election Polls, the News Media and Democracy.* New York: Chatham House, pp. 113–41.

Poynter Institute for Media Studies (1999) *Poynter Election Handbook. A Guide to Campaign Coverage*, St. Petersburg: Poynter Institute.

Raabe, J. (2005) *Die Beobachtung journalistischer Akteure. Optionen einer empirisch-kritischen Journalismusforschung* (*The Observation of Journalistic Actors: Options of an Empiric-Critical Journalism Research*), Wiesbaden: VS Verlag.

Rauch, J., Trager, K. and Kim, E. (2003) 'Clinging to tradition, welcoming civic solutions: A survey of college students' attitudes toward civic journalism', *Journalism & Mass Communication Educator*, 58(2): 175–86.

Rosen, J. (1995) 'Foreword', in A. Charity (ed.) *Doing Public Journalism.* New York: Guilford Press: v–vi.

Rosen, J. (1996) *Getting the Connections Right: Public Journalism and the Troubles in the Press*, New York: 20th Century Fund Press.

Rosen, J. (1999) *What Are Journalists For?* New Haven, CT: Yale University Press.

Rosen, J. (2006) 'The people formerly known as the audience', *PressThink*, 27 June. Available at http://journalism.nyu.edu/pubzone/weblogs/pressthink/2006/06/27/ppl_frmr.html (Accessed 8 March 2009).

Scholl, A. (2007) 'Review'. *Medien & Kommunikationswissenschaft* (*Media and Communication Studies*), 55(3): 460–1.

Scholl, A. and Weischenberg, S. (1998) *Journalismus in der Gesellschaft: Theorie, Methodologie und Empirie* (*Journalism in Society: Theory, Methodology, and Empirical Findings*), Opladen: Westdeutscher Verlag.

Schütz, W. (2007) 'Redaktionelle und verlegerische Struktur der deutschen Tagespresse (Editorial and publishing Structure of the german Press)', *Media Perspektiven*, (11): 560–88.

Seelye, K. and Sorkin, A. (2006) 'Knight Ridder newspaper chain agrees to sale', *New York Times*, 12 March. Available at http://query.nytimes.com/gst/fullpage. html?res=9A02E6DA1031F931A25750C0A9609C8B63 (Accessed 1 September 2009).

Stegers, F. (2005) 'Die Laien kommen (The Laymen are coming)', *journalist*, 8: 10–13.

Weischenberg, S. (1995) *Journalistik: Theorie und Praxis aktueller Medienkommunikation. Band 2: Medientechnik, Medienfunktionen, Medienakteure* (*Journalism Studies: Theory and Practice of Contemporary Media Communication. Vol. 2: Media Technology, Media Functions, Media Actors*), Opladen: Westdeutscher Verlag.

Weischenberg, S., Malik, M. and Scholl, A. (2006) *Die Souffleure der Mediengesellschaft: Report über die Journalisten in Deutschland* (*The Prompters of the Media Society: Report about the Journalists in Germany*), Konstanz: UVK.

Witt, L. (2004) 'Is public journalism morphing into the public's journalism?', *National Civic Review* 93(3): 49–57.

9 Public Journalism in Finnish Mainstream Newspapers

Laura Ahva

Public journalism in Finland has typically assumed forms in which the original ideas of the public/civic journalism movement—initiated in the United States by Jay Rosen and others—have merged with other reader-oriented aspirations of the newspapers. Newspapers that have incorporated a public journalism style have adapted the ideas to fit them to Finnish newsroom cultures and commercial needs. A study of public journalism in Finland is significant because it illuminates the reception and evolution of public journalism in the context of a Nordic welfare society. Some scholars argue that public journalism as a product of American context is ill-adaptable to other cultures (Richards 2000). However, Heikkilä and Kunelius (2003: 199) pose the counterargument that in the social sciences, we need to feed ourselves with others' ideas in order to avoid clinging onto our own immediate contextual restrictions. With the translation of public journalism from the American context to the Nordic one the question cannot be posed as 'does the idea of public journalism work elsewhere?' Rather, we can ask, 'what aspects of the Nordic culture do the idea and its application reveal?'

This chapter discusses the way in which public journalism has been absorbed into the existing media structures in Finland. To begin with, a strong tradition of newspaper readership provided a fertile ground for public journalism ideas in the mid 1990s, but the Finnish media landscape was facing broad changes when public journalism arrived. The overall media framework was moving away from the consensus-oriented and state-regulated system towards a more individual-oriented, liberal media model.

According to Hallin and Mancini (2004), the Finnish media system is a clear representative of the Democratic Corporatist Media Model, which is found in Scandinavia, Belgium, the Netherlands, Germany, Austria and Switzerland. These media systems are characterized by formalized journalistic professionalism, such as early institutional organization of the trade, commitment to professional standards and common public interest. Furthermore, mass circulation of the commercial press with high readership and coexistence of state-regulated media politics with liberal tradition of press freedom are features of the democratic-corporatist countries (Hallin and Mancini 2004).

However, factors such as globalization and increased deregulation have financially, technologically, culturally and politically reshaped Finland's media system. *Financially*, the field has been increasingly defined by competitive/industrial trends. Newspapers used to be the cornerstone of the Finnish media structure, but now they are struggling to maintain their circulation. The combination of the overarching business framework and the professional public service ethos requires an ongoing professional negotiation between the normative and financial features of journalism. Finnish newspapers were initially reactive in the *technological* changes that they implemented in relation to digitalization and the Internet, but now they search intensively for Web 2.0 solutions. The *cultural* trends mostly relate to consumer culture and the adjustment of newspapers to the fragmented lifestyle of present day consumers. Another cultural challenge is posed by the incremental change of Finland from a mono- to multicultural society. Similarly, the *sociopolitical* context has changed substantively during the past twenty years, with depoliticization and general passivity of civil society encouraging both the state and the press to develop interactive approaches of civic participation. Consequently, the public journalism approach has been developing during a period in which Finland's old order of democratic-corporatist system has commenced a long-term process of evolution.

This chapter provides an overview of how public journalism entered Finland. It will present the findings of a study on three Finnish newspapers that have applied public journalism, exploring current public journalism practices and texts and journalists' reflections about the roles of the readers and journalists in public journalism.[1]

PUBLIC JOURNALISM IN FINLAND

In the 1990s the concept of public journalism percolated from the United States to the Nordic countries. Three aspects of the movement acted as links in the transition: public journalism as a theoretical entity dealt with democratic theory and appealed to the academics; as a set of concrete and experimental practices it had appeal for professional journalists; and as an attempt to tackle the declining momentum of the newspaper business it also enticed newspaper managers. Public journalism thus differed from other alternative movements in journalism because it addressed different agents in the field of journalism within the same framework.

Although there has never been an institutionally supported international public journalism movement, like-minded initiatives have taken place in every continent. Public journalism was experimented in different countries either as the result of the work of individual journalists and editors eager to try new methods, for example in Sweden (Beckman 2003), or educators in charge of democracy supporting development and journalism education projects, as in Namibia (Shilongo 2005), or experimentally minded scholars wishing to see how the idea might work in their culture, as in Finland (Heikkilä 2001; Heikkilä and Kunelius 2003). In Finland, public journalism was first primarily discussed by the academics. At a time in which there was a paradigmatic and discursive change of the national culture from strong state-oriented 'planned economy' to more liberal 'competitive economy' (Alasuutari 1996: 104–21), the role of journalism in such changing conditions of democracy was obviously a fundamental question for academics. Media researchers became inspired by the ideas of public journalism and set up joint projects with newsrooms.

The first research projects were mostly carried out in newspapers and involved election coverage and local issues, such as city budgeting (Kunelius 2001). The first Finnish public journalism initiatives were practical experiments which utilized the idea of forming citizens' discussion groups and using these as journalistic resource (Heikkilä and Kunelius 2003).

The initial reactions of journalists towards public journalism were more reserved than those of researchers. Public journalism was first regarded as do-it-yourself journalism that undermined the authority of traditional quality journalism. However, the professional culture had already become more interested in critically evaluating its own practices, such as detachment from everyday life and dependency on institutional sources (Heikkilä 2001). In this context, the projects appeared reasonable. In addition, public journalism entered Finland during the economic recession that raised concerns about the erosion of the newspaper industry's traditionally strong subscriber base (Hujanen 2007). Thus Finland resembled the United States in that public journalism had a business-oriented dimension to start with. The early public journalism approach in Finland was characterized by normative–economic justification (Wahl-Jorgensen 2002) due to its promise to both enhance citizenship and boost readership. The experiments were built on a somewhat conflicting platform: journalists looking for opportunities to do better journalism and newspaper publishers looking for new ways to build loyal readerships.

In the initial experiments, citizens proved to be productive and competent—yet underused—participants in journalism. The projects indicated the need to develop new story formats and newsroom routines to grant participatory roles for ordinary people in journalistic products (Heikkilä 2001). Thereafter some of the methods of public journalism gained ground, and news organizations started to develop their own citizen-oriented approaches independently (Heikkilä and Kunelius 2003). To date, the active participation of the researcher community and the spread of the general consumer-coloured reader-orientation trend (Hujanen 2009) have kept the term 'public journalism' in the vocabulary of practising journalists. Moreover, the ideas of public journalism continue to reach the journalistic field also via the programs of journalism schools. Finnish public journalism can be therefore described as a rather mainstream activity that does not aim to radically challenge existing structures.

For a closer look at what public journalism has come to mean in Finland, I will next elaborate on recent forms and textual styles of public journalism in three Finnish newspapers in 2002–06. Understanding of public journalism within the media organizations is not very coherent and not all participatory practices are necessarily named as such. Nonetheless, a study of concrete practices and journalists' interpretations of them illustrate how Finnish journalists have domesticated the idea of public journalism.

PUBLIC JOURNALISM AS TEXTUAL PRACTICE

The three Finnish newspapers examined in this chapter—the nation-wide *Helsingin Sanomat (HS)*, regional *Aamulehti (AL)* and local *Itä-Häme (IH)*—are typical and well known Finnish newspapers. That is not to say that public journalism has penetrated the entire newspaper field in Finland. Rather, these newsrooms have taken a slightly more active approach to participatory practices than usual. The three newspapers offer a good sample of varying conditions in which pubic journalism has been applied and they represent different approaches for organizing public journalism within newsrooms.

Helsingin Sanomat (HS) is Finland's biggest quality daily and the leading national agenda setter. *HS* has applied public journalism in the form of distinct projects, mainly in relation to election coverage. During the Finnish parliamentary elections of 2003, *HS* based its pre-election reporting on the citizens' agenda rather than on the agenda of the political elite. Staff determined the citizens' agenda with a telephone survey, and the most important themes were covered in a series that featured ordinary citizens as their main sources. When *HS*'s political team covered the 2004 European Parliament election in cooperation with a national commercial television network, it featured four large discussion events in the indoor agora of the newspaper building. The newspaper invited candidates, experts and citizens to the events that were composed of discussion, interviewing and citizens' questions.

The regional *Aamulehti (AL)* newspaper has developed discussion-based reporting practices and story concepts. For example, *AL* organized an election tour in 2004 that featured public discussion events in the region's municipalities. The newspaper first sent its 'news van' team to towns to invite residents to suggest issues and questions, and a story based on the input was published to motivate further discussion. Later, candidates, representatives, local decision makers and voters would gather for face-to-face discussions. Another innovation was the 'value series' (2002 and 2004), which organized one-to-one encounters between citizens and decision makers. The concept worked in story pairs: the first story was based on citizen interviews with sources like nurses, farmers and high school students, and the second on the discussions between each of these citizens and a cabinet minister.

Itä-Häme (IH) is a local newspaper that has created a position for a civic reporter who is in charge of the organization's public journalism. Thus *IH* has approached public journalism via an individual, by assigning the responsibility to a specific journalist. The civic reporter usually writes two 'civic stories' a week. Either the story topics originate from the citizens, or citizens become active participants in the journalistic process. The civic stories can be categorized into four main groups: encounters between citizens and decision makers, stories about everyday life, activating or motivational stories, and answers to readers' questions.

This next section discusses the common storytelling elements that the three newspapers have employed in terms of their textual representations, story structures and designs. It offers a way to understand how the texts of Finnish public journalism stories promote civic engagement.

Relevance of Everyday Life

The clearest common feature in the public journalism stories is making citizens' everyday life relevant by bringing citizens' experiences to the focus and framing them as germane to the general interest. The idea of 'bottom-up' is very clearly present in the stories: the main story usually presents the citizen's point of view and the sidebar provides a more general angle to the issue. The story packages thus provide citizens the possibility to define issues first. Furthermore, practices such as *AL*'s 'news van' activities represent an attempt to approach ordinary people in their own environment and on their own terms so that the local perspectives and experiences reach the newsrooms. Also, *IH*'s concept and practice of the local civic reporter underlines the everyday element: in every 'civic story' there is a small information box indicating that the story has originated from the public, and that further citizen input is sought.

Connections Between Civic Life and Politics

The second common element in the public journalism stories is the link established between civic life and political life. This is apparent in the election stories, where the use of the voters' agenda as a backbone for pre-election coverage is an example of connecting the citizens' concerns to those of the political parties. Furthermore, politicians are often positioned in the stories as counter pairs for citizens. In the discussion events and encounters, citizens are encouraged to challenge the politicians from their position as voters. Public journalism stories also provide information about the political parties and candidates in a comprehensive manner and activate people to vote and take part. Overall the public journalism stories are characterized by an ethos that democratic and political participation, especially in terms of voting and public deliberation, is a desired civic act.

Citizens' Questions

Citizens' questions make up another usual element in the Finnish public journalism stories. A simple act of asking is used as a tool for involving, mobilizing and empowering citizens, as well as making their aspects part of the public discussion. In the texts, citizens' questions are presented either anonymously or in accounts of face-to-face situations. Some of the most successful uses of citizens' questions are written in a question and answer format. Questions that are based on the participant's own experience give concreteness to the story; the decision makers are invited to answer in a comprehensible manner. In some cases, however, the role and input of the citizen participant might get marginalized due to the unequal power balance that is innate in a meeting of a citizen and a top-level decision maker.

Possibilities for Dialogue

The news practices that most clearly aim for and enable dialogue are encounters, discussion events and group interviews. These meetings—mostly organized by the newspapers themselves—connect the citizens' experiences and concerns with the ideas of the authorities. At its best, this enables the emergence of dialogue and solution finding. The idea of problem solving that some theorists consider a central element in public journalism (e.g. Haas 2007) is most apparent in the encounter stories of the local newspaper. It seems that the local context and the fact that participants meet in the actual surroundings—be it a dangerous street crossing or a neglected playground—adds to the public pressure and thus possibilities for finding solutions. However, there are difficulties involved in printing such dialogue in newspaper stories, because the reciprocal nature of the real-life discussions does not easily translate into dialogic news text.

Citizens as Public Evaluators

Public journalism stories also represent citizens as agents who are proactive and capable of public discussion in terms of argumentation, critiquing or giving advice. Citizens are thus positioned as public evaluators. Citizens do not merely tell how they feel—they also explain *why* they feel that way or even suggest improvements. *AL*'s 'news van' stories invite citizens to present their concerns or comments freely. As a flexible format, the 'news van' stories provide room for different kinds of citizen contributions.

The common element in all these practices is the idea of transferring part of journalistic authority from reporters to citizens. Public journalism as textual practice works in favour of making citizens more active participants in the journalistic process, and also enables them to have dialogue with public authorities. This is manifested especially in citizens' questions, dialogue and public evaluation. Even if the current public journalism practice is diversified and the dialogical successes are often modest, the existence of these elements acts as evidence that public journalism has offered Finnish newspaper journalists means to regard the readers as capable public actors. Journalists have developed storytelling 'genres' which enable them to handle issues in a participatory way. While part of this emerging professional metalanguage would have no doubt emerged without public journalism, it is clear that in the experiments studied here, public journalism's normative vocabulary has had an effect on this development.

JOURNALISTS' VIEWS ON CITIZEN PARTICIPATION

Public journalism experiments have provided ground on which journalists have negotiated their views on both their own roles and those of citizens. Interviews with staff of the three newspapers revealed that the journalists identify six different participatory roles for readers in public journalism. The roles vary from symbolic to active and from the more traditional to participatory ones that challenge newspaper journalism conventions.

Sample Citizen

When journalists explain the need for increased citizen participation, a common motive is the wish to increase the presence of citizens on the newspaper pages. This position can be named as the sample citizen because it is based simply on the need to have examples of ordinary people in the stories. In this manner, citizens are sometimes used in a 'dramaturgical way', as one of the interviewees put it. In fact, actual citizen participation in this role is often rather limited. It might shrink into a mere posing for a photograph. The national daily, *HS*, often uses citizens in the example position. A concurring metaphor in the journalists' talk is that stories need to be told 'through people', in other words through frames that readers can recognize. This way of positioning the citizen is not considered a particularly new approach, and it is tied to the broad reader-oriented trend that emphasizes the use of individuals as interfaces of storytelling. This indicates that public journalism does not function in a vacuum, and that the broad trends of journalism become intermingled in practical work.

Providing Authentic Opinions

Another common way to justify citizen participation is the need to get 'citizens' voices' to the stories. This position provides a slightly more active role for the reader than the 'sample citizen'. In *AL* particularly, the idea of 'bringing forth citizens' voices' has become a slogan inside the newsroom, due to a view that citizen participation will bring 'authentic' comments and opinions to the stories. This perspective spurs newspapers to mobilize themselves with 'news van' tours, discussion events and similar activities so that citizens' opinions appear throughout the newspaper and not only on the letters-to-the-editor pages.

Ideas for Stories

A more demanding citizen role in public journalism is to provide story ideas. If viewed narrowly, this role is confined to readers sending in tips for stories. However, more broadly, all kinds of interaction between journalists and readers can tighten the connection with the audience and help in producing stories that are more rooted in the lives of regular people and not only in the realm of institutions. Journalists are not unanimous about how directly civic participation should affect a newspapers' contents. Some think that a news process should start from a clean slate, without pre-planning, while others think that the newspaper can and should decide the topic first and then invite people to comment—and if additional relevant issues come up in this process, the journalists should pick them up. The journalists thus all agreed that citizens played a role as a source for story topics, but debated the extent to which the topics should be purely citizen-based.

Representative Role

The fourth participatory citizen position in public journalism is the role of a representative. Journalists struggle to find such citizens' opinions and experiences that could be generalized in order to address a larger audience. Journalists attempt to resolve this dilemma by framing their interviewees as representatives. In public journalism, citizens are therefore often conceived as representatives of larger groups of people, for example their occupational group or neighbourhood. Seeing citizens as representatives enables journalists to validate individual citizen participation in journalism. As representatives people gain authority from the collective. In practice this becomes evident especially in the encounter stories in which the idea of representation is inbuilt: citizens meet ministers as representatives of their whole reference group.

The Everyday Expert

In public journalism, citizens are also experts on the everyday life, be it working life or family life. In the expert position, citizens are not merely used as elements in the stories; they are used as real sources of experience-based information that is relevant for public discussion. According to the interviewed journalists, newspapers need to be active in finding these but active citizens may also be regarded as too active and journalists become anxious about how representative those citizens' views are. In this sense, the legacy of democratic corporatism works against the idea of open citizen participation, since the past setting favoured the use of formally organized sources to provide representative political pluralism.

JOURNALISTS' VIEWS ON REPORTERS' ROLES

Public journalism has also pushed journalists to rearticulate some of the professional dimensions and their own identities as journalists (see Carpentier 2005: 214). The interviews identified five themes in how public journalism has affected professionalism.

Public Journalism as an Extension of Traditional Professionalism

There are journalists in all of the three newspapers who do not consider public journalism as a particularly significant professional challenge. They see it as a natural part or extension of traditional professionalism. For some of these journalists, public journalism is seen as an unnecessary buzzword, because good journalism already *is* public journalism; it has citizens in the focus. Others, by contrast, take a more supportive view that public journalism is a natural part of journalism, and there is no contradiction between the classical values of journalism and the public journalism values; they are both built on the premise of public service, a dominant value of the democratic-corporatist tradition. This discourse, thus, presents earlier and existing journalistic professionalism as an inclusive construct capable of adapting new approaches.

Helping and Supporting Citizens

A clearer case of rearticulation is apparent when professionals discuss their relationship with the audience. In public journalism, the journalist is positioned as a collaborator or helper. They speak of the need to 'support' citizens, even 'defend' them. The idea of helping can take different concrete forms. In interview situations where ordinary people meet decision makers, the journalists' role is to encourage the people to formulate and pose their questions. Helping may also happen 'textually' in a sense that stories are written with clear language and from the viewpoint of citizens. Stories with citizen angles are thought to be more relevant for the reading public than stories that cover political process as a game of a small inner circle. However, the idea of journalists as helpers retains an element of control. Journalists as professionals are still needed: the amateur/citizen cannot make it on her own in the public discussion. If the journalists' job previously was to 'help' the public by providing important information about the institutional people, since they possess the kind of information that does not traditioally reach the newsrooms. For example, the journalists in the local news paper *IH* expressed a wish to 'appreciate' and 'utilize' the knowledge an experience of ordinary people.

Posing Questions

An important participatory position that requires citizen expertise is the questioner. In this position the citizen is seen as a knowledgeable subject, capable of formulating her views into questions that may be better or more concrete than the questions posed by journalists. However, the position of the citizen/questioner does not always imply a high degree of activism. Citizens can, for instance, send their questions to journalists via email, allowing journalists to pose the questions while the citizens remain anonymous. This indirect practice excludes the element of tension that is often linked to face-to-face questioning. In these situations the presence of the citizen as the questioner becomes journalistically interesting. The participants—especially due to their positions as voters—have a special role to play in encounters with elected representatives. Thus, the role of the questioner can be a very powerful one: citizen participant is seen as a useful coworker for the professional journalist.

Readers as Public Actors

The final role for citizens in public journalism is connected to public agency. However, the role of the citizen as a public actor is considered controversial by journalists. On the one hand citizens are seen as active participants, but on the other hand as objects requiring activation. Despite the paradox, the logic is that if a newspaper wants to take citizens as participants in making journalism it cannot rely only on the ones that are already active. Instead, the newspaper needs to activate the public at large, because it benefits both the newspaper and the community. Moreover, journalists note that people who are willing to take part in the journalistic process often want to influence the direction of public discussion, publicize their cause or contribute in other ways to certain issues. The key is to understand that people do not want to participate *only* for the sake of journalism. The problem is, however, that this kind of civic activism is not always congruent with news values or professional norms, such as general significance or neutrality. Thus, dealing with active citizens is more demanding for journalists than to deal with 'sample citizens'. In sum, the stronger the citizen role becomes, the harder it becomes to handle journalistically.

Looking at the citizen roles perceived by Finnish journalists, one can see how the earlier professional culture provides the repertoires with which new challenges are understood. Aligning with the citizens can be seen as an asset in the traditional activity of keeping the public institutions in check, public life, their task now can be extended to 'helping' the citizens to participate and act. Therefore the idea of helping can be seen—paradoxically perhaps—as a way to retain the journalistic authority and competence that used to originate from remaining a distant observer.

Opening Up to the Public

The next cluster of rearticulations underlines interaction with the public. According to this discourse, journalism as a professional conduct needs to open up to make journalism more relevant, interesting and inclusive for the public. The need to open up is also justified by the previous isolation that journalists experienced. Usual terms linked to this discourse are 'meeting people' or 'being accessible'. By being more open to citizens' comments and participation, journalists get a 'reality check'. Public journalism projects have thus clearly encouraged journalists to remove their 'professional shell' to avoid 'barricading themselves in the newsroom'. This openness can be seen as an example of a broader trend in the welfare societies in which many previously closed professional and expert systems now have to claim their legitimacy through a language of transparency.

Journalist as a Discussion Moderator

Seeing the newspaper as a forum for public discussion is a classical professional ideal. This idea is extended in public journalism: discussion is not merely seen as an act that takes place after the publication of the news stories. Discussion moderation is considered to be part of journalists' professional capabilities. Discussion becomes an important method of information gathering and a way of making a story. A recurring metaphor in the interview material is the idea of bringing different participants together 'around the same table'. Discussion-based methods are, however, more stressful for journalists than traditional reporting. Indeed, the idea of bringing different sources to the same table and producing fruitful dialogue is considered a difficult task: journalists also need to be able to connect different participants with each other. Unsurprisingly, this aspect raises doubts among journalists. Previously, Finnish journalists were asked to provide a neutral interpretation of reality that would not offend any of the major (class-based) collective identities, but now they are called into a more complicated task of facilitating the interaction of complex sets of individually based identities and interests.

Being More Public

The title 'public journalism' suggests that the journalism profession should be more public. The Finnish journalists regard the idea in a dual manner. On the one hand, being more public is equated with increased publicity and promotion. This perspective stems from concrete experiences from public events, which aim to attract visibility and publicity for the newspapers and therefore also for the journalists in their roles as event hosts, interviewers or reporters. The journalists also experience increased pressures to identify themselves with the news organization and its brand. They do not consider this change in a positive light: it is not always nice to be a 'roving *Aamu-lehti*' correspondent or 'the face of the paper'. Some reporters, especially in the *AL* regional paper, think that public journalism has mixed journalistic work with marketing.

On the other hand, public journalism projects also evoke a deeper discourse in which the profession is seen as public in terms of being there *for* the public. This 'public professionalism' embodies all of the elements that have been discussed in this section: helping citizens, opening up to the public and fostering discussion. With these modifications to the professional role, the journalists can better achieve the aims of public journalism. This kind of publicness opens a reflective potential to two directions. In relation to the trends of the media industry, reporters articulate their critique by resorting to this demanding vocabulary of publicness. In relation to the audience, this version of publicness translates into a responsibility for acting as cocreators and participants in public dialogue.

CONCLUSION

Public journalism in Finland has evolved from researcher-led projects to independent, mainstream newspaper practices. Public journalism has bred new kinds of story elements aimed at bridging the gap between formal decision making and citizens, as well as encouraging active citizen engagement in the public discussion.

Public journalism has provided a possibility for the newsrooms to experiment with participatory methods and reflect upon the changing roles of the citizens as well as journalists. From the interviews, it becomes evident that some features in the professional culture encourage Finnish journalists to consider the ideas cautiously. For instance, some of the citizens' participatory roles are traditional and well in line with conventional newspaper practice, such as the idea of the sample citizen or the citizen as a provider of story ideas. In terms of the journalists' roles, the idea of public journalism as an extension to traditional professional journalism is a rather modest way of seeing the revitalizing potential of public journalism. However, seeing public journalism as an extension to professionalism is also an important reason why public journalism practice has gained ground among Finnish journalists. This is always a precondition for new ideals to be accepted.

Finnish public journalism experiences have also inspired journalists to reflect the role of the citizens and the journalists more intensely. The evidence that journalists are using citizens in roles such as the questioner or the expert show that public journalism practices have pushed the journalists to widen up their scope. Journalists conceive the readers as active public actors who can take part in the journalistic process together with professional journalists. This, in turn, poses challenges to the journalists' own position. Public journalism requires that reporters also act as helpers and discussion moderators and interact with citizens. Thus, the professional journalist is still needed to perform public service—a value embedded in the professional culture of Finnish journalists—but serving the public now requires assistance rather than distance. However, these impacts of public journalism on journalistic professionalism or readership are not uncritically regarded as completely positive. Finnish journalists criticize the marketing-style aspects of public journalism, a complaint that is also heard in United States (Haas and Steiner 2002).

Finland's Democratic Corporatist Media Model has offered a fertile ground for public journalism. The strong role of newspapers and the professional culture of journalists that value public service have created a setting in which newspapers have been willing to experiment with democracy supporting and participatory practices. Additionally, the fact that the media field is affected by various socioeconomic pressures has worked in favour of public journalism ideas to be developed in newspapers.

A trend towards reduced citizen engagement in politics and falling voter turnouts has encouraged newspapers to innovate activation projects. Adoption of public journalism in Finland is also connected to cultural changes, such as the individualized service culture. Indeed, the challenges of newspapers to maintain their market shares have caused the newspaper managers to think about various ways in which newspapers can become relevant for their readers—both as citizens and as subscribers. However, public journalism-style coverage has not proven to guarantee economic prosperity. In fact, as a labour intensive and costly approach, public journalism might even lose its appeal in the future.

Technological developments—such as email, Web questionnaires and online feedback features—have made reader–journalist interaction and participation easier. The research for this chapter was conducted at a time (2002–06) in which newsrooms had not yet fully realized the potential of Web-based participatory technologies. Current studies indicate that journalists are facing similar professional challenges with the handling of online audience materials to those experienced with the public journalism approach (e.g. Paulussen et al. 2007). Online audience participation is a trend that will intensify in the future, and therefore the lessons from public journalism practices are valuable for newsrooms that strive to fruitfully combine citizens' independent media production, such as citizen journalism and blogging, to the practices of the professional media.

At the moment, public journalism in Finland has less clear borders than in the late 1990s when the idea first circulated among academics. For example, newspapers do not necessarily label their approaches as 'public journalism'. In fact, there seems to be a trend to rename the approaches of the newspapers, to develop them into concepts, even brands such as the 'news van'. The global techno-economic trends have shaped journalism more generally towards practices that bracket out the structures of democracy and collective representation and underline individual experience and opinion. Public journalism has partly adapted to this framework. However, it still contains elements of resistance that stem from democratic theory and broader understanding of public service.

NOTES

1. This chapter is based on a larger empirical study of 165 public journalism news stories and interviews with forty journalists. For further details, see Ruusunoksa 2006.

BIBLIOGRAPHY

Alasuutari, P. (1996) *Toinen Tasavalta, Suomi 1946–1994 (The Second Republic, Finland 1946–1994)*, Tampere: Vastapaino.
Beckman, P. (2003) *Riv Stängslen! Medieran Som Mötesplats: Public Journalism i Svensk Tappning (Tear Down the Fences! Media as Meeting Place: Public Journalism in Swedish Practice)*, Stockholm: Sellin & Partner Bok och Idé AB.
Carpentier, N. (2005) 'Identity, contingency and rigidity: The (counter-) hegemonic constructions of the identity of the media professional', *Journalism*, 6(2): 199–219.
Haas, T. (2007) *The Pursuit of Public Journalism: Theory, Practice, and Criticism*, New York: Routledge.
Haas, T. and Steiner, L. (2002) 'Fears of corporate colonization in journalism reviews' critiques of public journalism', *Journalism Studies*, 3(3): 325–41.
Hallin, D. and Mancini, P. (2004) *Comparing Media Systems: Three Models of Media and Politics*. Cambridge, UK: Cambridge University Press.
Heikkilä, H. (2001) *Ohut ja Vankka Journalismi: Kansalaisuus Suomalaisen Uutisjournalismin Käytännöissä 1990-luvulla (Thin and Thick Journalism: Citizenship in the Practices of Finnish News Journalism in 1990s)*, Tampere: Tampereen yliopistopaino.
Heikkilä, H. and Kunelius, R. (2003) 'Ajatuksia lainaamassa' ('Borrowing thoughts'), in N. Malemin (ed.) *Välittämisen Tiede: Viestinnän Näkökulmia Yhteiskuntaan, Kulttuuriin ja Kansalaisuuteen (Science of Mediation: Perspectives of Communication to Society, Culture and Citizenship)*, Helsinki: Viestinnän laitos, pp. 179–204.
Hujanen, E. (2007) *Lukijakunnan Rajamailla: Sanomalehden Muuttuvat Merkitykset Arjessa (In the Borderline of Readership: The Changing Meanings of Newspaper in the Everyday)*, Jyväskylä: Jyväskylän yliopisto.
Hujanen, J. (2009) Informing, entertaining, empowering: Finnish press journalists' (re)negotiation of their tasks', *Journalism Practice*, 3(1): 30–45.
Kunelius, R. (2001) 'Conversation: A metaphor and a method for better journalism?', *Journalism Studies*, 2(1): 31–54.
Paulussen, S., Heinonen, A., Domingo, D. and Quandt, T. (2007) 'Doing it together: Citizen participation in the professional news making process', *Obervatorio*, 1(3): 131–54.

Richards, I. (2000) 'Public journalism and ethics', *Media International Australia,* (95): 171–182.

Ruusunoksa, L. (2006) 'Public journalism and professional culture: Local, regional and national public spheres as contexts of professionalism', *Javnost/The Public,* 13(4): 81–98.

Shilongo, P. (2005) *Echoes—Polytechnic Student News Service: Report of the Student Multimedia News Agency Pilot Project*, unpublished paper: Namibia and Finland.

Wahl-Jorgensen, K. (2002) 'The normative-economic justification for public discourse: Letters to the editor as a "wide open" forum', *Journalism & Mass Communication Quarterly*, 79(1): 121–33.

10 Citizen Voices
Public Journalism Made in Colombia

Ana Maria Miralles
(Translated by Angela Romano)

Colombia's experience of the practice of public journalism dates back to November 1998, when Citizen Voices (*Voces Ciudadanas*), the country's first public journalism project, was initiated by the Pontifical Boliviarian University (*Universidad Pontificia Bolivariana* or UPB) in Medellín. This chapter explores how UPB, largely inspired by models of public journalism from the United States, instigated the first public journalism activities in the country and has continued to lead exploration of how the principles and practices might help Colombia to address entrenched social problems. Despite the successes of Colombia's various public journalism projects, the chapter describes how the practice of public journalism continues to be driven by an academic/professional partnership, rather than by media organizations alone.

The concept of public journalism was introduced to Colombian academics in 1996, when UPB created a postgraduate training program called the Specialization in Urban Journalism. Public journalism became the key principle underlying the fields of the theory and investigation being taught. UPB's decision to focus its urban journalism specialization in this direction was brought to life by the belief that the media needed to be transformed so that it could be truly engaged in constructing a democratic public sphere. On a pragmatic level, UPB staff also recognized that public journalism offered something new to an academic program, as a complementary philosophy of journalism that had been formed not just in the halls of academia but also in newsrooms. Professors Cheryl Gibbs, then of Indiana University, and Barbara Zang, of Missouri University, were visiting academics who provided the educational program with insights about public journalism's theoretical foundations and practices.

Public journalism arrived in Colombia after a period of intense destabilization, resulting from attempts to curb drug trafficking and the persistent security problems faced by citizens. Journalism remained a risky profession, particularly for those who attempted to report about drug trafficking, guerrilla fighters and the paramilitary. During the 1990s, people who discussed the mass media usually addressed three major themes: journalists' self-censorship, the homogeneity of information available to society, and the expansion of media monopolies.

Journalists' self-censorship—which still continues—originates from political and economic pressures, arising from sources such as advertising companies' directors or affiliated political groups who may shape a media organization's editorial line. Self-censorship is also dictated by fear of the actors in Colombia's drug trafficking and the entailed armed conflict.

In observing the homogeneity of the information provided by the mass media, academics have noted a paradox: vibrant civil organizations arose in Colombia in the 1980s, but this did not translate in a greater representation of those new voices in the media scene. Journalists continued to seek the same official sources, interview the same people, and develop the same angles in reporting the information. After the political reform of 1988, which led to a system of voting for local mayors through popular election, journalists did not act as a conduit of information that might bring those in government closer to those who were governed. Academics were concerned not only by the lack of pluralism in perspectives about controversial issues, but also by the absence of debates that truly included the public as well as the homogeneity of the agenda set by Colombia's media.

The problem of media monopolies was already under scrutiny in 1996, a time in which the government was preparing to license Colombia's first private television networks. Only two national commercial networks were licensed in 1998, and this limited the variety of opinions provided by news and information programs in the television panorama. The media sphere was further restricted in 2001 when *El Espectador*—one of Colombia's most important and influential newspapers, which had been in circulation for 114 years—stopped publishing daily. It instead circulated on a weekly basis due to an economic crisis. There were also staff cuts in many other media organizations, with those in Bogota particularly badly affected (Gómez 2002). This slowed the local media in joining a partnership with the Citizen Voices project.

How did the academy manage to entice the mass media to practise public journalism? The answer in the case of the Citizen Voices project is *sui generis*. The students of UPB's Specialization in Urban Journalism were journalists and publishers of mass media organizations in Medellín, so when they completed their studies it was easy to suggest to them that they form a group which would introduce public journalism to Colombia. Due to the nature of these contacts, public journalism was initiated in the print media by the reporters, but in television it was led by the directors of news programs. Editors from the print media soon endorsed the idea and provided increasing support as the initiatives continued.

In the first ten years of Citizen Voices—1998 to 2008—the project passed through different phases and underwent a fundamental transformation. It moved from being a local venture in Medellín to becoming a project that promoted public deliberation at national level through its two latest phases, which considered respectively the constituency of education and the rights of people displaced by the armed conflict in Colombia.

THE COMMUNICATIONS MODEL OF CITIZEN VOICES

In the first ten years of the Citizen Voices project, a systematic strategy has been constructed to open mass media debates so that they include common citizens in public participation and deliberation. The next section describes the ten key elements in the Citizen Voices model. (Further details are available in Miralles 2001: Ch. 4.)

Configuration of Public Space

The Citizen Voices projects have been a joint effort of different media organizations with journalists and UPB to create debates of interest to a wide range of social sectors. Citizen Voices has not attempted to replace normal public politics, but it forms a special segment of political life that includes common citizens. Historically, there has been a division in the public sphere between common citizens and those who may be counted as elites. The distinctive characteristic of Citizen Voices is that it raises common people's voices in debate of public interest, with the different media and journalists working together to create public space for constructing Citizen Agendas. The mass media had never networked for a common purpose like this before in Colombia, particularly with such complex debates aimed at enabling citizens to construct their own agendas that would in turn impact upon the broader public agenda.

Positioning of the Subject or 'Focus'

Before public opinion can be formed, it is essential to call citizens' attention to subjects of public interest that may generate controversy and need to be resolved through debate. Without these elements, the news might be quickly disregarded and thus the issue would be ephemeral in the public mind. The mass media has enormous power to create scandals in the fields of politics and celebrity figures. The Citizen Voices team tried to use the media's ability to create outrage or an uproar, but with the purpose of putting this commotion to the service of democratic public debate. The uproar functions simply as a strategy that helps citizens to recognize the issue in a jungle of competing information, as a central subject that will sustain their attention so that they can commit themselves to considering the issue for a period of months.

The Citizen Voices team has also strengthened the position of citizens as subjects by using a basic strategy of directing *open-ended questions* to citizens. The intention is to construct the citizen as an interlocutor—an actual participant in dialogue—rather than see citizens only as passive victims of events or consumers of media information. Journalists involved in Citizen Voices had to change their language and use forms of address to convince the citizens to participate in the debates. For example, the media would publish a weekly question to try to activate citizens, who were invited to call a telephone hotline to provide responses and arguments. In the Citizen Voices team, one newspaper would play a leading role in inviting citizens to become involved, and UPB students would field the telephone calls. Journalists would continue placing the issue in the public arena all week to prolong the flow of citizen participation and to provide information that would keep the debate in the public agenda.

Information

In Citizen Voices, information is conceived as a *conductive wire*. Because of the long-term nature of the projects, dynamic journalistic production is required to develop the theme that is under discussion, to maintain public attention and to raise the visibility of the findings periodically. Additionally, one of the more important outcomes of the Citizen Voices projects was the creation of what we called a 'bank of journalistic subjects'. This bank contained details of all the opinions and proposals from citizens who had connected themselves to the project. The coordinators and Citizen Voices journalists analyzed these to try to identify latent subjects that might be used to set the agenda for media reports. Studying the ways in which citizens argue about various topics creates the possibility for journalists to identify issues and factors that might be leading citizens to feel anxious or concerned. Thus, by considering citizens as protagonists who are connected to the histories of particular issues, journalists can use these citizens' life experiences to look more meticulously into the background of issues and distil a deeper understanding of the problems of the greater collective.

Citizen Participation

The Citizen Voices project revealed the great capacity that the media has to mobilize citizen participation in the Colombian context. We conducted a survey of people who were involved in Citizen Voices, and they responded that journalists had high credibility in their eyes, which helped to contribute to the media's success in mobilizing the public. There were no antecedents in Colombia for the phenomenon of the mass media and journalists systematically summoning citizens to participate in public deliberation. Prior to this, citizen participation was usually roused by civil society organizations or occasionally by local governments. It was the first time that the mass media took a step beyond providing information and moved towards providing a platform for communication and deliberative interaction between citizens to construct Citizen Agendas. We did not initially anticipate the news media had such a capacity to motivate and assemble the public, due to the customs of a one-way flow of information, with the position of the dispatcher (journalist) and receiver (audience) being predetermined.

Debate

From the beginning, Citizen Voices embodied the notion of linking public opinion into democratic debate. Each Citizen Voices project developed the mechanisms of citizen deliberation, with the university taking a central position as the project coordinator. The journalists' role in the deliberation process has been to participate in these discussions as witnesses and to report on the results of the conversations of citizen groups. Some journalists were highly committed to deliberative practices, participating with questions for the citizens in public meetings and even becoming involved in the process of argument and reasoning. One of the main challenges for the media has been how to cover those citizen conversations, because journalists needed to record not just the comments of individual people but to capture the collective perspective. Journalists tended to single out some of the participants and conduct a conventional one-to-one interview. It was difficult for them to develop an understanding that deliberation involves a process and that after one meeting they could not expect clear signals—like the white smoke that is issued to indicate the result of the papal elections—of decisions or conclusions being reached.

Opinion Tendencies[1]

In the Citizen Voices projects, citizens respond to particular questions that the media posed to them each week, with academics trying to analyze and translate the tendencies that were occurring in citizens' opinions. The journalists did not participate in this analysis. Their role was to publish the results of the UPB's analysis and select citizens to ask about their histories and experience. This was the point where the projects began to make those citizens who participated visible. The analysis of the trends in public opinion provided the first indication of where Citizen Agendas were heading and this in turn issued a call for deliberative groups of citizens to continue exploring these subjects.

Visibility

In modern democracies, one of the conditions of the public is the principle of visibility (Rabotnikof 1993: 76), or how 'the public' (a community sphere comprising values, choices and actions) should be developed 'in public' (an observable space). In essence, if one accepts the principle that common citizens must play an active role in determining their own preferences (or agendas), then the process of constructing those preferences must occur in the full vision of the mass public. Here a distinction comes into play between 'mass' and 'public', as is identified by Vincent Price (1994). This helps us to understand that the active 'public'—or in this case, those citizens who participate in the Citizen Voices project—advance their deliberations in view of the remainder of the 'mass' community, who are largely an audience or spectators. In the Citizen Voices projects, a small group of citizens forms the public that creates perspectives that the rest of the masses can tune into by virtue of the *principle of the representativeness*. Citizens' positions are made visible only because of journalistic activities: interviews, feature articles and, occasionally, news stories.

Citizen Agenda

All the processes conducted in Citizen Voices projects are geared towards building Citizen Agendas on issues of public interest. The agendas of the projects are structured from three elements: the Preamble (citizens express their value position), the Critical Agenda (identifying what is going wrong) and the Proposition Agenda (citizens make proposals). Thus, the Citizen Agenda is a document that details and deepens the trends in public opinion that were expressed via the telephone hotline and, via the process of deliberation, it establishes the public's priorities in the topics being discussed. In our opinion, this exercise of power requires that citizens undergo a process that allows them to distil their own agendas and enter into a dialogue with the agendas of political power and the mass media themselves. It has been an historical weakness of citizens that as a public they have not formulated a clear system of preferences, and thus they have only been able to interact with the sources of formal political power in a disconnected and dispersed fashion, which has been less productive than an integrated approach.

Interlocution with Power

This is an important area, which we doubtlessly need to analyze far more. Once the Citizen Agenda has been established, there needs to be a space for formally delivering that agenda to the local or national authorities. To date, the journalists' role has been to summons the attention of the authorities who hold formal power and to guarantee that the Citizen Agenda is handed to them. The participating journalists in the Citizen Voices projects have fulfilled this task rigorously. They have thus assumed the responsibility, as far as their functions allow them, of advancing a successful process that kept the public engaged for several months. However, it is clear to the Citizen Voices coordinators and to the journalists who work to conduct a dialogue with those in power that the act of delivering the Citizen Agenda is an ongoing process. This process must be pursued by the citizens themselves, although this will probably most occur in conjunction with non-government organizations or political parties. This last point is the one that is most important to explore, at least in the Colombian context: how to revitalize and to propagate democratic ideas in the political parties so that they become civically engaged with serious processes like that of Citizen Voices?

Journalistic Pursuit

This is work that depends entirely on the journalists. We must recognize that, just as in the traditional media, this is one of the weakest points of our strategy. That weakness results from two fundamental causes. The first is that the journalists' giddy pace of work requires them to jump literally from one subject to another in terms of the topics that they report on. Consequently, journalists tend to neglect those subjects that require intensive investigation. The second is that if the citizens do not organize themselves to negotiate their agendas with those in power, it becomes very difficult for journalists to commit themselves to follow up the issues. Thus, the vigour with which journalists continue to pursue the issues depends on the ability of the Citizen Voices project to help citizens to construct mechanisms to follow up and progress their agendas. As I have mentioned previously, this has not happened yet due to the weakness of social capital in Colombia.

TEN YEARS VIEWED THROUGH THE REAR-VISION MIRROR

For ten years, the Citizen Voices project has worked with the journalistic corps that are known as the 'media of record', or in other words, media organizations with strong market penetration and political influence. In the localized projects, the notable television participants were the local channels of Teleantioquia television, Telemedellín and the opinion programs of Channel U. Participating Medellín-based newspapers included *El Colombiano*, *El Mundo* and *El Tiempo*'s local edition. Large radio stations that became involved were RCN, Caracol and Todelar. These organizations have been the more stable and consistent participants in the Citizen Voices projects. The two projects that were run at a national level included *El Tiempo* and *El Espectador* newspapers and RCN television as partners.

With the benefit of hindsight, it is possible to observe transformations in the nature of journalists' work during the course of the Citizen Voices deliberations, which ran for an average duration of about five months for each project. Those changes are summarized in the following paragraphs.

The Nature of the Process

The journalists had to understand the *nature of the process* of reporting on deliberation. In other words, they had to disregard the frenetic rate of normal news production and the ephemeral nature of the topics they previously addressed when they had undertaken conventional journalism, to be able to concentrate on a deliberative process that would develop over several months. This broke with the journalists' previous professional routine that involved switching to a new and different subject to report about each day, and required the journalists to persevere with a single theme for several months. This dimension of public journalism helps citizens to remain committed to following the topic. It is the best way to serve the pace of citizen deliberation, which is a process that is best forged over time and does not suit media traditions of 'breaking news'.

Listening to Citizens

Both the journalists and the students who participated in the projects experienced what it means to listen to citizens, in terms of their conversational style and the exercise of deliberation, in addition to conducting in-depth interviews. Journalists found it challenging to listen to common citizens rather than to sophisticated civil servants who often speak to the media on a daily basis. This required the journalists to spend more time with different citizens, to listen openly and to abandon the idea of hunting for the most lively quotes to publish in their stories. Instead, they had to exercise their capacity to understand and include the overall perspective of citizens. The main challenge to journalists' professional routines was precisely this task of learning to listen rather than to presume that they could preempt what their 'sources' were going to say.

News from the Street

Through the Citizen Voices project, the journalists went back to the streets. Academics and media professionals have regularly observed that journalists' work has become increasingly bureaucratized in recent decades. Journalists have lost contact with the people and instead established a relationship of dependency with the traditional political and economic sources to such a degree that one might think, perhaps with only a little exaggeration, that journalists no longer actively seek the news but that instead the elite sources deliver their news to the editing rooms. This propensity for journalists to rely on major politico-economic sources is reinforced by the activities of public relations units in different institutions that have an interest in making themselves visible through mass media. In public journalism, the reporters use the techniques of ethnography, such as walking through the streets in order to ramble in the *flâneur* style described by Marc Augé (1987): to observe, to talk with different citizens, and to leave aside their recorders and to listen some more.

Other Journalistic Texts

The journalists had to rethink and reframe the central objective of their texts: all elements of journalistic production would position the ordinary citizen as the key protagonist. This meant challenging the traditional protagonists of the news, who are those official and elite sources mentioned previously, and beginning to ask how citizens produce news or whether the citizen perspectives are better represented in alternative formats such as interviews and feature stories. Turning to the citizen protagonists for information helped the journalists to understand citizens' communicative codes, which are very different to the communicative codes of traditional sources. Additionally, there were two major changes in the way that journalists prepared their reports.

The first change for journalists was to conceive the information so that their reports still adhered to the traditional concepts of including the five Ws and one H (the who, what, when, where, why and how) in each story, but so that they also provided citizens with the data and perspective that would enable them to participate in deliberation. That meant providing more detail about the background and context of the project's topics. This was not always achieved, nor is it clear whether these informational formats had any influence on participants in the deliberations. There are several reasons for this.

- These reports did not always coincide with the timing of the deliberative meetings and the participants did not always have timely access to the stories. This meant that the participants were less able to offer further inputs that might stimulate follow-up journalistic reports;
- The journalists did not always manage to devise new ways of approaching and structuring the information, and thus they often maintained traditional reporting formats;

- The data that journalists presented as input for the deliberations did not differ from traditional paradigms for interpreting the issues;
- Initially, neither the UPB staff nor the journalists could distinguish the difference between those various journalistic formats that might promote civic participation and those formats that were simply informative. As they became more experienced, journalists paid more attention to how they invited the public to participate, with a change of the type of language they used in order to motivate members of the public to call the weekly telephone hotline.

Second, the journalists were asked to change their perspective about information and to narrate the stories from the viewpoint of the citizenry. This implied that journalists provided the ordinary citizens with a voice as the subjects of interviews, feature stories and news article. They additionally recorded the opinion trends as they arose from citizen deliberation on the project topics. The journalists thus sought citizens who were participating in each project to interview them about their perspectives. It was vital that the UPB staff, as the project coordinators, provided the information about these citizen contacts and stimulated the journalists to pursue them. It was challenging for journalists to shift their mindset away from interviewing ordinary citizens with the sole goal of producing news stories, and to instead see the media production processes as a component of the overall practice of public deliberation. A good example of the journalists' change in perspective can be seen at the culmination of one of the first projects, *Citizen Voices: Viva the City Centre*, when *El Colombiano* newspaper published a headline and lead that reported the citizens' action in presenting the Citizen Agenda to the Mayor of Medellín. In this story, the citizens were the active protagonists and the authorities the passive subjects of action (*Periódico El Colombiano* 1999: 2D).

Valuing Public Opinion

The journalists had to appreciate and value the processes of creating public opinion as a fundamental part of democratic deliberations. The inclusion of ordinary citizens via the paradigm of the citizen participation has become an ideal that the journalists have assumed with total integrity. Prior to this, newsroom staff had shown a certain contempt for the processes of public opinion formation, because journalists worshiped the cult of 'facts' and saw opinion as something that should be relegated to actors outside the media. Public journalism implies that the journalists understand the importance of public opinion, which Giovanni Sartori (1994) describes as the interactions between information and opinion.

A Space to Discuss the Profession

As the projects progressed, the journalists participated in weekly meetings with colleagues from other media linked to Citizen Voices. This provided them with the power to pause, so that they could discuss the theory and strategies of public journalism and debate ethical issues. Some journalists recognized that these discussions were not taking place in their newsrooms, due to the swift pace of their work and their immersion in professional routines. The Citizen Voices projects offered them a space to deliberate about the city, citizenship and the media. Above all, journalists recognized that they could work together, even with their 'rivals', in the interests of the city.

The Journalists become Part of the Project

Journalists broke the habit of only gathering information from those conventional sites where they have traditionally expected to find news. In the Citizen Voices projects, journalists attended the citizen's deliberative groups, which lasted between two and three hours, to observe developments in the deliberation process. Not all journalists attended these meetings. None attended each and every group. Overall, however, journalists recognized that one of the media's more pernicious habits is to look only at the result of a process, and not observe how decisions were made and how the process was played out. By attending the deliberations, journalists did not simply seek a source to interview about the result of discussions. They also developed an understanding about how collective visions are constructed through deliberation.

Not all the media organizations and journalists had the same levels of commitment to the Citizen Voices projects, and therefore there were unequal levels of engagement with the citizens. However, all media organizations and journalists were still considered equal partners in Citizen Voices. UPB did not assume the classic role of academics as critics or evaluators who tried to teach the journalists what they have to do, but instead it has been collaborative work among peers. For ten years, journalists reported on Citizen Voices from a position *inside* the project, rather than the traditional journalists' position as an external observer. The journalists approached UPB, took notes with the students who monitored the citizen's telephone hotline, looked for trends in citizens' opinions and went to the streets to find the citizens' views themselves. This was possible thanks to an ongoing, daily process of communication between the Citizen Voices coordinators and the project leaders within each mass media organization. This dialogue was articulated by a powerful force: the enthusiasm for discovering the citizens' contributions, for verifying directly that citizens were not apathetic about topics of communal interest that were presented in the media, and for revealing journalists' capacity to be convenors of citizen participation.

Table 10.1   Summary of Citizen Voices Projects in Colombia

Project	Objective	Length	Agenda
Citizen voices on security and coexistence Medellín, 1998	To deliberate with citizens about how to obtain a peaceful coexistence in a city wracked by conflict	5 months	A Citizen Agenda was given to the city's mayor
Citizen voices: Viva the city centre! Medellín, 1999	To construct a Citizen Agenda for revitalising the downtown (inner city) district	4 months	A Citizen Agenda was given to the city's mayor
Citizen voices by the reconstruction of Armenia Armenia, 1999	To engage earthquake victims in designing a blueprint for reconstructing the destroyed city	5 months	A Citizen Agenda was given to the authorities overseeing the reconstruction
Citizen voices on parking meters Medellín, 1999	To engage citizens in resolving problems of maintaining public thoroughfares	2 months	A Citizen Agenda was given to the city's mayor
You decide! Citizen voices Cali and Medellín, 2000	To construct an agenda of issues for the mayoral election	8 months	The agenda was circulated among citizens and mayoral candidates
Citizen voices: Raising your voice Medellín, 2001	To assess the mayor's Development Plan in light of Citizen Agendas on development	1 month	A Citizen Agenda was given to the city's mayor
Citizen voices: Viva soccer Medellín, 2002	To debate with fans and other citizens on how to overcome violence at soccer matches and to celebrate the sport harmoniously	8 months	A Citizen Agenda was given to the city's mayor
Citizen voices on the quality of life Medellín, 2005	To deliberate with citizens about poverty and possible solutions	5 months	A Citizen Agenda was given to the city's mayor
Citizen voices on the quality of the education Colombia, 2006–07	To construct Citizen Agendas on education for the next 10 years	5 months	A Citizen Agenda was given to the Ministry of National Education
Citizen voices of people displaced by force Colombia, 2008	To allow people displaced by Colombia's internal conflict to construct an agenda of demands for basic rights	4 months	A Citizen Agenda was given to the Constitutional Court

IMPACT OF CITIZEN VOICES

In spite of all the benefits that have arisen from citizen participation and management of the political agenda, the Citizen Voices project has had less impact than might be expected in transforming journalistic professional culture. There are three reasons for this comparatively low bearing. First, the high rotation of journalists means that many who have been trained in the nature and practices of public journalism often move to new positions, other media organizations or even different professions. Each time this happens, the Citizen Voices team faces the challenge of preparing a new contingent of journalists to undertake projects. Second, the greediness of the marketplace has led media managers to trim personnel numbers and double the duties of the remaining journalists. As a consequence, journalists find it harder to dedicate their time to the Citizen Voices projects. Third, the problem arises from structural causes. As Michael Schudson has already noted (1999: 112), without changes in the system of media ownership or the commercial logic of media proprietors, the reforms of public journalism will largely be conservative, without any radical transformation of journalistic practices or systems for constructing a public agenda with citizens.

In contrast to this commercial logic, the Citizen Voices project is aligned philosophically with the World Social Forum (WSF). The annual WSF deliberations, initiated in Porto Alegre, Brazil, offer an alternative to the formulations of the industrialized countries that are expressed through the World Economic Forum in Davos, Switzerland. The WSF has a general motto: 'another world is possible'. For those in the field of communication, this raises the proposition that 'another communication is possible'. In Latin America it is recognized that community radio and television, as well as Internet communications, have huge potential to offer the citizenship outcomes that are rarely achieved via large commercial media. In general, the expectation is that public journalism will involve the creation of new media, which have different directives and owners, thus overcoming the dilemmas of balancing commercial and communitarian concerns.

Nevertheless, the greatest impact of these projects has been in the academy. They have inspired the interest of many universities and departments for teaching mass media across Latin America. In the ten years of Citizen Voices, the UPB academics involved in the projects have presented at workshops, courses and conferences throughout Latin America. They have conducted research that to date has led to four books, various book chapters and numerous academic journal articles. Many students from several Latin American universities have undertaken theses about public journalism and some universities have introduced the subject into their curriculum. This suggests that one major difference between the public journalism movement in the United States and in

Latin America has been that the experience of the latter has shown how the transformation of the media can come from the education of future professionals.

It remains necessary to keep focussed on the Citizen Voices projects themselves as exercises in deliberation and to develop new daily information strategies inspired by the values of public journalism. This will help to ensure greater sustainability of public journalism in newsrooms that are entrenched in the commercial and political interests of certain community sectors. Accordingly, UPB academics are recommencing research about journalists' professional routines. The aim is to invigorate the system of cooperation between journalists and the university that was initiated through Citizen Voices, in order to identify new styles that will enable journalists to modify their standards for reporting and journalistic narratives so that they are more inclusive of the plurality of voices in our societies.

Our greatest contribution is arguably a revision of the theoretical perspective on public journalism and journalism in general. Launching the Citizen Voices project allowed us to refine our ideas about how democracy is really constructed with the *demos* (the people) via the performance of public journalism's communication strategies. In the beginning, we shared the vision of our North American colleagues, and placed much emphasis on building consensus from the deliberations. In common with Jay Rosen, we began by building our theoretical structure from Habermas' visions on deliberative democracy. Nevertheless, ten years later, this has changed due to our contact with the citizens and our own academic analyses of the traditional behaviour of the media in market-centred societies, which we compared with the findings of political philosophers and reflections about how the common good is constructed in modern communities.

From this, we have concluded that one of the main functions of the reporter and the media in general is to investigate and make visible the dissent in our societies. This does not mean, as many believe, that the media promotes chaos. Here it is important to differentiate clearly between the preoccupations and concerns of the political arena and the journalistic arena. Although consensus, which can be broadly understood as social agreements, are crucial for governance to occur, the construction of a true democracy requires that there is permission to publicly express dissent and disagreements. As Chantal Mouffe (2000) asserts, democracy is constituted through dissent and not consensus. (See pages 8 of 9 of this book for a further discussion of this.)

UPB scholars who are studying public journalism now focus their work on how dissent contributes to the formation of democracy. This will probably result in a reconsideration of the participation patterns and styles of deliberation that have occurred to date, because we should not forget that for Mouffe and other theorists of radical democracy, deliberative democracy tries to rise above these differences and not exploit them for political ends.

NOTES

1. In *Journalism, Public Opinion and the Citizen Agenda*, I spoke of 'consensus' of opinion, but today I prefer the term 'opinion tendencies'. Increasingly the Citizen Voices project has identified that the central role of mass media is more to make disagreement visible than to construct consensus, with the arena politics itself being a field of consent and dissent. I am currently finishing a book on the media, dissent and consensus, in which I draw from the learning of ten years with Citizen Voices.

BIBLIOGRAPHY

Augé, M. (1987) *Travesía por los Jardines de Luxemburgo* (*Crossing the Luxembourg Gardens*), Barcelona: Gedisa.
Gómez, I. (2002) *Libertad de Expresión, Herida de Muerte por la Crisis Económica* (*Freedom of Expression, Mortally Wounded by the Economic Crisis*), Bogotá: Foundation Antonio Nariño.
Miralles, A.M. *Periodismo, Opinión Pública y Agenda Ciudadana* (*Journalism, Public Opinion and the Citizen Agenda*), Bogotá: Editorial Norma.
Mouffe, C. (2000) *La Paradoja Democrática* (*The Democratic Paradox*), Barcelona: Gedisa.
Periódico El Colombiano (1999) 23 August: 2D.
Price, V. (1994) *Opinión Pública* (*Public Opinion*), Barcelona: Paidós.
Rabotnikof, N. (1993) 'Lo público y sus problemas: Notas para una reconsideración ('The public and its problems: Notes for a reevaluation), *Revista Internacional de Filosofía Política* (*International Journal of Political Philosophy*) (2): 75–99.
Sartori, G. (1994) *¿Qué es la democracia?* (*What is Democracy?*) Bogotá: Ediciones Altamir.
Schudson, M. (1999) 'What public journalism knows about journalism but doesn't know about "public"', in T.L. Glasser (ed.), *The Idea of Public Journalism*, New York: Guilford Press, pp. 118–33.

Part III

Other Deliberative Models for Peace, Participation, Development and Empowerment

eless and marginalized people them-
the first level, participation may be
marginalized people sell the maga-
urs when professional journalists
inalized people, thus circulating
e. At the third and most com-
less or marginalized people to
publication. This may include
als, define its identity in the
its written and visual con-
udience.
sinesses are self-sustain-
m government, private
publication focuses on
hat kind of audience
s presentation style,
alized stakeholders
ld communities,
not just through
perating in the
illustrates the
at is the best
alized peo-
ut actions
hat exi
erati
ne-
press
vel of
these

...paper
...ot only
...of growth
...pers or maga-
...es also by other
...to improve these
...st commercially suc-
...s founded in London in
...name in the United King-
...eyday in the 1990s, but it still
...ek.

...entrepreneurs. Social entrepreneurs
...ither (i) use entrepreneurial strategies for
...als or (ii) seek profits with the goal of help-
...nities or achieving social good (Ledbetter 1997).
...ial entrepreneurs, with both economic and social justice
...reet press apart from most of the mainstream and commu-
...lia. Another defining characteristic of street publications
...employment for homeless or other disadvantaged people.
...nbers of the International Network of Street Papers allow
...er disadvantaged vendors to keep a large percentage—on
...r cent—of the cover price of the publications that they
...TBI have been lauded for the way in which they are per-
...power marginalized communities, but this chapter argues
...utcomes of such initiatives are not always clear cut. This
...es how the street press's role as social enterprises creates
...out the appropriate balance of what I call the 'three Ps' of
...ntation, participation and profit-making.
...n is the level of professionalism or 'slickness' in the news-
...e product, in terms of the quality of its writing, editing,
...g. The level of professionalism is influenced by the editors'
...but what kind of product will attract and hold the target
...ion.

f the
dick
ared
buy
the
od-
nd
ne-

Participation is the inclusion of hor
selves, and can occur at three levels. A
confined solely to having homeless or
zine to the public. The second level occ
write many stories about homeless or mar
their views and issues in the public spher
mon level, the street press encourages home
participate in organizing and producing the
helping to set the newspaper or magazine's go
marketplace, determine its news agendas, create
tent, circulate the publication, and read it as an

Profit-making refers to the extent to which bu
ing and can operate independently of handouts fr
enterprise or charities. The degree to which a street
profit-making will heavily influence choices about w
it will target, the types of stories that it will present, i
and the levels of participation that homeless or margin
are allowed to engage in.

This chapter explores the potential for media to bu
encourage political activism and promote active citizenship
their content, but through their actions as economic bodies o
public sphere. The chapter focuses on *TBI*, because its story
tensions that exist within the street paper movement about wh
media model for helping the homeless, poor or other margin
ple—and indeed the wider community—to identify and carry
that will improve their lives and societies. The disagreements
within the street paper movement and the disparities in their op
can also be witnessed in community and alternative media more ge
(Van Vuuren 2008: 16). However, the economic goals of the street
and their operations as social entrepreneurs have added another le
division, ambiguity and complexity about the best way to organize
types of publications.

THE BIRTH AND GROWTH OF *TBI*

TBI was conceived in the early 1990s after a trip by the cofounder o
Body Shop cosmetic giant, Gordon Roddick, to the United States. Rod
claims he was approached in New York by a man who he initially fe
was a mugger, but who actually only wanted to ask the businessman to
a copy of *Street News* (Studholme 1992: 26). *Street News* was one of
first and most prominent street papers to emerge in the United States. R
dick asked John Bird, an old acquaintance with experience in writing
printing, to set up a similar venture in London. The aim was to offer hor
less and vulnerably housed people an alternative to charity and begging

TBI was launched as a monthly newspaper in September 1991. Bird aimed to attract an audience of mainstream eighteen- to forty-year-olds through a modern, urban design and a mix of features on social/political issues, celebrity interviews, reviews and entertainment listings. A section of *TBI* was also to be devoted to the issues and creative contributions of homeless people. Despite the newspaper's relatively unsophisticated presentation and content in its initial years, there was a strong public response in London to the overall principle of helping homeless people, who would sell the publication for 50p and keep 40p. *TBI* was so popular that it started publishing fortnightly at eleven months, also shifting to a magazine format at the same time.

TBI's circulations and scale of operations grew exponentially for the first several years of its life. Bird says he was 'astonished' when the magazine achieved a turnover of £1 million in 1993, after his initial expectations that he would be working with thirty to fifty homeless people in central London (Graham 2009: 12). That year the magazine turned into a weekly, and a separate Scottish edition was launched, later to be followed by editions in Wales, North England and the South West. *TBI* is now a firmly established player in Britain's publishing scene, and both Bird and the magazine have won much praise and many accolades over the years.

The Big Issue Foundation was established as a charity in 1995. The Foundation is funded from grants, donations and post-investment profits from *TBI*'s operations, with the aim of providing support and connection to services that will help the vendors reconstruct their lives and move away from homelessness.

Despite its laudable mission, it is questionable as to how much the *TBI* venture allows homeless people themselves to be agents in the process of determining the nature of change in their lives and societies. In exploring this question, it is important to consider the three main ways in which street papers like *TBI* can stimulate awareness and action to improve the lives of disadvantaged or marginalized people. The first way is to provide a venue for raising the voices, opinions and agendas of disadvantaged or marginalized people. The goal is usually to increase public awareness of homeless and/or marginalized people or integrate them into mainstream society. Some publications are more deliberative in nature, and attempt to sustain a dialogue that enables disadvantaged and marginalized people to name and frame issues on their own terms, and to play a substantive role in identifying the root causes and potential responses to these issues. The second way is to offer disadvantaged and marginalized people a venue to express themselves by creating the editorial content. The third way is to create enterprises that allow disadvantaged and marginalized people to be key players in building their own financial stability, confidence and workplace skills. The next section of the chapter addresses the challenges that publications like *TBI* face in achieving a reasonable balance between these three types of action, and how these quandaries relate directly to the three Ps of presentation, participation and profit-making.

HOW CONTENT ENGAGES COMMUNITY

Some street papers focus exclusively on stories about the experiences, causes and means of addressing homelessness. By contrast, *TBI*'s founders were determined from the outset that the publication's contents would not specifically be *about* the homeless. Nor were they seeking to *address* a readership of homeless people, but instead they would target the general public. 'We're not interested in a ghetto paper, with homeless people talking to homeless people,' Bird said soon after *TBI*'s launch (*The Independent* 1992a: 15). He described *Street News* as 'boring and inferior' (*Straits Times* 1994), claiming that *TBI*'s market research in the United States had revealed that people only bought *Street News* because they felt sorry for vendors; 'as soon as they buy it, they shove it in the nearest litter bin' (Wittstock 1991). Instead, Bird claimed that *TBI*'s objective was to work *for* and *with* homeless people by creating a paper that they would then be 'proud to sell and the general public is proud to buy' (Wittstock 1991).

Despite this aspiration to provide a newspaper that would sell on its own merits, *TBI* started with a small and relatively inexperienced editorial team, and its early issues were described by many as 'patchy', with stories 'like a student rag' (e.g. Pilkington 1992: 29). However, the reporting rapidly improved, so that *TBI* developed a reputation for its in-depth feature articles on social, environmental, cultural and political issues.

Much was made in its early years of the fact that *TBI* had exposed a number of stories that were overlooked by the mainstream media, although in reality, most of its exclusives were arts and entertainment stories. Because of the magazine's charitable nature, many British celebrities and public figures contributed articles to *TBI* or granted interviews to its reporters ahead of journalists from the mainstream media. One example was when the media-shy English alternative rock band, The Stone Roses, granted an exclusive interview to *TBI* in 1995 in the lead-up to a US tour. It was the Roses' first interview after a five year silence, and the only interview conducted in Britain on the release of their 'Second Coming' album. Explaining their decision, singer Ian Brown said: 'Somebody was gonna make money selling papers with us on the cover. . . . Why not do something for someone who could really use the money?' (Snyder 1995: E1). *TBI* increased its print run in the week that the interview was published, with the exclusive story pushing up sales by 40 per cent (*Campaign* 1995: 10). *TBI* also regularly uses stories about celebrities and other 'pop culture' icons to promote worthy topics. Examples include Oscar-winning actress Helen Mirren's musing on fuel poverty and the airing of fashion designers' views on politics and social change.

Thus *TBI* does sometimes 'break' stories and regularly discusses marginalized communities and sociopolitical issues. However, it arguably does not do this substantially more often than other British media organizations whose design, content and approach appeal to an educated and culturally progressive audience. Clever use of social icons and 'pop culture' can certainly help to advance public understanding of issues that might otherwise seem dull and weighty. Again this is a familiar strategy in mainstream media organizations that target a cosmopolitan audience. Although Bird purported in the 1990s that *TBI* looked and felt 'like something on the edge' (Meikle 1995: 6), his editor and director of the time, Joanne Mallabar, argued otherwise. 'Aside from the poor-quality paper, its celebrity interviews are often indistinguishable from articles in the mainstream press,' Mallabar (1998) noted.

Factors that distinguish *TBI* from other mainstream publications are relatively subtle (with the exception of its 'City Lights' and 'Alternative Roots' pages, which are discussed further below). Compared to most mainstream publications, far more *TBI* stories focus on how people or organizations are attempting to resolve different issues. In doing so, they provide communities not just with an explanation of what 'the problem' is, but various approaches to understanding the causes and potential solutions. Every few weeks, *TBI* prints a 'themed' issue, which presents a cluster of stories about a particular issue. These can vary considerably from lighter themes, like fashion or food or theatre, to more 'weighty' ones, such as mental health, needy children and the environment. The individual stories that are printed in the themed issues rarely differ greatly from those that might potentially appear in the mainstream media. However, the combination of several stories together provides readers with images of different dimensions of the problem and different ways of tackling them. Although *TBI* does not usually take an active role in attempting to mediate a coherent discussion between stakeholders, such material can support and motivate deliberation and action in communities.

TBI's stories about homeless people and issues affecting them tend to take a different character. Prior to launching *TBI*, Bird claimed that *TBI* would 'challenge prejudices and preconceptions expressed about the homeless' (Wittstock 1991). This was a significant goal, given the very limited range of stereotypes that appeared in the mainstream media. Academic studies in the United States indicate that the media in that country commonly portray homeless people as 'drunk, stoned, crazy, sick and drug abusers', and that the 'preoccupation' with this 'socially dysfunctional portrayal' leads to a general distortion of the issue of homelessness (Min 1999: ix). Given the broader similarities of media cultures in Britain and the United States, it can be presumed that such 'preoccupations' have dominated Britain's mainstream media too.

TBI innovated with content by, about and for the homeless. This was reflected in the main feature of the first issue, which was provocatively headlined 'Why don't the homeless just go home?' Within a few years, however, Bird had reduced the amount of space devoted to the writings of the homeless about homelessness to make *TBI* more culture oriented, a decision that was reportedly driven by market research (Carvel 1994: 13).

Although *TBI* runs occasional features on issues relating to homelessness, the perspectives and insights of homeless, ex-homeless or marginally housed people were generally confined to the two-page 'City Lights' pages and vendor profiles at the back of the publication. 'City Lights' includes poetry, photographs, drawings, and fiction and nonfiction essays. These pages offer homeless people an opportunity for self expression. The stories demonstrate the diverse backgrounds and experiences of homeless people and raise community awareness that almost any type of person might unexpectedly become homeless. Previously *TBI* also profiled a 'star' vendor in each issue, with a photograph, interview and testimonies from the vendor's regular customers. The vendor profiles were phased out several years ago in a revamp of the back pages, although profiles still intermittently appear amid other stories within the magazine.

In her analysis of street newspapers, Danièle Torck analyzed *TBI* and three other street papers from France, the Netherlands and United States in 1999 and 2000. She found that in all four, the pages by the homeless and stories about the homeless were dominated by personal narratives and expression of feelings—How did I get into this situation? How do I experience this situation?—rather than facts or issues (Torck 2001: 384). Although such stories aim to be different from the mainstream, Torck argues that they reflect 'the social ethos that traditions, politics and media have created around poor and homeless people' (Torck 2001: 385).

In contrast to the focus of 'City Lights' pages on experiences and narratives, the newer 'Alternative Roots' page—also at the back of the magazine—spotlights people whose actions and philosophies have aimed to address social problems. The 'Alternative Roots' page now appears in the back pages instead. 'Alternative Roots' publishes stories from a range of community activists, many who have experienced homelessness themselves, and the page describes active efforts to address various issues that contribute to or result from homelessness.

Apart from these dedicated pages, *TBI*'s focus on a broader audience means that there is only sporadic and sometimes disjointed discussion that includes homeless people themselves in exploring the responsibility, self-initiatives, social changes and resources needed for their empowerment. Regular readers would have the opportunity to form a coherent picture over time of the different issues involved in tackling homelessness as a larger phenomenon. However, occasional readers would be left with a piecemeal perspective or, depending on which issues they purchase, scant understanding at all.

In evaluating *TBI*'s performance, contextual issues need to be considered. *TBI* might be criticized as providing inadequate and insufficient inclusion of the homeless given its goals of countering the misconceptions that hamper public responses to homelessness. However, in the context of how little is published in the British mass media about homeless people and their issues, it might conversely be seen as making a substantial and much-needed contribution.

THE HOMELESS AS MEDIA MAKERS

The central mission of many street publications is to include homeless people themselves in creating the publications. Drawing homeless people into the heart of a media organization's operations allows the possibility of what John Hartley (1997) calls 'colonizing' the public sphere. Colonization is more than merely having the words or ideas of representatives of minority groups included in media stories or public discussions. It involves a broader kind of access that enables those groups to influence the terms in which issues are raised, the frequency that they are talked about, who gets to speak about them, and how the issues are framed and presented. Canadian mental health advocate, Pat Capponi, also argues that including homeless people in creating a well-respected publication that focuses on their issues provides therapy for people who have lost everything. She describes those street publications that exclude homeless people from the writing and editing processes as 'cutting their legs out from underneath them' (Brown 2002).

Prior to *TBI*'s launch in September 1991, its founders indicated that the publication's profits would be used to train homeless people as writers, photographers, computer operators, desktop publishers and office workers. Vendors were to be channelled into special courses set up by organizations that provided services to homeless people, such as Shelter, Centrepoint, London Connection and New Horizon. Some would contribute to *TBI* itself, although due to the limited number of places within the organization, the publication also intended to help place 'graduates' elsewhere (Wittstock 1991).

TBI did indeed run some workshops. Sometimes it even attracted celebrated media figures, such *Marie Claire* editor Glenda Bailey, who talked with homeless writing groups about how to write for women's magazines. However, despite the initial aims to include homeless people in *TBI*'s creation, it instead established and maintained clear-cut boundaries between editorial staff and vendors. From her position as *TBI*'s former editor and director, Mallabar (1998) observed that the attempt 'to marry charity and business' led to internal culture clashes.

> Distribution staff working on the frontline with vendors sneered at what they called the 'ivory tower' of management and journalists on the top floor. . . . Vendors had all but vanished from the landscape, restricted to the distribution counter and formal monthly meetings with editorial, where they were able to express their—invariably negative— views of the magazine.

The experience of countless community-based media organizations around the world indicated that *TBI* was bound to experience such stresses due to the tensions between encouraging stakeholder participation and creating a professionally presented product to attract a mass audience. However, most community media organizations rely heavily on unpaid labour and need only to generate sufficient funds to cover their operating costs for publishing or broadcasting plus sometimes the salaries for a few paid managers or technical staff. The conflicts are potentially much greater at street papers, because as social enterprises they must find sufficient funds not just to cover the operating expenses of publishing, but to also provide the surplus that enables vendors to pocket a substantial percentage of the sale price.

The challenges of creating a professional product are also greater for street papers than for many other community and alternative media, because distinctive issues arise in engaging homeless people in such ventures. Even Michael Burke, an engineer who cofounded Canada's long-running *Street Feat* paper, describes homeless people as 'fairly dysfunctional' and notes that 'it is very hard to get them organized' (Brown 2002). Fifty per cent of the *Street Feat* team is made up of poor and homeless people. Burke recognizes that they have difficulty making a commitment to the routines required by media organizations because they struggle with the basics of daily survival and lack access to facilities that writers regard as basic, such as housing, telephones and computers (Brown 2002). Given the transience of many homeless people's living circumstances, there can also be a very high turnover of homeless contributors to street papers. *TBI* focuses on professional presentation and generating income to provide vendors with direct revenue plus profits that enable vendor support and other services through The Big Issue Foundation; this logically leaves little time or energy for integrating homeless people into the realms of content creation and management. As an entity that is primarily a publishing business, the focus is on empowerment through entrepreneurship and profits rather than through participation and expression.

The conflicts that Mallabar observed within *TBI* are thus symptomatic of the natural variations that exist in the street paper movement and communities about the appropriate balance of the 'three Ps' of professional presentation, participation and profit-making. For healthy and democratic deliberation to occur, however, street papers need to establish lines of communications and organizational structures that provide the means for the publication's staff, homeless people, homeless advocates and other stakeholders to express and manage their differences. Van Vuuren sums this up in her conclusion that the *content* of community and alternative media alone is not a good measure of the sector's capacity to enhance civil society. The focus also should be on *organization* of the various elements involved in creating that content (Van Vuuren 2008: 149). In short, such organizations must not only be professional in how they present their content but also in how they provide training and support that helps to build the confidence, competence and capacity of volunteers and/or staff. The organizations furthermore need to be professional in how they forge networks with stakeholders and overcome barriers to participation.

THE POWER OF PUBLIC PRESENCE

Although *TBI* does not offer homeless people many chances to participate in the magazine's creation or content in comparison to many other street publications, it has given homeless people greater public voice and visibility via the position of its vendors in the streets. Prior to *TBI*'s birth, the relationship between homeless people and general public was both limited and tarnished. This was due in a large part to the disproportionate notoriety of a minority of homeless people who were prominent in the public eye due to demeaning, disruptive or demanding behaviours. *TBI* vendors, by comparison, are conspicuously nonthreatening. Homeless people who wish to obtain the badge that authorizes them to sell *TBI* must sign a code of conduct, which requires them to refrain from a range of behaviours that might lower the reputation of *TBI* and its vendors. This includes, among other things, not buying or consuming alcohol or illegal substances, using aggressive or threatening behaviours, using offensive language, obstructing the public, busking or begging while wearing the badge. The vendor's position of selling a socially legitimated product in public also issue an invitation for vendors and the general public to talk with each other. When *TBI* was first introduced, many vendors indicated the 'relief of being able to talk to ordinary people who, before the excuse of purchasing the paper, merely averted their eyes in embarrassment at their predicament' (*The Independent* 1992b: 4).

Testimonies published in *TBI* and elsewhere often point to fact that the exchanges between vendors, customers and other passersby go far beyond discussions of the product being sold. Many vendors and customers develop nuanced relationships through extensive interactions over time. Published testimonies indicate the extent to which these relationships often come to be highly valued by the parties on both sides. These face-to-face interactions can potentially allow participants to develop deeper and wider understandings of homelessness, its causes, potential solutions and complexities than they might acquire from the more distant experience of reading a journalistic article.

THE MEDIA AND SOCIAL ENTERPRISES

Although all street press include a social and commercial/entrepreneurial dimension, publications vary dramatically in the degree to which they prioritize socially mediated versus profit-driven outcomes. Britain's *TBI* is among the relatively few street press that are financially self-sustaining, presenting itself as 'a business solution to a social problem' (*TBI* 2009). Bird argues that the 'power of a business is to improve and transform the lives of people' through a relationship of 'taking'. He contrasts this with charity, which he describes as being only about 'giving'.

> Unless you involve the people in their own redemption, they will never
> be redeemed. I have always worked with the simple idea of giving
> homeless people not just opportunity but responsibility. . . . I give to
> the homeless and take from them, so they become useful to me and
> other people (Graham 2009: 12).

TBI has been described as the most prominent example of 'caring capitalism' in the UK (Hibbert, Hogg and Quinn 2002: 289), but despite this,
antipathy from some quarters of the street press is so strong that the magazine was once dubbed a 'poverty pimp' (Boden 1998). This concern was
expressed particularly intensely when Bird attempted to set up a *Big Issue*
in the United States in 1998.

The American *TBI* was not a commercial success, and only circulated in
Los Angeles for one year. In that time it came under fire for allegedly being
'a sensationalist publication that champions capitalism' (Brown 2002).
Chance Martin from *Street Sheet* argued that by catering to the rich with its
celebrity interviews and advertisements for jeans and cosmetics, the LA version of *TBI* supported the agenda that creates homelessness (Brown 2002).

American critics questioned both the trade-off of homeless participation
for profit and the fairness of distribution of profits. Some argued that publications like *TBI* reduce the homeless to a source of cheap distribution for
a commercial product. For example, Paul Boden (1998), a worker at the San
Francisco Coalition of the Homeless, asked why funds that are currently
directed to The Big Issue Foundation's activities are not used to pay vendors
a living wage with benefits. 'You can bet their advertising staff are paid and
paid well,' Boden said. 'No street newspaper can claim the vendors leave
poverty with the money they get from selling the paper' (Boden 1998). In a
letter to Bird, Jennafer Wagonner, the founder and editor of the local street
paper, *Making Change*, similarly asked:

> How is this corporate philosophy any different from that of compa-
> nies who hire day labourers, leaving them without civilized benefits
> like health care, inside/upward mobility, livable wages, co-operative
> administration or profit-sharing with employees?

Waggoner furthermore expressed doubt about the underlying rationale of
TBI and similar 'corporate social service structures' (Waggoner 1998). She
argued that homeless services should not just treat people like clients, but
incorporate them as policymakers and planners of relief efforts. 'If it is
about product, anyone could have homeless people out selling things like
toothpaste or laundry detergent,' she said. 'It's about having a voice' (*Making Change* 1998).

The American critics raised a valid critique of the magazine's overall
operations. *TBI* is a mainstream institution that primarily promotes rehabilitation of homeless at an individual level. In its British operations, *TBI*

rarely contests the underlying corporate and political structures that have reduced the supply of affordable housing and contribute in other ways to homelessness. *TBI*'s stories certainly do not provide a cost analysis of the organization's own commercial operations compared to its outputs.

Although *TBI*'s vaunted success is attributed to a viable business operation, this neglects the fact that in its first years of life *TBI* was dependent on donations totalling £500,000 from Roddick and The Body Shop (Graham 2009: 12; Meikle 1995: 6). Added to this, *TBI* 's initiatives have been underpinned by numerous and sizeable grants and donations from governments and private enterprise, as well as support from other charities. It also relies on continuing payments by members of the public for a magazine whose sale is based on charitable impulses as much if not more than demand for the actual product alone. Problems in *TBI*'s commercial structure have emerged since 2002, leading it to shed most of its editorial staff in London and Wales. The London *TBI* is produced by a team that straddles the London and Manchester (*TBI in the North*) offices, and the Welsh *TBI* (*TBI Cymru*) is produced by *TBI Scotland*'s team in Glasgow. If people in Britain are to make informed choices about buying *TBI*, they need to weigh up the costs and benefits of *TBI*'s current model of business enterprise. Are the outcomes better than those that might have resulted had this enormous pool of money, talent, time, voluntary contributions, paid labour and public good will been marshalled and put to use in other ways?

If the public's ability to deliberate on their own role in *TBI*'s activities is limited, then the capacity of homeless people for deliberation about their participation is even more constricted. Bird talks of involving homeless people 'in their own redemption', but *TBI*'s management clearly defines and delimits the terms for their participation. There is no doubt that Bird and *TBI* staff hold genuine concerns about the well-being of the homeless and have constant opportunities to interact with homeless people and take their views into account. Despite this, Bird and *TBI* staff do not include homeless people in making decisions about the magazine's business structure and goals nor its creation or content. While a homeless person can contribute to the two-page 'City Lights' section, any individual's contributions can only be occasional at best, given that there are many hundreds of thousands of homeless Britons who might potentially submit their creative works to *TBI* for consideration.

CONCLUSION

In her analysis of street papers, Teresa Heinz (2004: 539) points to their deliberative potential: 'Street papers demonstrate how effectively alternative publications can serve as mouthpieces for marginalized groups. As they educate readers, street papers are bases for further community building and political activism.'

As one of the world's most prominent street papers, *TBI* is notable for many remarkable achievements, most particularly in marshalling massive community resources and using the communications media to stimulate action to help improve homeless people's lives. Despite many initial warnings to Bird that a magazine for the homeless was destined to fail, it has not just survived but its success has led to versions being set up in Australia, Ethiopia, Japan, Kenya, Malawi, Namibia and South Africa. Further ventures are also mooted for Pakistan and India.

Each issue provides some representation of homeless people and their concerns. Although such coverage is often relegated to a few of the back pages, it provides a consistent space, in contrast to the relative absence of homeless people in other British media. Its slick writing style and use of celebrities and pop culture has built *TBI* a solid following among people who might not otherwise read a publication that regularly includes the experiences and perspectives of homeless people. Thousands of homeless are provided each year with an opportunity to raise their income and rebuild self-confidence, marketable skills, communications capacities, and social connections. Further support comes through the outreach services provided through The Big Issue Foundation, which has also conducted many campaigns to help prevent homelessness and promote awareness of particular priority issues. One of *TBI*'s important and generally unacknowledged achievements is the increase in interactions between vendors and passersby, which have allowed for a greater number of open, sustained dialogues between the homeless people and the mainstream public. These interactions benefit not just the direct participants of these exchanges, but homeless people overall, as it increases the visibility and public understanding of homeless people more broadly.

All operational choices made by *TBI* and other street publications must have their pros and cons, and this chapter exposes and examines some of them. Social entrepreneurialism in the media is a relatively new phenomenon, and the movement has had only a few decades to consider how to balance their need for financial resources against their social goals and the many boundaries created by the social, political and economic environments that they operate in. If the street press is to achieve further progress in helping the homeless and other marginalized people, there must be further deliberation on the nature and balance of the 'three Ps' of professionalism, participation and profit-making.

BIBLIOGRAPHY

Boden, P. (1998) 'The British are coming!', *Street Sheet*, February. Available at http://www.ainfos.ca/98/jan/ainfos00301.html (Accessed 1 September 2009).
Brown, A.M. (2002) 'Small papers, big issues', *Ryerson Review of Journalism*, Summer. Available at http://www.rrj.ca/issue/2002/summer/373/ (Accessed 1 September 2009).

Campaign (1995) 'ABC sales figures show jump in *Big Issue* circulation to 100,000', 17 February: 10.

Carvel, J. (1994) 'Homeless find their voice in the street', *The Guardian*, 22 February: 13.

Graham, N. (2009) 'A streetwise seller of self-help strategy', *Financial Times* (Money supplement), 9 May: 12.

Hartley, J. (1997) 'An Aboriginal public sphere in the era of media citizenship', *Culture and Policy*, 8(2): 43–64.

Heinz, T.L. (2004) 'Street newspapers', *Encyclopedia of Homelessness*, vol. II, ed. D. Levinson, Thousand Oaks, CA: Sage: 534–9.

Hibbert, S.A., Hogg, G. and Quinn, T. (2002) 'Consumer response to social entrepreneurship: The case of the Big Issue in Scotland', *International Journal of Nonprofit and Voluntary Sector Marketing*, 7(3): 288–301.

The Independent (1992a) 'A bigger issue every time: *Big Issue* magazine', 19 February: 15.

The Independent (1992b) 'London's homeless sell a success story—*TBI* monthly newspaper', 5 August: 4.

Ledbetter, C. (1997) *The Rise of the Social Entrepreneur*, Demos: London.

Lorber, J. (2009) 'Extra, extra! Homeless lift street papers, and attitudes', *New York Times*, 13 April: 5.

Making Change (1998) 'TBI and homeless industries', 3 March. Available at http://www.ainfos.ca/98/mar/ainfos00044.html (Accessed 1 September 2009).

Mallabar, J. (1998) 'Has the issue become too big?' *Independent on Sunday*, 18 October. Available at http://www.independent.co.uk/arts-entertainment/has-the-issue-become-too-big-1179143.html (Accessed 1 September 2009).

Meikle, J. (1995) 'Homeless paper seeks social projects cash', *The Guardian*, 22 November: 6.

Min, E. (ed.) *Reading the Homeless: The Media's Image of Homeless Culture*, Westport: Praeger.

Pilkington, E. (1992) 'The word on the street—*TBI* newspaper', *The Guardian*, 9 March: 29.

Povoledo, E. (2009) 'As bigger publications falter, "street papers" cling to their niche', *International Herald Tribune*, 4 May: 14.

Snyder, M. (1995) 'Stone Roses' comeback has smell of success: Legal Hassles over; new album is out', *San Francisco Chronicle*, 25 January: E1.

Straits Times (1994) 'Papers sold by homeless a hit in UK', 4 August.

Studholme, A. (1992) 'It's big on the streets', *The Evening Standard*, 19 November: 26.

TBI (2009) 'Big Issue history'. Available at http://www.bigissue.com/History_34.php (Accessed 1 September 2009)

Torck, D. (2001) 'Voices of homeless people in street newspapers: A cross-cultural exploration', *Discourse & Society*, 12(3): 371–92.

Van Vuuren, K. (2008) *Participation in Australian Community Broadcasting: A Comparison of Rural, Regional and Remote Radio*, VDM Verlag Dr Müller: Sarbrücken.

Waggonner, J. (1998) 'To Big Issue Street newspaper: By Jennafer Waggoner (NASNA)', 14 January. Available at http://hpn.asu.edu/archives/Jan98/0305.html (Accessed 1 September 2009).

Wittstock, M. (1991) 'Newspaper with street cred—'TBI' set for September launch', *The Times*, 16 August.

12 Inspiring Public Participation
Environmental Journalism in China

Jiannu Bao

This chapter is a study of the role of Chinese environmental journalism in enhancing and supporting public participation in environmental areas. It defines the meaning of public participation in the Chinese context, and examines how the Chinese news media has facilitated public participation in environmental issues at the following three levels:

1. Informing and educating the public about environmental issues;
2. Observing and inspiring discussion and action by presenting diversified views and conflicting interests;
3. Facilitating informed participation in government decision making on projects that have environmental impacts.

After presenting a summary of how environmental journalism has developed in China since the 1970s, this chapter will analyze the news coverage of two significant environmental cases. The first case study explores the reporting of a controversial proposed dam construction next to the site of the world cultural heritage-listed Dujiangyan Water Conservatory Project in southwestern Sichuan province. The second case study analyses the news coverage of the public protest against the construction of a US$1.5 billion Paraxylene (PX) petrochemical plant in the southern coastal city of Xiamen and the subsequent government concession to relocate the plant. These two cases show the extent to which the Chinese news media can facilitate public participation so that citizens can influence government actions. They also illustrate the importance of the news media's relationship with the government and environmental non-government organizations (NGOs) in the process of enhancing public participation in environmental matters.

ENVIRONMENTAL JOURNALISM IN CHINA

Environmental reporting was limited in China until the mid-1990s, but in the twenty-first century it is emerging as a distinctive form of public journalism as the media seek a third way between the Communist Party line and the market. The hallmark for the emergence of environmental reporting was the launch of a specialized bi-weekly magazine *Environmental Protection* in 1973, and the specialist *China Environmental News* newspaper in 1984, both in Beijing. As affiliated media outlets owned and run by the then State Environmental Protection Administration (upgraded to the Ministry of Environmental Protection in 2008), their mission was limited to publicizing and explaining government policies and actions.

Environmental reporting has developed rapidly since then. By the late 1980s, national newspapers had commenced regular environmental columns. Radio and television stations joined the print media in producing special environmental programmes in the mid-1990s, in addition to routine news coverage of environmental issues. Since the late 1990s, environmental websites, run by various stakeholders, have flourished. Environmental issues have now become an everyday topic in the news media.

The 'form' of environmental writing and reporting also proliferated over this period. Early environmental reporting was mainly in the form of 'literary nonfiction' by newspaper journalists, with their stories being published in major literary journals (Zhang 2007). This form of writing dominated environmental reporting in the 1980s, and it continued to flourish in the early and mid-1990s. Since then news coverage of environmental issues has increased beyond straight news stories to include spot news, features, and profiles and commentaries that add life and colour to environmental reporting.

The content in environmental reporting and writing has also increased in variety. In the 1970s, news was mainly about the subsidence of metropolitan Shanghai and treatment of three kinds of industrial wastes—sewage, exhaust and residues. On 5 March 1979, the Chinese official Xinhua News Agency filed a report, 'Sandstorms press on towards Beijing', in the form of a 'Letter from a Journalist'. For the first time, the news media publicly acknowledged and addressed the sandstorms that had been striking the Chinese capital for years and, more importantly, the cause of the problem—desertification. Desertification and deforestation thereafter became a major theme in environmental reporting and writing in the 1980s and 1990s.

Another milestone in Chinese environmental reporting in China occurred in 1998, when large-scale floods caused huge human and economic losses that alerted the nation to the need for ecological balance in the process of China's industrialization. Topics on sustained development and ecological balance started to increase in the news media, accompanied by discussions on global warming and climate change in the next few years. Incidents such as frequent algae outbreaks in major Chinese lakes, the explosion of a major chemical plant in northeast China in 2005, and a plague of two billion rats that invaded a major lake in central China in 2007 have further intensified discussions on environmental and ecological problems. They have been linked to ideas of environmental economy, green consumption and lifestyle, environmental philosophy, bio-diversity, environmental safety in urban planning, and appropriate exploitation and use of natural resources.

ENVIRONMENTAL JOURNALISM AS A FORM OF DELIBERATIVE JOURNALISM

Environmental reporters relied intensely on the strategy of 'emotional call-out' to attract attention to issues in the 1980s, but shifted to an approach of presenting 'rational thinking' on issues in the 1990s. They have moved further to 'taking a global perspective' from the turn of the new century (Zhang 2007). Realizing that too much 'exposure' of environmental problems without offering possible solutions can only drive people to depression and despair, the media have set out to engage the public in discussion of what can be done to remedy the impaired environment. Proposals were discussed in the news media for activities that citizens could be involved in, such as reducing the use of plastic bags and setting air conditioning in public buildings to no lower than 26° Celsius in the summer. At a more technical level, the news media circulated ideas such as the 'ecological compensation mechanism'[1], 'green choice'[2] and 'green loan'[3] from developed countries, which subsequently were institutionalized in government policy. The idea of 'ecological compensation', for instance, originated from a call-in participant in an environmental radio programme hosted on China Central Radio Station by seasoned journalist, Wang Yongchen.

Environmental reporting in the Chinese news media in the 1980s and 1990s focussed on events, activities and campaigns. Extensive coverage came only on occasions like 'World Water Day' and 'Tree Planting Day', or annual themed campaigns organized by high-profile government institutions like the 'China Environmental Protection Centenary Tour' and 'Up Close to Forests'. Now the news media take more initiative in setting their own agendas, seeking to shape public opinion and influence the government and corporate sector.

The role of environmental journalism has also evolved. While continuing to inform and educate the public on environmental issues, the news media are also inspiring and engaging people in discussion and action. They observe struggles from grassroots individuals and communities. They present different voices from various societal agencies including experts, academic institutions, environmental NGOs and the general public. They reveal conflicting interests and frameworks for understanding of different parties involved.

One example of this kind of reporting includes stories about the fight of a rural woman, Wei Dongying, against local chemical plants polluting a major river where she and her husband used to fish for a living. Wei kept an 'environmental diary', recorded the changing water condition of the river, took photographs and kept polluted water samples as evidence, to get local environmental authorities to take action and tackle the problem. Another example is the stories about a plastic lining project in Imperial Summer Palace in Beijing in 2003, which inspired discussions on preservation and protection of cultural heritages in the news media nationwide. The discussions finally led to a public hearing, the first ever on an environmental case.

Environmental reporting in China has acquired distinctive attributes that support public deliberation. These characteristics match those noted by veteran American journalist Michael Frome, who describes environmental journalism as:

> writing with a purpose, designed to present the public with sound, accurate data as the basis of informed participation in the process of decision making on environmental issues. . . . It is more than a way of reporting and writing, but a way of living, of looking at the world, and at oneself. It starts with a concept of social service, gives voice to struggle and demand, and comes across with honesty, credibility, and purpose (Frome 1998).

The emergence of environmental reporting as a distinctive form of deliberative journalism results from the interplay of three factors in the Chinese context. The first is the increasing demand for sound and accurate information about the deteriorating environment, and for possible ways to address problems. This has been coupled with increased citizen demand to participate in decision making on issues that may impact on their local environments. Surveys indicate that the environment is the third most concerning issue to Chinese citizens, after the issues of inflation and food safety. Such problems are inevitable given China's recent, rapid industrial development.

The second factor that promotes a deliberative approach to environmental reporting is the increased propensity for the news media to pursue social responsibility goals by 'standing up' for citizens in the face of corruption, social injustice or other problems. While this results in part from the journalists' active expression of their civic responsibility and social conscience, it is also supported by the profit-driven media market. Since 1992, the government has liberalized controls on the media, both in terms of the content of stories that can be published and the commercial ownership of media organizations (Pan 2000; Zhao 1998). Reporting on pressing environmental issues and incidents is an easy way to attract an audience, which results in increased subscriptions and/or advertising income.

The third factor that promotes deliberative environmental reporting is the central government's support for public participation in environmental protection. The central government, and the Ministry of Environmental Protection in particular, has encouraged public participation and media exposure of environmental problems, which have been caused to a large degree by the frenzy of local governments to boost local economies at almost any cost and corporate enterprise's lack of social responsibility.

Despite liberalization of the media environment, the central government still maintains tight control over media conversation about particular topics that might be regarded as 'sensitive', especially those that might affect social stability or provoke riots or unrest. Against this background, there is little control over environmental reporting, which the Communist Party regards as a relatively 'safe' topic.

The central government furthermore sees public participation in decision making and action on environmental issues as being relatively low risk. Encouraging the public to be active in environmental politics is viewed as a good starting point for improving socialist democracy and social justice. By affirming and encouraging media discussion and public participation in environmental politics, the government is able to point to successful enactment of laws and regulations that enshrine principles of public participation.

While the government takes a dominant position in determining the public policy and framework for action on environmental protection in China, both the public and the media play a crucial role. Qu Geping, the founding president of the Chinese State Administration of Environmental Protection, sums this up in his observation that 'China's progress in environment protection over the last 20 years has been driven by public opinion informed by the media. While the public is the power generator, the media is the driving force' (Wang 2005: 2).

PUBLIC PARTICIPATION: THE ULTIMATE FORCE IN ENVIRONMENTAL PROTECTION

Public participation by individuals, institutions and communities in environmental areas can occur at three levels:

1. The public becomes aware of environmental issues as a result of education campaigns, abides by government environmental policies for sustained development and adopts an environmental friendly lifestyle;
2. Individuals and communities negotiate with the government on decision making on environmental issues as parties with conflicting interests;
3. The public have the right to decide what kind of living environment they have for themselves and their descendents (Hu 2006).

Success in achieving these three levels of participation is seen an endorsement of the Constitution, which stipulates the rights of citizens to know, to participate, to express opinions and to check on government power in various public environmental affairs.

Legislation and government regulation have been strengthened since the turn of the twenty-first century to enhance public participation in decision making and action on environmental issues. China's highest legislative body adopted the Environmental Impact Assessment (EIA) Law in 2002, the first law to endorse public participation in environmental concerns. The EIA Law requires that all relevant parties, including experts and the general public, evaluate the likely impacts of development projects, programs and plans on natural and human environments. The State Administration of Environmental Protection also requires that all EIAs include public participation and obliges government departments to publish information on environmental issues. China's cabinet, the State Council, released documents in 2006 and 2008 stipulating that public consultations must be held in cases when a project will have an impact on the public's environmental interests and entitling the public to government information on environmental projects of public concern.

This has not guaranteed an easy path to public participation, let alone public inclusion in decision making and action. Current laws and regulations fail to specify the scope of public participation or define acceptable means and channels for public participation. Moreover, the alliance formed between the local governments hungry to build the gross domestic product (GDP) within their region and maximum profit-seeking corporate enterprises have made public participation in environmental areas even more challenging. People therefore experience extreme difficulties in airing their voices or ensuring their concerns are dealt with. As a result, complaints to government agencies about environment-related issues have increased by 30 per cent annually from 2005 to 2007. Many of them have led to 'mass incidents', as in the case of public response to the Xiamen PX project (Hu and Yang 2008). Yet, as leading Chinese environmentalist Ma Jun notes, public participation is a must in breaking such interest group alliances to achieve environmental protection (Ma 2007).

CAMPAIGN TO SAVE A WORLD CULTURAL HERITAGE SITE

One significant case of journalism provoking mass deliberation and action occurred in 2003 after the Dujiangyan Administrative Bureau proposed to construct a dam next to Dujiangyan, a 2,500-year-old water conservatory system that is still in use today. Dujiangyan was listed as a world cultural heritage site by UNESCO in 2001 and is renowned worldwide for its non-damming devices for water diversion, automatic flooding control and irrigation.

The dam project was expected to help control water levels for the Zipingpu Reservoir, which was built only a few kilometres from Dujiangyan as a hydropower generator in 2000 despite much controversy. The dam proposal was rejected by most experts because it would severely damage Dujiangyan's water diversion device, the crucial part of the world heritage water conservatory system. The Administration Bureau dumped these experts, appointed new ones, and commenced preparatory work for dam construction. The Administration Bureau insisted on going ahead with the dam because the Zipingpu Reservoir could only operate at half its hydropower generating capacity until a new reservoir was built to divert water for it.

Zhang Kejia, a veteran journalist from the Beijing-based *China Youth Daily*, learnt about the dam construction from a local expert on cultural relic preservation. Zhang immediately passed the news to Wang Yongchen, a seasoned environmental journalist from the Chinese Central Radio Station in Beijing. The two journalists visited the dam site on 26 June 2003. Rather than simply taking a traditional journalistic approach and making the controversy on the dam project public by telling 'both sides of the story' immediately, the pair decided to establish a network of concerned parties to take a more deliberative approach to the problematic dam construction. Zhang set out to enlist UNESCO Beijing Office to help lobby for the dam project to be halted. She hoped that high-level institutions could stop the dam construction in a top-down fashion.

Zhang's strategy worked. The controversy over the dam construction caught the attention of the Chinese Ministry of Construction, which oversees major construction projects across the country and started to look into the matter. Zhang published her story with the headline 'UN Concern of New Dam to be Built in World Heritage Site Dujiangyan' on 9 July. Zhang presented in her story the controversy about how the dam construction would damage Dujiangyan. The fate of the historic water conservatory irrigation system, a well-known tourist attraction, captured public attention.

While Zhang was seeking UNSECO support in safeguarding Dujiangyan, Wang took full advantage of her own Green Journalist Saloon to circulate information and her own story on the dam project among environmental journalists. The news spread. In the next few weeks, more than 180 media outlets—national and local, official and market-oriented, from in and out of the province—reported on the dam project and its inevitable damage to the heritage site. The extensive media coverage including that of the official China Central Television Station (CCTV) and Xinhua News Agency presented views from all parties concerned, which inspired further discussions and debates among the general public about the alternative courses of action. Opposition to the dam construction became the predominant sentiment within the community and the provincial government announced on 29 August 2003 that the dam project was to be terminated.

Zhang and Wang played a crucial role in preserving the Dujiangyan water conservatory system, 'the battle for defending Dujiangyan', as many called it (Zhang 2003). One of their strategies was to marshal organizations and community groups that would have an interest in the dam issue, and to encourage them to take action. As mentioned above, two of the more prominent were UNESCO's China agency and the Green Journalist Saloon.

Wang points out that the second strategy was to avoid reporting that was simply 'for' or 'against' the project. The media, instead, became a platform where diversified views from all sides were presented and their merits evaluated. Discussion and debates went beyond the pros and cons of a certain major project to raise questions about how to make the process of decision making more democratic and transparent. More importantly, the news media called for a new type of mechanism in public decision making—one which encourages and engages people from different societal sectors in discussion and action as equal citizens (Wang 2008).

This case is believed to be the first time in modern Chinese history that the media have directly influenced the government in decision making on a major project. The case stands as a model as to how the Chinese news media can elevate environmental issues onto the social agenda in a manner that is socially and politically acceptable in order to seek solutions to problems.

XIAMEN PETROCHEMICAL PROJECT

In November 2006, construction work of a 10.8 billion yuan (US$1.5 billion) Taiwanese-funded paraxylene (PX) petrochemical project started in the southern coastal city of Xiamen in Fujian province. The project under construction was expected to produce 800,000 tons of paraxylene and generate revenue of 80 billion yuan (US$10.8 billion) a year, almost one quarter of the city's GDP. However, there was no coverage of the project in the news media.

Zhao Yufen, a chemistry professor from Xiamen University, spearheaded a proposal to relocate the PX project when she was attending the annual session of the Chinese People's Political Consultative Conference (CPPCC) in March 2007 in Beijing. This followed the failure of her previous efforts to lobby the top Fujian provincial and Xiamen city government officials. Her greatest fear was the threat that leaks, explosions or natural disasters might create for the area's 100,000 residents. Her proposal was signed by 105 CPPCC members.

The proposal was made public by the *China Youth Daily* on 15 March. *China Business*, a Beijing-based market-oriented weekly newspaper, followed up with an in-depth, front-page story on 19 March. Both stories focused on Zhao's proposal to relocate the project. Both quoted Zhao in explaining the health risks of paraxylene and concerns about the paraxylene petrochemical complex being only 350 metres from a newly built major residential area while similar petrochemical plants are usually 100 kilometres from residential areas in international practice. The stories were picked up by commercial news websites which further circulated the news. One story in the Guangzhou-based *Southern Metropolitan News*, a market-oriented paper that has a reputation for crusading journalism, even offered a list of suggestions for Xiamen residents about legally permissible ways to oppose the project.

In the following month, no local Xiamen media outlets—official or market-oriented—explained the situation to residents. A feature story called

'Shadow of Chemical Industry over Island City' was published in late April by *Phoenix Weekly*, a Hong Kong-based news magazine that also circulates in major Chinese cities. However, copies of the issue were taken off the shelves in Xiamen immediately by the magazine's distributors under the pressure from the local government. Given the lack of information in the local media, Xiamen residents increasingly turned to Internet forums and chatrooms, particularly the popular community forum known as 'little fish forum', to discuss their worries about the project's environmental impact.

Millions of residents received a mobile/cellular telephone message from *Southern Metropolitan News* in mid-May, warning that paraxylene could cause 'cancer' and 'fetus malformation' and calling on residents to 'Safeguard Xiamen' through public opposition to the project. Once again, the local news media remained silent.

Media outlets in Xiamen finally started to respond on 28 May, when the *Xiamen Evening News* published a 10,000-character article by the city's chief environmental officer. This lengthy article assured the public that the project had passed its EIA and met the most advanced safety standards. It appeared that the paper was telling the official story under the instruction of the Xiamen city government. However, two days later, the city government held a five-minute news briefing, announcing that the PX project would be suspended and there would be further study of environmental concerns as part of the EIA for urban planning. No details were given, and the public was not convinced. More than 5,000 residents went to streets to demonstrate against the project on 1 June, and another large protest took place on the following morning.

The State Environmental Protection Administration stipulated on 7 June that an overall urban planning EIA of the project was required before the paraxylene or any other petrochemical project could proceed further. The EIA included a call for public opinions and suggestions plus a public hearing on the future of the PX project. An overwhelming majority of the resident representatives who attended the public hearing opposed the project. In contrast to the period prior to the demonstrations, the local Fujiang and Xiamen media followed news about the EIA and other developments closely until January 2008, when a final decision was made to relocate the project.

The project was relocated to Zhangzhou, a smaller city about 100 kilometres from Xiamen, with construction starting in February 2009. Local officials avoid the use of the word paraxylene and refer to the project as 'a major petrochemical project'. No news of the construction was reported in the following months by local news media in Zhangzhou, Xiamen or the provincial capital of Fuzhou. However, news media organizations from Guangzhou—the *Southern Weekend*, *Southern Metropolis News*—and other media outlets from out of Fujian reported on the project's development. News coverage indicated that the local Zhangzhou city government was blocking news about the project's relocation, for fear that residents in Zhangzhou would respond in the same way as Xiamen residents.

The news media coverage of the petrochemical project and the responses and participation of Xiamen residents says a lot about the relationship between the government and the media in China today. The market-oriented news media outlets have contrasted the official news media in terms of their approach towards the matter. While all the official news media organizations—national or local—except the Beijing-based *China Youth Daily*, kept silent on such issues or ignored them, the market-oriented news media chose to expose the issues. This coverage by the market-oriented newspapers and news magazines enabled residents in Xiamen to learn more about the project, which inspired and encouraged local discussion and action. While the silence of the official news media is attributable to self-censorship, it must also be understood that the market-oriented media were motivated, at least in part, by the commercial interests of exploring a newsworthy issue to attract more readers and build the newspaper or magazine's reputation.

While a few media organizations in Beijing, Guangzhou and Shanghai actively involved themselves in the coverage of the issue, no voice was heard from local news media in Xiamen, or from media organizations from Fujian province at large, except the top Xiamen environmental official's article in the *Xiamen Evening News*. It is an explicit rule in China that media organizations, the official media institutions in particular, are not supposed to criticize government authorities which they are subordinate to because they are part of government institutions themselves. However, it is not rare for national news media organizations to report on sensitive issues in provinces or cities away from their home bases. In the case of coverage of the Xiamen petrochemical project, those influential media organizations in Beijing, Guangzhou and Shanghai—largely market-oriented despite their links to local governments in one way or another—succeeded in informing the public about topics they were entitled to know about.

As the events unfolded, the news media covered not just the residents' concern about environmental and health risks in Xiamen; they also discussed the significance of public participation in decision making. The Xiamen event is seen as a turning point in public participation in China. It is the first time since the founding of the People's Republic of China that citizen action has succeeded in influencing government decisions on a major project. The event 'has helped establish a new type of activism, which focuses on a single issue in order to change government habits and the law' (Tang 2008). As the City Government's deputy secretary-general said: 'The government and the citizens have grown up together in the course of the event.'

It has to be noted that the news coverage was not flawless in terms of providing scientific and accurate information on the technical aspect of the Xiamen paraxylene project. The Beijing-based *China Youth Daily* and the *China Business* relied on a single source, the chemistry professor Zhao Yufen, for explanation of the potential environmental and health risks, instead of seeking further sources for accuracy, context or other possibilities. The news media generally ignored different opinions in internet forums and chatroom discussions that contrasted with the professor's account of the health threat, such as her claims that paraxylene was a high cancer risk and that the international standard for buffer zones was 100 kilometres. The news media instead exaggerated its teratogenic effects. This is a serious failing in an issue that demanded high levels of accuracy and precision while seeking to inspire democracy in decision making. It indicates that the Chinese news media still has a long way to progress in its application of deliberative principles.

ALLIANCE OF JOURNALISTS AND NGOS

As environmental reporting has developed, a group of devoted and distinguished environmental journalists has emerged. The most widely known include Wang Yongchen from China Central Radio Station, and Zhang Kejia from the *China Youth Daily*. Journalists like them who have been prolific reporters of environmental issues commonly develop a close and sometimes symbiotic relationship with NGOs. On one hand, journalists rely on the NGOs for story ideas, information and analysis. Zhang Kejia notes that the news media look to NGO's activities and agendas for interesting and newsworthy stories that can be beneficial to the course of the environmental protection in the country (Zhang 2006). On the other hand, NGOs often need media publicity to achieve their goals and agendas.

Wang Yongchen ventured into environmental reporting in 1984. Her radio programmes seek to engage the public to discuss and act on environmental issues and facilitate government policies and actions in environmental protection. Wang founded the environmental organization known as Green Home in 1996—which subsequently registered as an NGO in 2007—to raise public awareness of environmental issues and engage them in discussion and action by organizing tangible action. She is also an organizer of the Green Journalist Saloon. The Saloon convenes monthly free lectures on a wide range of topics related to environment reporting. Its purpose is to influence and build the capacity of journalists, whose reports may potentially influence and build the capacity of a wider public.

Therefore, Wang has a dual identity. She is a public figure in her own right for her activism in environmental protection and is also prominent as a journalist who has won numerous national prizes for environmental reporting. For the many environmental journalists who work in the media and are also active in NGOs, a conflict of interest may arise between the role of advocate/activist on the one hand and the requirement to be an objective journalist on the other. This conflict is one that deliberative journalists often have to negotiate (see pp. 231–233 of this book). 'This is not an ideal situation, but it is a social reality at the moment', Wang says in an interview. 'Journalists should speak for the public instead of a few certain organizations or institutions after all' (Weng 2005).

Such an integrated and interwoven relationship between the news media and NGOs is originated in the unique features of Chinese media in its relation to government administration. The news media are among the few channels available to Chinese NGOs for promoting their agendas in environmental protection. It is also strategic for NGOs to form alliances with the Chinese news media organizations, because they enjoy a special status as part of the governmental institution. The media are able to shape public opinions that are very likely to attract the attention from government administrations, which have the power to allocate resources and help solve problems. Furthermore, journalists and NGO leaders act as public intellectuals. 'This is a unique Chinese phenomenon, but it has its deficiencies,' said Liang Xiaoyan, one of the four organizers of Friends of Nature, the first environmental NGO in China, at the 2006 China Environmental NGO Annual Conference on Sustainable Development. 'We need to develop a wider range of channels and means to expand corporation in areas of environmental protection' (Liang 2006).

CONCLUSION

Environmental reporting in China has taken a big step forward in recent decades, from merely informing and educating on environmental issues in the late 1970s and the 1980s to inspiring and encouraging the public discussion and action today. This is partly a result of media industry reform in China since the mid-1990s, which encourages and even compels media institutions to diversify their content and seek larger audiences in order to earn more advertising revenues. It is also a result of the gradually improving political environment for the Chinese journalists. Both the official and the market-oriented media are still subject to Chinese Communist Party and government controls. However, these controls have been loosened so that the media are not merely a mouthpiece of the party and government. They are able to reflect and represent diversified views of social groups with different interests. Journalists enjoy far more freedom in covering environmental issues than they do in other areas of political life. Their ability to write reports that promote deliberation has been indirectly strengthened by environmental laws that enshrine the public's rights to know and participate in decision making.

Environmental journalists seek a third way between the Communist Party and the market, balancing social responsibility with the imperative to maintain economic profits. They share the Central Chinese Government's mission in environmental protection for sustainable development. The media, especially the market-oriented media, seek to stand for social justice, and defend environmental rights of the public as a form of civil rights. However, it is increasingly difficult for the news media to perform its duty as corporate enterprises form an alliance with local governments to achieve maximum economic profits at the expense of environment. This chapter indicates the importance and potential of China's media in persisting with attempts to inspire and facilitate public participation not only in environmental issues but in all areas of political and public life.

NOTES

1. The ecological compensation mechanism is an institutionalized practice for maintaining a balance of interest between parties of conflicting interest (a balance between those who attempt to protect, who damage or who profit from the environment) mainly by economic means so as to improve or restore the function of the ecological system.
2. The expression 'green choice' refers to a consumer's choice of commodities that are produced by non-polluting or less polluting manufacturers.
3. The 'green loan' is a term used to explain the policy of banks to give loans to enterprises only when they meet the standards for environment protection set by governmental environmental authorities.

BIBLIOGRAPHY

Frome, M. (1998) *Green Ink: An Introduction to Environmental Journalism*, Salt Lake City, UT: University of Utah Press.

Hu, K.P. (2006) *Role of Environmental NGOs and News Media in China in Facilitating Administration of River Reaches and Public Participation* (《中国的环保 NGO 和新闻媒体在推动流域管理和环境保护公众参与中的作用》). Available at http://www.greengrants.org.cn/poster/show.php?id=3719> (Accessed 10 January 2009).

Hu, K.P. and Yang, D.P (2008) 'China's green long march: Proceeding amidst crisis and opportunities' (《中国的绿色长征: 在危机与转机中前行》), in D. Yang (ed.) *2008 Green Book of Environment: Crisis and Turning of China's Environment* (《中国环境的危机与转机》), Beijing: Social Sciences Academic Press.

Liang, X.Y. (2006) 'Chinese characteristics in the relationship between the news media and environmental NGOs in China' (《媒体和NGO 关系的中国特殊性》), 2006 Chinese Environmental NGO Annual Conference on Sustainable Development, Beijing, December. Available at http://www.eedu.org.cn/ngo/communion/studies/200701/ngo_11836_5.shtml (Accessed on 16 January 2009).

Ma, J. (2007) 'Environmental Protection and Public Participation' (《环境保护与公众参与》), Speech at the Lingnan Discussion Forum (《岭南大讲堂》), Guangzhou. Available at http://theory.southcn.com/llzhuanti/lndit.gzlt/content/2007–07/09/content_4203224.htm (Accessed 6 January 2009).

Pan, Y. (2007) 'Speech at a symposium to commemorate the 15th anniversary of the launch of "Green Leave" magazine'. Available at http://www.news.xinhuanet.com/environment/2007–02/05/content_5696528.htm (Accessed on 22 December 2008).

Pan, Z.D. (2000) 'Improvising for reform activities: The changing reality of journalistic practice in China', in C.-C. Lee (ed.) *Power, Money and Media: Communication Patterns and Bureaucratic Control in Cultural China*, Evenston, IL: Northwestern University Press, pp. 68–111.

Tang, H. (2008) 'Xiamen PX: A turning point?', *China Dialogue*. Available at http://www.chinadialogue.net/article/show/single/en1626 (Accessed on 27 December 2008).

Wang, L.L. (2005) *Green Media: Environmental Communication in China* (《绿媒体: 中国环境传播》), Beijing: Tshinghua University Press.

Wang, Y.C. (2008) 'A biological perspective of news media coverage of water resources development' (《水资源报道的生态观》)', *Chinese Journalists* (《中国记者》), (5).

Weng, S.Y. (2005) 'An idealist environmentalist' (《理想的环保主义者》), *Decision Making* (《决策》), (3). Available at http://www.csid.com.cn/NewsInfo.asp?NewsId=6153 (Accessed 20 December 2007).

Zhang, K.J. (2006) 'NGOs and the media share social responsibility', Discussion at the Symposium on How Can Environmental NGOs Work with the Media?', Tsinghua University, Beijing. Available at http://hinature.5d6d.com/thread-154–1-1.html (Accessed on 8 February 2009).

Zhang, W. (2007) 'The rise of green journalism and green journalists' (《绿色新闻与中国环境记者群之崛起》), *The Journalist Monthly* (《新闻记者》) (5). Available at http://www.cjr.com.cn (Accessed 20 December 2007).

Zhang, W.O. (2003) 'Behind the "Battle for Safeguarding Dujiangyan"' (《"保卫都江堰" 背后—公众力量影响工程决策》)' *Southern Metropolitan News*, 26 September. Available at http://news.sina.com.cn/c/2003–09–22/0956795690s.shtml (Accessed 2 February 2009).

Zhao, S.Y. (1998) 'The public is the ultimate force in tackling severe environmental problems in China: Pan Yue' (《潘岳: 解决中国严峻环境问题的最终动力来自公》), Xinhuanet. Available at http://news.xinhuanet.com/politics/2007–04/01/content_5920062.htm (Accessed 8 January 2009).

Zhao, Y.Z. (1998) *Media, Market, Democracy in China: Between the Party Line and the Bottom Line*, Urbana: University of Illinois Press.

13 Peace Journalism in Indonesia

Gita Widya Laksmini Soerjoatmodjo[1]

> It was as if we were reporting a sport event, where both parties tried to keep the scores—on how many people murdered or injured, houses burned down, religious facilities destroyed.
>
> —Novi Pinontoan, Maluku journalist

This chapter describes how peace journalism, among many other initiatives, was used to build peace in the spice islands of Maluku after a series of bloody conflicts between Christians and Muslims commenced in 1999. This chapter highlights the importance of institutional building to ensure sustainability of peace in the area. Finally, this chapter attempts to project what is needed to continue supporting peace journalism initiatives as conflict potentials continue to lurk. The chapter draws from interviews that I conducted with journalists in Maluku, plus knowledge obtained through my role as a researcher for the Institute for Press and Development Studies (*Lembaga Studi Pers dan Pembangunan*, or LSPP), which is one of several non-government organizations (NGOs) which have promoted peace journalism in Maluku archipelago.

HISTORICAL CONTEXT

Indonesia may well be one of the most diverse and complex melting pots on earth. This country comprises 13,670 islands spread over an area the size of Europe. It is also home to 300 ethnic groups speaking some 365 local dialects.

The Maluku violence followed soon after the end of the thirty-two-year presidency of Soeharto and his authoritarian 'New Order' government. Indonesia had enjoyed economic growth but efforts to create a thriving civil society and independent media were repressed during the 'New Order' period. In the post-Soeharto *reformasi* (reform) era, Indonesia enjoyed greater media freedoms and diversity. There was an exponential increase in the number of independent radio stations, newspapers, magazines, television stations and online news portals (Romano 2003: 35–6).

Such unprecedented media growth was difficult to manage. The rapid growth led to such job market competition that many media organizations hired journalists with few or no qualifications or experience. This factor and journalists' focus on satisfying public thirst for information in an era of unaccustomed freedom led to problems in ethical and professional standards, most evident in a rise in biased and sensationalist coverage (Romano 2003: 65–6). This became very apparent as the media reported violent ethnic, religions, and political conflicts that erupted in Aceh, Maluku, East Timor, Irian Jaya and Kalimantan after the end of the Soeharto regime.

THE MALUKU CONFLICTS

This chapter focuses on the Maluku islands, a place that Gerry van Klinken (2007) describes as the site of the most terrifying communal conflicts in post-Soeharto Indonesia. All the islands in Maluku were a single province until 1999, when the regencies of North Maluku and Central Halmahera were split off as the separate province of North Maluku. The capital city, Ambon, remains the Maluku province's main urban area and was the focal point for much of the violence that commenced in 1999. While there were other major non-separatist conflicts in Indonesia in that period, the extreme nature of the Maluku violence meant that it dominated the headlines for more than five years.

According to Brigit Bräuchler (2003), Ambonese of both faiths practised a system of *pela gandong*—peaceful coexistence—under which mosques and churches were built together for generations. The idea of *pela gandong* was buried underneath the rubble as Ambon became a divided city in 1999. Although Ambon only covers an area of 377 km² (130 sq mi) and hosts only 206,210 inhabitants, the city was split along religious lines. Muslims occupied one end of town and Christians the other. Along the middle was a no-man's-land that acted as a partition line. Bräuchler describes how in 2000 armed soldiers kept a tense watch next to the barbed wire and the checkpoints (Bräuchler 2003). Around them, most buildings had been razed, while those still standing were little more than burnt-out shells. Graffiti on the wall of a ruined department store boldly pronounced: 'Muslim power vanquishes the Nazarenes.' Another countered: 'Christians conquer Muslim pigs' (Bräuchler 2003: 123).

The conflict started when fighting broke out between gangs of young men in the Batumerah transport terminal in the heart of Ambon on 19 January 1999, which was also Idul Fitri, the holiest day in the Islamic calendar (Van Klinken 2006: 131). What started as an argument between a Christian bus driver and Muslim passenger rapidly escalated into a fight between largely local groups of Christians and Muslims (ISAI 2004), spreading quickly throughout the city, especially its lower-class areas, and to the surrounding islands (Van Klinken 2006). The vicious fighting was often between neighbouring villages or between Christian Ambonese and largely Muslim Ambonese newcomers, but was spoken of in religious terms, of Christians (predominantly Protestant) versus Muslims (Van Klinken 2006: 131). Fire was a major weapon; homes and houses of worship were torched by the hundreds. Fighting extended to many places in the south of the Maluku archipelago. In the first year of the spiralling violence, 3,000 to 4,000 people died and an estimated 123,000 and 370,000 were displaced from their home regions (Van Klinken 2006).

In the early days of the conflict, local media organizations frequently stopped reporting for periods of time because of physical threats or warnings from the stakeholders in the conflict. In early 1999, no local radio stations in Ambon were broadcasting (ISAI 2004).

The fact that Idul Fitri was the opening day of the conflict attained considerable significance. Rumours that houses of worship had been burned down or that worshippers were massacred while at prayer instigated new acts of violence for more than a year. The year was characterized by intense fighting, often erupting around dates with religious significance, such as the Muslim Idul Adha festival, the Christian commemoration of Good Friday and the day after Christmas. In January 1999, no one outside the police and armed forces had modern firearms and only a few used primitive homemade guns, but by December both sides had acquired semiautomatic rifles from sources that have remained largely unidentified. Clandestine workshops were producing sophisticated rifles that used military ammunition. Homemade bombs were in abundant supply. The conflict led to the loss of thousands of lives, the destruction of thousands of houses, the segregation of Muslims and Christians and an increase in the number of displaced people to approximately 500,000, including the expulsion of all Christians from the Banda Islands.

With the arrival of the newly formed *Laskar Jihad* (Holy War Warrior) militia groups in South Maluku in May 2000, religious tensions rose further. Another huge conflict erupted in June 2000, claiming about fifty lives. In the same month, then-president Abdurrahman Wahid declared a state of civil emergency, and by July, there were approximately 14,000 troops in Maluku. The military solution was adopted after strong urging by local Ambon elites, especially but not exclusively the Muslim ones. It implied a serious reversal of the democratic progress that had been achieved elsewhere in Indonesia.

The violence began to subside in 2002, with a turning point being the December 2001 meeting between approximately 200 Muslim and Christian leaders to explore the possibility of reaching reconciliation. A further breakthrough was achieved in February 2002 with the government-sponsored peace talks. The two sides agreed on eleven points, of which the most important were to cease violence, return the internally displaced people (IDPs) to their homes, and respect the rule of law. The situation became calmer in the province, with the exception of Ambon city, and people started to return home. In spite of numerous negotiations and the February 2002 peace agreement, tension on Ambon Island remained high until late 2002, when a series of spontaneous 'mixings' between previously hostile groups lead to a sporadic but generally increasingly stable peace.

Tensions again rose in Ambon in the lead up to 25 April 2004, the anniversary of a proclamation of a South Maluku Republic in 1950 by secessionist forces. A series of bombings re-inflamed tensions between communities in the province, claiming thirty-eight lives and displacing more than 10,000 people (Norwegian Refugee Council 2005: 51). However, since then, Maluku has been relatively peaceful.

CONFLICTS AND THE MEDIA

Indonesian media reports have repeatedly noted that unsubstantiated and exaggerated gossip and rumours played a crucial role in the Maluku violence. Unfortunately, both local and national media were split into two opposing parties and their coverage dangerously fuelled the conflicts. The Media Watch team at the Institute for Free Flow of Information conducted a study of *Adil, Aksi, Tekad* and *Detak*, which found that the four national tabloids used inflammatory words such as 'butchering field', 'crusade', 'holy war' and even described Maluku as 'the second Bosnia' (Putranto 2004). Some other national newspapers took sides in the conflict or presented a limited range of perspectives. For example, *Republika*, a major Islamic newspaper, also spoke for and defended the interests of Islamic parties in the Maluku conflict, initially taking a cautious line but later presenting the situation as a Christian attempt to eradicate Muslims (Stanley 2006: 200).

The local media in Maluku were also significantly affected by the violence, as the media organizations were split along religious lines, just as the city of Ambon was. Bambang Wisudo—national newspaper reporter, Maluku Media Centre supervisor and also peace journalism trainer—notes that such a split was long-rooted in its history. Religious inclinations were evident in the region's first newspaper, *Ambon Vooruit*, published in 1917 and other publications that followed in the Dutch colonial era. This propensity crystallized further in post-independent era (Wisudo 2006). During Soeharto's regime, partisan characteristics were suppressed as the media were obliged to fully support the New Order government, its developmental ideology and its strict taboos on reporting that might arouse ethnic, religious or other intergroup tensions (Romano 2003: 45–6).

At the time the violence started, the Jawa Pos Group, one of the nation's largest media corporations, had recently completed its takeover of the daily newspaper, *Suara Maluku*, which operated in the Halong area with twenty-five reporters, of whom ten were Muslims and the remainder Christians (Wisudo 2006). Other dailies that published locally were *National* and *Pos Maluku*, while the weeklies were *National, Malindo, Karabesi* and *Tabaos*—all weekly publications. The state-owned radio and television services, RRI (*Radio Republik Indonesia*) and TVRI (*Televisi Republik Indonesia*), had local stations operating in the region, represented by RRI Ambon, RRU Tual (South East Maluku), RRI Ternate (North Maluku) and TVRI Ambon. The private station, *Duta Musik Serasi* (DMS) Radio, also operated in Masohi (Central Maluku).

Local journalist Rudi Fofid worked for the *Tabaos* weekly at the time, and was also close with the *Suara Maluku* crew. He recalls that when the conflict commenced, he was in his newspaper's office, waiting for his friends so that they could go out to pay courtesy visits to their Muslim friends who celebrated Holy Idul Fitri. He remembers that Muslim and Christian journalists felt close to each other at the time. He and his colleagues—both Christians and Muslims—called and checked each other's situations and discussed how to write about this kind of event (Fofid 2009: pers. comm.). Despite this, in the next two weeks, the news about the conflicts was spread locally by RRI Ambon and TVRI Ambon, nationally by Jakarta-based media and in mailing lists or online media. According to Fofid (2009: pers. comm.), these reports were riddled with bias.

Suara Maluku temporarily ceased publication, because of concerns about journalists' safety. As most of the newspaper's journalists were Muslims, they could not go to the office since it was located in Halong, which was considered a Christian area. Even if it had published, there was no one to distribute *Suara Maluku*. All of its newspaper agents and kiosks were run by people from South Sulawesi and South East Sulawesi, who were Muslims, and it was unsafe for them to enter a Christian area to pick up the newspapers.

Suara Maluku resumed its publication after the holiday in the beginning of February 1999, with the spirit to rectify the biased coverage. However, Muslim journalists from *Suara Maluku* found it difficult to pass the various checkpoints and through the religious-based territorial divisions to travel from their homes to their office. In an attempt to overcome the problem, they created a strategy so that journalists located on either the Christian or Muslim 'side' could send their reports via facsimile. Colleagues living near the office received the faxes and transcribed and edited them for publication (Fofid 2009: pers. comm.).

Problems began when Muslim and Christian journalists were disappointed as their faxed reports were not published or were distorted. Fofid explains that journalists working in the office were de-motivated by this new job as typists. If the facsimiles were unclear, they simply threw them away (Fofid 2009: pers. comm.). This was a contributing factor to growing religious-based divisions between Christian and Muslim journalists (Maluku Media Centre 2009).

The obstructions to travel and communications led to the birth of the *Ambon Ekspres* newspaper on 2 July 1999, during one of the most intense periods of conflict. Most of the *Ambon Ekspres* editorial staff were former *Suara Maluku* journalists who had resigned due to pressures related to the conflict. Even though both newspapers were owned by the Jawa Pos publishing group, the division created a culture whereby *Suara Maluku* promoted Christian concerns and *Ambon Ekspres* expressed Muslim perspectives.

The Ambon-based correspondent for the online *TempoInteractive* news portal, Yusnita Tiakoly, recalls that the waves of conflict in the area increased the gap between the two groups, as most of the journalists or their families were victims of the riots and lived in areas dominated by particular religions (Tiakoly 2009: pers. comm.). Another Ambonese reporter, Saswaty Matakena, was one such journalist. She lost her house and all her possessions when they were engulfed by fire. She admits that she used to create provocative news reports, because her experience distorted her objectivity (Matakena 2009: pers.comm.). Another local journalist, Lucky Sopacua, was publicly harassed and labelled a provocateur by Suara Perjuangan Muslim Maluku (SPMM) Radio, a local radio station established by *Laskar Jihad* (Sopacua 2009: pers. comm.).

Journalists' physical circumstances also reduced their capacity to cover both sides of the story. Lucky Sopacua explains that due to communal hostilities, Muslim sources would usually only agree to be interviewed by Muslim journalists, and vice versa (2009: pers. comm.). This compromised journalists' ability to check facts and the accuracy of their resulting stories.

On the flip side, the partisan news was making good money as coverage of the bloody incidents was in high demand. Yusnita Tiakoly remembers people photocopying newspaper pages with stories of violence, brawls and destruction, and then selling the copies (2009: pers. comm.).

A number of media analysts have documented the deep divisions that continued to widen the split between Muslim and Christian journalists (e.g. Eriyanto 2003). In this context, a number of individuals and organizations joined forces to try to promote peace journalism as a means for reestablishing peace.

INTRODUCING PEACE JOURNALISM

The term 'peace journalism' can be traced back to the 1970s and the work of Johan Galtung, Professor of Peace Studies and Director of the TRANSCEND Peace and Development Network. Galtung (2000) argues that when journalists report on conflicts, it would be more productive to focus on possible remedies and proactive preventive measures than on violence, negative events and siding with a particular protagonist.

Peace journalism seeks to minimize the rift between opposing parties by not repeating 'facts' that demonize particular parties or set the stage for conflict (McGoldrick and Lynch 2001). Before crafting any story, a peace journalist will ask: 'What can I do with my intervention to enhance the prospects for peace?' The ethos of peace journalism is to use the choices made in editing and reporting to create opportunities for society at large to consider and value nonviolent responses to conflict (McGoldrick and Lynch 2001).

Peace journalism is a broader, fairer and more accurate way of framing stories, drawing on the insights of conflict analysis and transformation (McGoldrick and Lynch 2001). The peace journalism approach provides a new road map for tracing the connection between journalists, their sources, the story they cover and the consequences of their reporting—the ethics of journalistic intervention. It opens up a literacy of nonviolence and creativity as applied to the practical job of everyday reporting.

Peace journalism is not based on idealistic hopes for a conflict-free future. It requires journalists to have the skills to analyze and recognize the endemic and structural nature of many conflicts in the world but nonetheless to seek to identify and promote constructive responses. Galtung (2000) criticizes what he calls war or violence journalism, in which the media tends to dehumanize the enemy, privilege elite views and focus on the events of war/conflict rather than political context, preceding history, aftermath or devastating human consequences.

Table 13.1   Peace/Conflict Journalism and War/Violence Journalism

Peace/Conflict Journalism	*War/Violence Journalism*
I. War/Violence Orientated Focus on conflict arena, 2 parties, 1 goal (win), war general zero-sum orientation Closed space, closed time; causes and exits in arenas, who threw the first stone Making wars opaque/secret 'Us-Them' journalism, propaganda, voice, for 'Us' See 'Them' as the problem, focus on who prevails in war Dehumanization of 'them'; more so the worse the weapon Reactive: waiting for violence before reporting Focus only on visible effect of violence (killed, wounded and material damage)	**I. Peace/Conflict Orientated** Explore conflict formation, x parties, y goals, z issues general 'win, win' orientation Open space, open time; causes and outcomes anywhere, also in history/culture Making conflict transparent Giving voice to all parties; empathy, understanding See conflict/war as problem, focus on conflict creativity Humanization of all sides; more so the worse the weapons Proactive: prevention before any violence/war occurs Focus on invisible effects of violence (trauma and glory, damage to structure/culture)
II. Propaganda Orientated Expose 'Their' untruths/help 'Our' cover-ups/lies	**II. Truth Orientated** Expose untruths on all sides/uncover all cover-ups
III. Elite Orientated Focus on 'Our' sufferings; on able-bodied elite males, being their mouthpiece Give name to their evil doers Focus on elite peace makers	**III. People Orientated** Focus on suffering all over; on women, the aged, children, giving voice to voiceless Give name to all evil doers Focus on people peace makers
IV. Victory Orientated Peace = victory + ceasefire Conceal peace initiative, before victory is at hand Focus on treaty, institution, the controlled society Leaving for another war, return if the old flares up again	**IV. Solution Orientated** Peace = non violence + creativity Highlight peace initiatives, also to prevent more war Focus on structure, culture, the peaceful society Aftermath: resolution, reconstruction, reconciliation

Note: This table has been copied from Galtung (2000) with permission of Johan Galtung.

According to McGoldrick and Lynch (2001), if a country is moving toward democratic government, then a free and accountable media—one that monitors rights abuses and promotes divergent opinions—can help deter a return to violence. A biased or hate-mongering media can sabotage almost any other peace building effort (McGoldrick and Lynch 2001).

The role of media in conflict resolution is deceivingly complex. One useful tool in understanding the role of journalists is to view the media as several stages in a continuum of intervention, as mapped in Figure 13.1. This continuum can help interested parties determine how to approach and effectively use the media. It is also useful to conventional journalists who wish to examine their work and its potential impact.

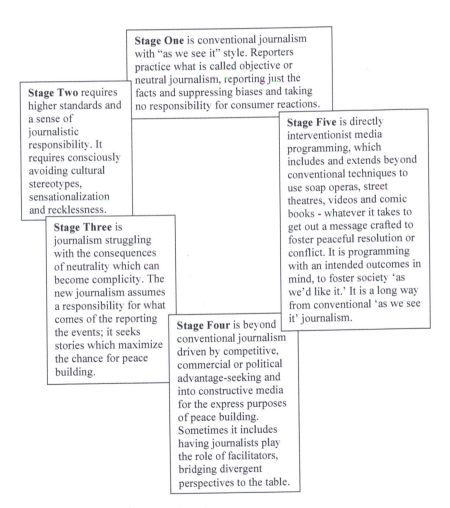

Stage One is conventional journalism with "as we see it" style. Reporters practice what is called objective or neutral journalism, reporting just the facts and suppressing biases and taking no responsibility for consumer reactions.

Stage Two requires higher standards and a sense of journalistic responsibility. It requires consciously avoiding cultural stereotypes, sensationalization and recklessness.

Stage Three is journalism struggling with the consequences of neutrality which can become complicity. The new journalism assumes a responsibility for what comes of the reporting the events; it seeks stories which maximize the chance for peace building.

Stage Four is beyond conventional journalism driven by competitive, commercial or political advantage-seeking and into constructive media for the express purposes of peace building. Sometimes it includes having journalists play the role of facilitators, bridging divergent perspectives to the table.

Stage Five is directly interventionist media programming, which includes and extends beyond conventional techniques to use soap operas, street theatres, videos and comic books - whatever it takes to get out a message crafted to foster peaceful resolution or conflict. It is programming with an intended outcomes in mind, to foster society 'as we'd like it.' It is a long way from conventional 'as we see it' journalism.

Figure 13.1   Stages of intervention

Note: This figure has been abridged from Howard (2001: 13) with permission of Ross Howard.

INTERVENTIONS FOR PEACE IN MALUKU

Many training initiatives have been directed towards Maluku journalists in an attempt to ameliorate the conflict. For example, the US-based NGO Internews brought a number of radio journalists to Jakarta to attend intensive, ten-day 'Reporting for Peace' workshops run by Fiona Lloyd. This training provided practical and analytical skills to journalists. These workshops were 'Stage One' interventions or 'conventional journalism' with 'as we see it' style.

Other initiatives tried to reach Stage Three, where journalists assume responsibilities for what comes of reporting the events—they seek stories which maximize the chance for peace building. At a meeting at the Indonesian Press Council—involving NGOs, journalists, media watch institutions, chief editors and the military—the Alliance of Independent Journalists (*Aliansi Jurnalis Indpenden*, AJI) conducted an assessment of Maluku journalists' needs. The AJI assessment indicated that it was necessary to undertake an intervention into Maluku that treated Maluku journalists as both professional journalists and victims of the conflict. Based on their core concerns and expertise, AJI and the LSPP formed a partnership to conduct peace journalism training. AJI organized events and mobilized its members to participate in peace journalism training, and LSPP focussed on developing materials, manuals and other resources. LSPP's trainers fanned out across the country, with AJI helping to spread the word about training activities. With the assistance from the British Council Indonesia, LSPP also invited peace journalism experts, Jake Lynch and Annabel McGoldrick, to promote some form of journalism capable of contributing to the wherewithal of society at large to discuss, devise and apply nonviolent responses to conflict—a perception which preceded any specific knowledge of the term peace journalism.

This program began with preparation of training manuals, *Peace Journalism: A How-to-Guide* (*Jurnalisme Damai, Bagaimana Melakukannya*) and *Peace Journalism: Facilitator's Guidebook* (*Jurnalisme Damai: Panduan Fasilitator*). LSPP organized a train-the-trainers workshop in Yogyakarta in February 2000 to facilitate better understanding of peace journalism. In collaboration with the British Council, British Embassy, and Conflict and Peace Forum (UK), a round table discussion was organized, with chief editors of national mass media organizations and professional associations in Jakarta. Following this, peace journalism training programs were launched in Ambon and other locations of intercommunal violence, Pontianak, Palu and Papua.

This training was completed with a field visit in November 2000, where a group of reporters visited Central Sulawesi's provincial capital, Palu, to experiment with peace journalism and explore ethical issues for journalists covering conflicts. Explaining her reason to participate, *Kompas* journalist Maria Hartiningsih stated: 'I saw a lot of innocent people become victims in this situation, especially women and children. I have a spirit to do something to contribute to the reconciliation of this nation' (Hanitzsch, Loffelholz and Mustamu 2004).

After the training and field visit, a meeting was set up for thirty-one Maluku and North Maluku journalists and media executives on 25 February–1 March 2001 in Bogor. The three main agendas were to raise the participants' consciousness as ordinary people involved in the conflict, to increase their professional consciousness as journalists, and to provide a technical introduction to peace journalism. Participants were selected on the basis of representativeness of the existing media in both regions. It was the first time that some of the participants had interacted with each other since the conflict erupted on 19 January 1999, aside from passing greetings that they exchanged when they ran into each other in government offices. As an indication of the tensions between them, some of them refused to share rooms with participants from a different religion, until the organizers insisted that they abide by the accommodation arrangements (Wisudo 2006).

The meeting ended with a joint commitment from Maluku journalists to uphold professionalism and ethics, put an end to war journalism, and try to practise humanitarian journalism. The term humanitarian journalism was used instead of peace journalism because Muslims in Maluku deemed the word 'peace' to be a Christian-related term. All participants signed a Statement of the Joint Commitment, and a small team was assembled to work with the AJI executive board to initiate follow-up training and activities and a special media centre.

Following the Bogor meeting, the participants tried to implement peace journalism in Ambon despite initial difficulties. Both Christians and Muslim journalists resumed interaction, but steps towards further professional cooperation proved more challenging. It was still hard for journalists to provide balanced reports and check facts. Local journalist Insany Syahbarwaty, who started working in February 2001, describes such problems, saying it was difficult for her to access the Christian perspective because of her Muslim background (Syahbarwaty 2009: pers. comm.).

Despite these obstacles, NGOs, government officials and military authorities observed an incremental change in the performance of Ambon's media. TVRI Ambon, which had previously sided with Christians, started to report news from Muslim communities. To overcome the problems of the territorial division, TVRI reporters agreed to cover issues occurring in their own territory and then exchange reports with journalists from the other side in 'neutral' territory, such as the governor's office, each afternoon. During this phase, Ambonese journalists phased out labels for the communal groups—such as *Merah* (Red) for Christians and *Putih* (White) for Muslims.

A further meeting was carried out in Central Sulawesi province, with thirty-eight participants, twenty-six of whom took part in Bogor meeting. The meeting of 27–30 May 2001 focused on technical matters to upgrade the participants' capabilities in peace journalism. The meeting took place in both the cities of Palu and Poso—which had experienced widespread violence between Christians and Muslims—to help participants learn how to observe communal conflict and identify characteristics that might have been shared with the Maluku conflict. Participants were shown the strategies that AJI-affiliated journalists in Palu used to distance themselves from the conflict so that they could cooperate and maintain their access to the conflicting parties, regardless of the religious background of reporters. The Palu–Poso meeting reinforced the commitment expressed in Bogor, and participants urged AJI to immediately facilitate further activity in Maluku by establishing a media centre.

The Maluku Media Centre (MMC) was founded in October 2001 on a shoestring budget from donor institutions and the government (Wisudo 2006). The MMC was a joint initiative of AJI Indonesia and the Baku Bae peace movement to reconcile Muslim and Christian journalists. It was set up in the neutral zone at Mardika, to provide a place for journalists to meet freely and trade information, reduce occupational hazards and improve relations (ISAI 2004). AJI selected Bambang Wisudo as the MMC project manager, who facilitated interaction between Christian and Muslim journalists. Wisudo (2006) noted that as their contacts increased, journalists from different religions began to crack jokes with one another freely and show other signs of more harmonious relations. Wisudo also sought to rebuild the trust of government and NGO sources in journalists, and to establish the MMC as a recognized venue where sources and journalists could meet safely.

In addition to its foremost function as a place of interaction and dialogue, the MMC gradually provided training workshops and its own news coverage on the situation in the province to national and international media. The MMC and its publications helped to intensify debate among journalists, who discussed and evaluated the quality of current affairs reporting and exchanged criticism in informal dialogues. The MMC encouraged the media to produce balanced reporting and assist them in basic practices of checking information.

Physical barriers still hinder reporters from reaching sources in the opposite side, and the MMC is expected to facilitate journalists to help one another to exchange information. The MMC attempts to establish a situation where information can be exchanged in a natural and incidental way, increasing the number of sources from both sides who make themselves accessible to both Christian and Muslim journalists. It continues to work on building the trust between journalists and the government, NGO activists, the military and the police to support peace process.

Local journalist M. Azis Tunny describes the impact of the MMC's establishment at a personal and professional level. Tunny started his career as a journalist in early 2002 with MMC as his news 'beat' or 'round', and says he is grateful for this, as it shaped his aptitude for applying peace journalism principles. He also observes that more and more media organizations, including his own, are recruiting both Christian and Muslim journalists and basing their operations in the neutral zone of Mardika (Tunny 2009: pers. comm.).

The MMC also supported the government-sponsored peace talks in Malino. Prior to the 2002 peace meetings, journalists gathered at the MMC and expressed their commitment to supporting the success of the meeting, and consequently there were no significant reports in the Maluku press that opposed the actual talks.

After the Malino peace agreement, both Christian and Muslim journalists in Ambon were able visit and cover each faction's area in groups, even though neither of the communal groups were interacting freely at that time. Maluku journalists were increasingly accessing sources from other group leaders. The interaction between journalists increased further. For example, *Suara Maluku* journalists began visiting the *Ambon Ekspres* office, which was located in the front of Al Fatah mosque, to meet their former colleagues. Wisudo (2006) evaluated that the media in Maluku had completely abolished the remaining vestiges of partisan and sectarian bias, to provide balanced and objective reporting.

LOOKING AHEAD

Although there have been no formal quantitative studies to try to measure the nature of Maluku media's reporting before and after the peace journalism intervention, the qualitative evidence points to favourable results. Local journalists themselves note an improvement. Observing the situation in 2003, John S. Uhurella found that the news had improved and journalists were more responsible (ISAI 2004). Local journalist Novi Pinontoan (2009: pers. comm.) thought that after the initiatives, stories about the conflict focussed on the incidents but no longer emphasized differences of group identity or used provocative words that might incite religious hatred.

Bimo Nugroho argues that when the conflict commenced, the local media capitalized on war journalism, but when the prolonged unrest damaged both the local economy and political stability of Maluku, this undermined the populace's purchasing power and weakened the media's advertising base (Nugroho 2006). In short, with war journalism, the media saw some short-term increases in sales but in the longer term were digging their own graves. Pinontoan (2009: pers. comm.) agreed that this no-win situation was another reason for supporting peace journalism, as the conflict only brought destruction and damage to all aspects of life.

Local journalists also speak highly of the reporting strategies involved in peace journalism. Syahbarwaty affirms that peace journalism helps her to analyze the possible impacts of an event, to see things with greater consciousness and to use these insights to raise the conflicting parties' awareness of the conflict's effects (2009: pers. comm.). Tunny says that peace journalism opens the door for the media to be able to retain its independence while also supporting the peace process as part of their responsibility towards humanity (2009: pers. comm.). Sopacua similarly argues that even though media should remain neutral, in times of conflict, the media should provide solutions to promote peace—and this is the role of peace journalism (2009: pers. comm.). Fofid has coined the term 'neutral–active' to describe how the media should be neutral while also pushing all parties to actively build peace (2009: pers. comm.).

Despite such positive comments, not all journalists in Maluku feel completely equipped to handle situations as they arise. When the conflict reignited in April 2004, several journalists said that they did not feel sufficiently capable to adequately address the resurgences (ISAI 2004). Several other editors in Ambon also stated that they would not report on incidents that might cause further unrest (ISAI 2004).

It is instructive to consider the results of a recent AJI survey (2008), which found that 54 per cent of respondents disagreed with the statement that the Ambon conflicts were escalated by media coverage. Of the fifty respondents, forty-three had commenced working for the media after 2002, or in other words after the peace agreement had signed, and only seven had directly experienced the conflict or observed the media coverage as practising journalists. AJI analysts suggest that this indicates a generation gap exists between those conflict 'veterans' and more junior colleagues, who had not been exposed as journalists to the realities of covering bloody conflicts (AJI 2008). It raises questions about whether and how the knowledge and experience gained from the peace journalism initiative is being transferred between generations of journalists.

This highlights the importance of sustainable and ongoing peace journalism training for the media. History is prone to repeating itself for those who do not learn from it.

NOTES

1. Former LSPP executive director and peace journalism facilitator Hanif Suranto contributed significantly to this chapter by providing resource materials, contacts to be interviewed and his own personal experience. Ignatius Haryanto, also a peace journalism facilitator and the current LSPP executive director, offered his valuable comments and helped to edit this chapter. This chapter could not have been written without their assistance.

BIBLIOGRAPHY

Aliansi Jurnalis Independen (2008) *Pendapat Jurnalis Ambon terhadap Isu Media* (Opinions of Ambon Journalists about Media Issues), unpublished report, AJI, Jakarta.
Bräuchler, B. (2003) 'Cyberidentities at war: religion, identity and the Internet in the Moluccan conflict', *Jurnal Indonesia*, 75: 123–151.

Eriyanto (2003) *Media dan Konflik Ambon: Media, Berita dan Kerusuhan Komunal di Ambon 1999–2002* (Media and Conflict in Ambon: Media, News and the Communal Unrest in Ambon 1999–2002), Jakarta: Kantor Berita 68H, Majalah Pantau and the Media Development Loan Fund.

Hanitzsch, T., Loffelholz, M. and Mustamu, R. (eds) (2004) Peace journalism in Indonesia', in *Agents of Peace—Public Communication and Conflict Resolution in an Asian Setting* Jakarta: Friedrich Ebert Stiftung.

Howard, R. (2001) 'Media and peacebuilding: Mapping the possibilities', *Activate (From Headlines to Front Lines: Media and Peacebuilding)*, (Winter): 12–13.

Galtung, J. (2000) 'Reporting conflict: The low and the high', a working document for Der Begriff Fortschritt in Unterschiedlichen Kulturen, GTZ and the Goethe-Institut. Available at www.fortschritt-weltweit.de/dokumente/wirkung/fortschritt_wirkung_peacejournalism.pdf (Accessed 1 September 2009).

Institute Studi Arus Informasi (ISAI) (2004) *The Role of Media in Peace-Building and Reconciliation: Central Sulawesi, Maluku and North Maluku*, Jakarta: International Media Support (IMS).

Maluku Media Centre (2009) *Antara Kriminalitas dan Ketidakpahaman—Kasus Jurnalis Maluku (Between Criminality and Misunderstanding—The Case of Maluku Journalists)*, Jakarta: AJI and Free Voice.

McGoldrick, A. and Lynch, J. (2001) 'What is Peace Journalism?', *Activate (From Headlines to Front Lines: Media and Peacebuilding)*, (Winter): 6–9.

Norwegian Refugee Council (2005) *Internal Displacement—A Global Overview of Trends and Developments in 2004*, Geneva: Global IDP Project.

Nugroho, B. (2006) 'Writing the Dark Side: Publishing about Violence in Indonesia' in Coppel, Charles A. (ed) (2006) *Violent Conflicts in Indonesia: Analysis, Representation, Resolution*, New York: Routledge, pp. 206–16.

Putranto, A. (2004) '*Jurnalisme damai dan jurnalisme perang*' (Peace journalism and war journalism), *Kompas*, 9 February.

Romano, A. (2003) *Politics and the Press in Indonesia*, London: Routledge-Curzon.

Stanley (2006) 'The media as a control and as a spur for acts of violence' in Coppel, C.A. (ed.) *Violent Conflicts in Indonesia: Analysis, Representation, Resolution*, New York: Routledge, pp. 195–205.

Van Klinken, G. (2006) 'The Maluku wars: "Communal contenders" in a failing state' in Coppel, C.A. (ed) *Violent Conflicts in Indonesia: Analysis, Representation, Resolution*, New York: Routledge, pp. 129–43.

Van Klinken, G. (2007) *Perang Kota Kecil: Kekerasan Komunal dan Demokrasi di Indonesia* (Small Town Wars: Communal Violence and Democratization in Indonesia), Jakarta: Yayasan Obor Indonesia .

Wisudo, P.B. (2006) *Struggle between War and Peace Journalism: A Lesson from Maluku*, Manila: Paper for Workshop on Peace journalism in the Philippines (unpublished).

14 Traditions of Public Journalism in India

Pradip Thomas

The founder of the investigative newspaper and online portal *Tehelka*, Tarun Tejpal (2003: 125), describes the moral reasons for his organization conducting Operation West End, the most explosive sting operation ever mounted in India. The operation resulted in serious allegations of corruption in the procurement of defence equipment and led to resignations of senior political and military functionaries including the president of the then ruling party and the defence minister:

> When we launched Tehelka in 2000 we made some immodest claims. We said we wanted to rediscover the distinction between journalism, public relations, and entertainment—a distinction that had been blurred in the 1990s by a combination of satellite television, colour pages in the newspapers, and the first giddiness of liberal consumerism. And also by the co-options of politics and business; by the end of the 90s every senior journalist, every publication, could be identified with a political party or a business house. We said we too loved trivia, we too had friends among politicians and businessmen, but we believed that *the core of journalism was a very serious one. It was built on the bedrock of uncomfortable questions*, not comfortable alignments, nor pretty sentences or pretty pictures (Tejpal 2003: 125, emphasis added).

Tehelka paid a high price for this operation. It became victim of a government-fronted witch hunt, its staff levels dropped from 150 to six, and key journalists faced death threats and went into hiding. The ethics of a sting operation that involved money, whisky, five-star hotels and prostitutes, rather than the sting's momentous findings, became the focus for both government and journalism. *Tehelka* only enjoyed a reversal in fortunes after the Congress government came to power in 2004.

Throughout it all, Tejpal stood by what he had said after *Tehelka* 'broke' the initial story by screening it in the ballroom of the Imperial Hotel in New Delhi:

At the press conference after the screening, we had made it clear that as far as we were concerned our role was over. We had followed what had seemed like a good story—it had turned out to be better than just a good story. We had broken it at the moment it was ready and now we were out of it. The truth and morality of the story concerned us; the politics of it did not (Tejpal 2003: 121).

In a real sense, the gap between the original intent and the inexorable pace of circumstances that overtook *Tehelka*'s journalists highlights in relief some of the key issues facing public journalism.[1] What are the objectives of public journalism? Is it merely to redeem mainstream journalism that, in popular perception, has lost its way in its many entanglements with the market and politics, or are the objectives more radical and linked to the redemption of communities and democracy itself? Tejpal and *Tehelka*'s story reveals the limits of public journalism, in this case in a context riven by multiple interests and one in which corruption has infected the body-corporate and is part of a way of a life that is frequently defended in public.

THE LIMITS TO PUBLIC JOURNALISM

Are there limits to this sort of journalism and would it have made a difference if *Tehelka* had invited the public to be involved in a campaign against public sector corruption? I am of the opinion that public campaigns related to systemic issues such as corruption work best at a local level. It is when people are convinced that an anticorruption drive will result in transparent expenditures of public money and that this will lead to better infrastructure, access, job security—that such a campaign will make a difference. Corruption as a national issue cannot be dealt with by the public precisely because it is deep-rooted and cuts across every public sector, state government and political party. *Tehelka* would not have been able to mobilize the nation because the 'morality' of this issue is multilayered and multi-accentual. Corruption in a defence deal is far removed from the day-to-day corruption that impacts on people's lives and that is of concern to people.

The *Tehelka* case is now recognized as a 'critical incident' that impacted on Indian journalism practice. Not only did it turn the issue of corruption into a national media debate, but it provided the first indications of the potential of the Internet for public journalism. 'For the first time journalists started getting ideas about "belonging" to a larger community rather than merely their publication' (Atre 2009: 18). The fact that 'journalistic authority' was renegotiated as a result of *Tehelka* is as important a contribution as its original sting operation. The non-involvement of the public in this media operation does not invalidate *Tehelka*'s. Instead, it shows that different types of public journalism based on different levels of citizen involvement can contribute to awareness, education, empowerment and social change. To absolutize one type of journalism over the other takes away from the dynamism that is inherent to different types of public journalism.

One of the issues that can be highlighted from the *Tehelka* episode is whether that type of public journalism, in a complex country like India, can ever result in lasting changes to structures, processes and ways of life. John Durham Peters (1999: 99–103) is convinced of the impossible nature of the public journalism project because of the congenital unattainability of democracy as a viable, all-encompassing, large-scale project. He lists four key obstacles to public journalism—democracy's limits given that as per its origins in small-scale settings, it was not meant to deal with the ordering of life in large-scale societies; the intricacies of human nature; old and new structures of exclusion; and people's loss of credibility in politics. He also queries dialogue and its limits given its centrality to the public journalism ethic:

> The vastness of the world outside, the antics of human behaviour, the stubborn structures of the market and the state, and the difficulty of knowing what to believe are more than challenges to the dream of public journalism; they provide and always have provided both the challenge to and the topic of journalism itself (Peters 1999: 115).

While this interpretation can be critiqued for its overt pessimism, it highlights some of the fault lines that continue to bedevil public journalism practice. The *Tehelka* example reveals that there are limits to democracy in the world's largest democracy.

Having said that, there are examples of civic movements from below in India, most notably the Right to Information (RTI) movement that began in a few rural Rajasthan villages and became a national force. Its results included the Right to Information Act (2002) and the enactment of similar acts in most if not all states in India. While the RTI movement can be described as the valorization of the common good and an example of the exercise of substantive democracy, there are not very many examples of this kind in post-Independent India. The RTI movement's success does suggest that issues such as corruption are better dealt with by people for whom the exercises of corruption are a daily reality that has affected their quality of life. Such people have a greater moral authority to deal with the corrosive influence of corruption than say the urban middle classes who tend to accept the prevailing system.

THE MANY INTERPETATIONS OF PUBLIC JOURNALISM

While I argue that *Tehelka* is an example of public journalism, the meaning of the term public journalism is imprecise and multi-accentual. It can describe a variety of journalistic traditions that are attempting to reinvigorate civil society, reinstitute democratic politics, establish multiple public spheres and redeem mainstream journalism that is easily corrupted and influenced by lobbies linked to commerce and politics. There are those who believe that the objective of public journalism is to work towards fulfilling the traditional ideals of journalism—an objective, nonpartisan journalism wedded to the middle ground of ideas and committed to a watchdog function. The accent is on an apolitical role for journalism to ensure that key liberal ideals such as fair play, equality and democratic equilibrium are maintained. Another objective is to provide impartial information from a variety of perspectives that consumers can use to form understandings and interpretations, and make rational choices. Here public journalism clearly has an educational function. It is the means for mediating civilizational values and a tool for understanding contemporary societies and the threads that make it up in a fast changing world.

Some variants of public journalism take the view that it is not as much the middle ground that should be the focus of public journalism but the strengthening of communitarian values that have become eroded in the context of industrialization, individualism and neoliberalism. This understanding of public journalism sits comfortably with theories of communitarianism (such as those of Amitai Etzioni and Charles Taylor). Here the journalist is not the detached observer but deeply involved in providing options and solutions in the making of the good society. In the words of the communication ethicist Clifford Christians (1999: 77), 'the communal character of our moral interpretations enables public journalism to come to grips with the common good. Our references to moral matters involve the community. A self exists only within "webs of interlocution"'.

Others believe that public journalism can only be exercised when the structures of journalism are sufficiently independent and run on cooperative or small business lines as opposed to a journalism that is part and parcel of mega-media empires. At the same time there are those for whom public journalism is clearly opposed to mainstream journalism and works on a different ethos and business model. Since advertising pays for most mainstream journalism, there are expressions of public journalism that are subscriptions-based or dependent on public or private grants or based on support from special interest groups. The ethos can deliberately embrace user-generated content as is the case with netizens in the context of citizen journalism such as *OhMyNews* and *Malaysiakini*.

Keeping these ideas and the *Tehelka* case in mind, the next section will explore the possibilities and limits of sustainable public journalism in India.

GANDHI AND THE TRADITIONS OF PUBLIC JOURNALISM

While the reinvention of mainstream journalism in line with public journalism is best seen in the approach taken by the Chennai-based English

with issues that are of concern to indigenous people. However, the *Prabhat Khabar* example does suggest that issues related to scale, as Peters has pointed out, are indeed critical to public journalism. The more local the journalism, the better its chances to function in the interests of its public. This could include consistently highlighting local issues, becoming a reliable forum for creating and maintaining local identities, acting as the location and conduit for training and mobilization, and valorizing public voices and the common good. Another interesting dimension to *Prabhat Khabar* is the fact that it has adapted to people's diverse needs for journalism. While the need for advocacy is keenly felt, its readers also wanted news on entertainment, economics and information on general issues of both a serious and trivial kind. The newspaper also had to deal with competition and advertisers, and evolve a newspaper that catered to diverse interests (see Ninan 2007). Sevanti Ninan's study of the regional and local press in the 'Hindi heartland' makes the point that local circumstances, including the advent of local self-government and inroads made by the rural market, provided the reasons for the localization of news and for the emergence of local public spheres. While most local editions included news by citizen journalists, for the most part, this news did not unsettle the constancy of feudal relationships in these areas.

PUBLIC JOURNALISM TRADITIONS IN INDIA

The macro-public that was *Tehelka's* audience, by contrast, is unmanageable, riven, different, and complex, and does not agree on the foundations of a good society. While corruption certainly features in the public narrative of India, it is an issue that is part of a larger discourse that is slippery, to say the least. However, there has been space for a public journalism in India that has dealt with issues of national import. For example, India witnessed an explosion of public journalism in the years following Emergency rule (1975–77), a period characterized by dictatorship, arbitrary arrests, deaths in custody and authoritarian rule. This period is regarded as the golden age of Indian investigative journalism and a number of news magazines were established during this era.

The journalist and ex-government minister Arun Shourie was perhaps the most notable example of an investigative journalist who was also deeply committed to changing society for the better. Among his many exposés was his early 1980s coverage of the plight of 'undertrials', or people detained in jail pending their trials. They accounted for close to 53 per cent of the prison population in India in the late 1970s, and many had spent years awaiting trial. The immediate story was how policemen had blinded 'undertrials' in the Bhagalpur jail in Bihar. Shourie's exposure led to a decrease in the period of detention for 'undertrials' and the release of many thousands who were kept under one pretext or another:

One of the interesting aspects of Shourie's approach to public journalism was that he actively sought the help of citizens in the creation of a larger environment for justice. Writ petitions filed at the Supreme Court by ordinary citizens had the needed effect.

> Orders followed for immediate release of prisoners detained beyond the maximum period for which they were liable if convicted; and of those who had served six months without filed charges, except when held for murder or gang robbery. The court further demanded that all filed charges be investigated within two months, and pending cases by disposed of in six months; and that lawyers be provided at state expense for all prisoners held more than 90 days. Within six months some 40,000 'undertrials' were discharged—29,000 in Bihar alone (Rai Foundation N.D.).

The veteran journalist B.G. Verghese (2003: xlix) describes the vocation of Teesta Setelvad, another combative journalist and editor of *Communalism Combat*, in similar terms:

> [W]hat is practiced here is avowedly advocacy and crusading journalism which is not to be judged by the standards of general interest media. It not merely narrates the story but goes on to pursue it to its logical conclusion in search of legal and political redress. It is the deeper investigatory and evidentiary quality of the reporting that singles it out. Here, the journalist is manifestly an activist and clearly on the side of the victim, striving to counter the rot in the mind before it spills out in blood on the street.

KHABAR LHARIYA AND PUBLIC JOURNALISM IN RURAL INDIA

Perhaps the most edifying and comprehensive account of public journalism in India is contained in Farah Naqvi's book, *Waves in the Hinterland: The Journey of a Newspaper* (2007). The narrative describes the stories of two publications run by women in Chitrakoot, Uttar Pradesh, the now defunct *Mahila Dakiya* and the thriving *Khabar Lhariya*. Started by a group of poor, rural, low-caste women, it has broken down the myths and barriers related to women in journalism and most importantly contributed to awareness among the doubly disadvantaged Dalit women, who occupy the lowest rungs of society in the entire country. Naqvi describes Chitrakoot as the 'war-zone of feudal India' (2007: 20), where gender-based violence is commonplace and caste-based atrocities are everyday.

Kalpana Sharma (2008) describes how the journalists:

> have struggled to understand politics, economics, history, have trudged hundreds of kilometres in their districts to see for themselves what is happening on the ground, have learned through mistakes how to

double check all the facts before committing to print—in other words, everything that a journalist must learn. The result of all this is evident in the confidence in these women journalists. When we met them in Mumbai, they spoke of the different stories that they investigated, of how they decide each fortnight which story should come on page one, of how district reporters from major Hindi newspapers initially ignored them but now try to steal their information without giving them the credit, of how they have learned to hold their own at press conferences, and why today even district officials, who did not earlier give them the time of day, are willing to speak to them on the phone.

While *Khabar Lhariya* has definite feminist objectives, it is also read by men and has crucially contributed to the empowerment of poor communities, and in particular, women:

> While most local papers continue to portray women either as pin-up girls or, at best, as sorry subjects of the latest sensational rape story, KL is about women and human rights. While mainstream Sankritised Hindi is considered the language of the educated and powerful, it chooses to write in a dialect. It writes for people with low levels of literacy when the rest of the world writes for the literate few. Unlike most media products, which even as they go regional and local, continue to cater to a target audience with purchasing power, KL writes specifically for the poorest of the poor. . . . while most publications are written by 'others' for a target audience, KL is written by the target audience itself. . . . (Naqvi 2007: 14).

The most important impact of *Khabar Lhariya* is that it has contributed to the creation of 'interpretive communities' within Dalit, Kol, Muslim and lower-caste/tribal households—communities that are habitually ignored and not recognized contributors to the life of the nation. *Khabar Lhariya* has empowered these communities, provided education and created awareness on issues such as governance, transparency, accountability and citizenship. In turn, local exercises of power by empowered communities have led to the recognition of the worth of the narratives that define locality. There has also been recognition of individual identities. Nirantar (2008), the organization that produces *Khabar Lhariya*, notes that:

> all the members of the team have become reflective about their gender, class and class identities, and the way in which this moulds their lives and work. Take for example Kavita, who was married at 14. In spite of much resistance to her studying, and financial constraints, she studied at a residential school and completed her education. After almost ten years of being in a marriage where she had no support or respect, she was able to make the decision to leave and live independently. Shanti,

another senior member of the team, is from the Kol community, a scheduled tribe. She had had no access to education as a child, and began to study in her mid-thirties. This had a huge impact on her life: it gave her a confidence she never had before, and allowed her to take up a job, become informed and articulate and give her a mobility that she had never experienced.

THE CONTEXTS OF PUBLIC JOURNALISM IN INDIA

Globalization

While all sectors of India's media have witnessed massive growth over the last decade, growth has been predominantly in media as a business. While key newspapers such as the *Times of India* previously had a commitment to 'development journalism', the circulation and expansion wars led to such objectives being jettisoned in favour of consumerism, entertainment, glamour and the stock market. India's most prominent 'poverty' journalist, P. Sainath (2006), who incidentally used to write for the *Times of India*, has memorably described this change in objectives:

> Farm suicides in Vidarbha crossed 400 this week. The Sensex crossed the 11,000 mark. And Lakme Fashion Week issued over 500 media passes to journalists. All three are firsts. All happened the same week. And each captures in a brilliant if bizarre way a sense of where India's Brave New World is headed. A powerful measure of a massive disconnect. Of the gap between the haves and the have-mores on the one hand, and the dispossessed and desperate, on the other. . . . When 322 of 413 suicides have occurred since just November 1, you'd think that is newsworthy. When the highest number, 77, take place in March alone, you'd believe the same. You'd be wrong, though. The Great Depression of the Indian countryside does not make news.

Bringing a rare candour and sensitivity, Sainath has exemplified public journalism at its best. In his articles on life and death in remote parts of India beyond the pale of development, he writes about people's daily struggle to eat a square meal and the contexts of their suffering that include exploitation by moneylenders, caste conflict, the degradation of public services, and endemic corruption in the provision (and non-provision) of public services. As he points out:

> You can have the mandatory 2,400 or 2,100 calories a day and yet be very poor. India's problems differ from those of a Somalia or Ethiopia in crisis. Hunger—again just one aspect of poverty—is far more complex here. It is more low-level, less visible and does not make for the

dramatic television footage that a Somalia or Ethiopia do. That makes covering the process more challenging—and perhaps more important (Sainath 1996: 3).

Sainath's journalism includes advocacy, a commitment to the training of rural journalists and consciousness-raising on issues especially linked to the downside of globalization.

Hindu Nationalism

In the context of the rise of Hindu nationalism in India, the journal *Communalism Combat* has played an important role in challenging the ideologies of exclusion that are at the very core of the Hindutva movement. Teesta Setelvad has taken her role as a public journalist seriously and has repeatedly exposed the perpetrators of communalism in India. In that process, she has enlarged the boundaries of public journalism. Writing on the Hindu–Muslim riots that led to the deaths of scores of Muslims in Mumbai in the early 1990s, she reveals what it takes to be a public journalist when there is a deafening silence from the key institutions meant to deal with a breakdown in law and order:

> Throughout the weeks of December 1992 and January 1993 our home . . . along with those of at least eight other journalists in Mumbai served as mini-control rooms where distress calls were received and then relayed to the police. Otherwise, the authorities were not inclined to heed complaints coming from a certain section of the population— Muslims (Setelvad 2003: 135).

What is interesting is that the debates and discussions on the merits and demerits of Hindutva have not only taken place in some mainstream newspapers and magazines but also in the vernacular press, particularly in South India. Geetha observes that there is a vibrant public sphere and an extant public journalism in the context of small literary journals in Tamilnadu:

> Debates regarding Hindutva and its meanings in the Tamil context have been legion in what is known as the 'little magazine' circuit. Little magazines are small, literary journals, which chiefly address each other. There are at least over 50 of these, and often the same set of people write in them . . . This last decade, most of the little magazines have been critical of Hindutva, with some leading intellectuals associated with some of the more stridently anti-case and anti-Hindutva magazines (for instance, *Pudiya Tadam* and the more catholic *Pudiya Kattru*) supporting and endorsing minority rights (Geetha 2005: 122).

The Internet and Public Journalism

The Internet has contributed towards many forms of emancipatory communications via blogs, citizen journalism and other technologically mediated means. However, in India, there are any number of applications under the citizen journalism umbrella and it is not clear whether these, taken in their entirety, contribute significantly to the cause of public journalism. User-generated content and networking offer opportunities to extend the quality and reach of public journalism, but the Internet in India resolutely remains an urban medium.

India's largest citizen journalism portal, *Merinews*, is often cited for its role in extending access and enabling dialogue. While there is a lot of discussion on the site including attempts to create a citizen's charter, one of the issues is whether it really is nothing more than another channel for middle-class opinion making, rather than a space for inclusive deliberations on key issues facing the nation. *Merinews* online is accompanied by a monthly publication that includes the best of *Merinews*. A cursory scan of the *Merinews* site (6 February 2009) revealed the following:

1. The web-page layout and sections—world, India, sports, business, entertainment, lifestyle, potpourri, reviews—and the news under each of these sections are 'mainstream'. It would seem that it is organized to compete with mainstream online news providers.
2. While there is a section on citizen journalism and how to submit articles, so it is clear that *Merinews* accepts articles on all sorts of issues from citizens, if one were to be cynical this is a relatively inexpensive way of filling in the web pages.

There is little indication of its role in advocacy or whether it contributes to the making of a more democratic society in India. While *Merinews* was involved with the World Social Forum that was held in Delhi in 2006, it is arguable as to whether it really is a form of public media or really a business model. There are other sites such as *GroundReport* and the Indian version of *Instablogs* that have a commitment to engagement and public journalism.

While the Internet enables social networking on a large scale, localized versions seem to offer better possibilities for the operationalization of public journalism objectives. Sonwalker and Allan (2007) have described the role played by citizen journalism in North-East India, an area consisting of seven independent 'tribal' states that have been locations for various 'insurgencies' and independence movements against the Indian government. One of the major issues in this region is that of 'impunity' and the Indian army. A contemporary struggle waged offline and online is on the repeal of the draconian Armed Forces (Special Powers) Act (AFSPA) of 1958 that gives the army the right 'to shoot, arrest or search without warrant'. Sonwalker and Allan (2007) write of citizen journalism initiatives related to *Manipuronline.com*, *E-Pao.net*, *Kanglaonline.com* and the *SangaiExpress* that have played a role in supporting the cause of a Manipuri hunger-striker Irom Sharmilla Chanu against the AFSPA as an example of the capacity of citizen journalism 'to bear witness to human suffering'.

CONCLUSION

Public journalism defines an attitude, a stance, a commitment to using journalism as a vehicle to advance public causes, and thereby contribute to the exercise of substantive democracy. Traditions of public journalism are materialized at a variety of levels—from *Tehelka* located in the capital city, Delhi, to grassroots women journalists in a remote part of rural Uttar Pradesh. Each of these traditions of public journalism contributes in small and large measures to the project of democratization in India. This project is shaped as much by the ripple effect of exposés such as that of the *Tehelka* defence deal and the many conversations that it has prompted throughout the country, as much as by the committed journalism of Dalit women and citizen bloggers.

The meaning of public journalism is imprecise, although as I have argued, its multi-accentuality is its strength. This impreciseness does not take away from the fact that there are many examples of public journalism in India that have contributed and are contributing to democracy and engaging with its public in ways that are redefining both the scope and nature of journalism and democracy. As Keane (1991: 190) observes, 'Freedom of communication is not something which can be realised in a definite or perfect sense. It is an ongoing project without an ultimate solution. It is a project which constantly generates new constellations of dilemmas and contradictions'.

NOTES

1. The term public journalism is not widely known in India. This chapter uses the term simply as a useful summary for various deliberative journalism practices that have philosophical similarities to public journalism.

BIBLIOGRAPHY

Atre, J. (2009) 'Red hot chilli papers: the sensational rise of muckraking in India' (1–29), Paper presented at the Annual ICA Meeting, New York, May 2009. Available at http://www.allacademic.com/one/www/www/index.php?cmd=www_search&offset=0&limit=5&multi_search_search_mode=publication&multi_search_publication_fulltext_mod=fulltext&textfield_submit=true&search_module=multi_search&search=Search&search_field=title_idx&fulltext_search=Red+Hot+Chili+Papers+%3A+The+Sensational+Rise+of+Muckraking+in+India (Accessed 1 September 2009)

Chapman, J. (2007) 'Arundhati Roy and the Narmada Dam controversy: Development journalism and the 'new international public sphere'?, *International Journal of Communication*, July–Dec. Available at: BNet, http://findarticles.com/p/articles/mi_m1AIY/is_2_17/ai_n25015852/pg_1 (Accessed 1 September 2009)

Christians, C.G. (1999) 'The common good as first principle', in T.L. Glasser (ed.) *The Idea of Public Journalism*, New York: Guildford Press, pp. 67–84.

Geetha, V. (2005) 'Gender, identity and the Tamil popular press', in N. Rajan, (ed.) *Practicing Journalism: Values, Constraints, Implications,* Thousand Oaks, CA: Sage, pp. 115–24.

Greenough, P.R. (1983) 'Political mobilisation and the underground literature of the Quit India movement, 1942–44', *Modern Asian Studies*, 17(3): 353–86

Harivansh (2005) 'Prabhat Khabar: An experiment in journalism', in N. Rajan (ed.) *Practicing Journalism: Values, Constraints, Implications,* Thousand Oaks, CA: Sage, pp. 46–62.

Iyer, R (ed.) (1990) *The Essential Writings of Mahatma Gandhi*, Oxford, UK: Oxford University Press.

Keane, K. (1991) *The Media and Democracy*, Cambridge, UK: Polity Press.

Naqvi, A. (2007) *Waves in the Hinterland: The Journey of a Newspaper*, New Delhi: Nirantar/Zubaan.

Nirantar (2008) '*Khabar Lahiriya*: Impact'. Available at http://www.nirantar.net/khabar_impact.htm (Accessed 1 September 2009).

Ninan, S. (2007) *Headlines from the Heartland: Reinventing the Hindi Public Sphere*, Thousand Oaks, CA: Sage.

Peters, J.D. (1999), 'Public journalism and democratic theory: Four challenges', in T.L. Glasser (ed.) *The Idea of Public Journalism*, New York: Guildford Press, pp. 99–117.

Rai Foundation (N.D.) 'From yellow journalism to advocacy journalism', *Media Evolution*. Available at http://www.rocw.raifoundation.org/masscommunication/MACM/mediaevolution/lecture-notes/lecture-08.pdf (Accessed 1 September 2009).

Sainath, P. (1996) *Everybody Loves a Good Drought*, London: Review.

Sainath, P. (2006) 'India shining meets the Great Depression', *India Together*, 2 April. Available at http://indiatogether.com/2006/apr/psa-depress.htm. Accessed 1 May 2009.

Setelvad, T. (2003) 'Communal violence: From select pogroms to full blown genocide', in B.G. Verghese (ed.), *Breaking the Big Story: Great Moments in Indian Journalism*, New Delhi: Viking and Penguin Press, pp. 132–50.

Sharma, K. (2008) 'A trailblazer by Dalit women scribes', OneWorldSouthAsia, http://southasia.oneworld.net/Article/a-trail-blazer-by-dalit-women-scribes (Accessed 1 September 2009).

Sonwalker, P. and Allan, S. (2007) 'Citizen journalism and human rights in northeast India', *Media Development*, 3. Available at http://www.waccglobal.org/en/20073-media-and-terror/462-Citizen-journalism-and-human-rights-in-north-east-India.html (Accessed 1 September 2009).

Tejpal, T.J. (2003) 'Tehelka: Hitting dirt, getting hurt', in B.G. Verghese (ed.), *Breaking the Big Story: Great Moments in Indian Journalism*, New Delhi: Viking and Penguin Books, pp. 112–31.

Verghese, B.G. (ed.) (2003) 'Introduction', in *Breaking the Big Story: Great Moments in Indian Journalism*, New Delhi: Viking, Penguin Books, pp. vii–L.

15 In the Hands of the People
Citizen Media for Revitalizing Puerto Rico's Poor Communities

Angela Romano and
Anette Sofía Ruiz Morales[1]

Prensa Comunitaria (Community Press) has ambitious goals for its work in Puerto Rico's disadvantaged communities. When *Prensa Comunitaria* formally registered as a non-government organization with the Department of State in the Commonwealth of Puerto Rico in 2004, its stated mission was 'to create and develop community mass media enterprises in the hands of disadvantaged communities and their leaders as tools to improve their socio-economic status'. Its threefold aims are to revitalize the communities and their leadership, to increase the accessibility and use of communications technologies, and to stimulate economic development.

This chapter describes how *Prensa Comunitaria* was set up by residents of economically disadvantaged communities as a unique model of community social enterprise in Puerto Rico. *Prensa Comunitaria* steps beyond the Puerto Rican traditions of using the media as a tool to either promote national development or the commercial interests of media proprietors. The chapter examines *Prensa Comunitaria* as a model for helping people in poorer communities to establish their own agendas and platforms for collective discussion and action within and between communities.

CONTEXT OF MEDIA OPERATIONS

There are clearly many activities and issues in Puerto Rico's economically disadvantaged communities of public importance that are worthy of media attention. Puerto Rico itself is one of the most dynamic economies in the Caribbean. As an unincorporated territory of the United States, Puerto Ricans have many of the same political entitlements as residents of the US mainland states and open access to US financial markets. The island has strong political institutions, a stable political and economic history, and an enormous tourism industry based on its cultural richness and natural beauty.

Even with these advantages, Puerto Rico faces substantial economic challenges, and 45.5 per cent of residents lived below the poverty line in 2007 (Bigshaw and Semega 2008: 21). Only 60 per cent of the population has a secondary school education (Bauman and Graf 2003: 3). Furthermore, the education system has not generated a labour force that is prepared for today's economy, and the poorest households continue to face critical challenges in terms of educational attainment, employment and economic activity (Ladd and Rivera-Batiz 2006; Red de Fundaciones 2007; Sotomayor 2004). Communities with limited economic resources also face problems of economic and social inequalities (including insufficient and inadequate housing, lack of basic services and infrastructure, and poor access to private and public resources), domestic violence and family-related problems, limited public health services, violence and drug dependence (Red de Fundaciones 2007).

Does Puerto Rico have a media that might tell stories that capture these communities' spirit and essence, or their successes and struggles? For a state with a population of just under four million and a land mass of 9,104 km^2 (3515 sq m), Puerto Rico has a remarkable proliferation of mass media services. Puerto Ricans are served by three national daily newspapers with a circulation of over half a million copies, five weekly national newspapers, twenty-two regional newspapers, sixty-eight television stations (although four of them monopolize 85 per cent of the audience), 120 radio stations, thirty-six magazines and specialized journals, and three international wire services; also, 50 per cent of households have access to cable or satellite (Caribbean Business 2006; CIA World Factbook 2009; Morales 2008: 17). More than one third of the population has access to the internet and nearly half to a personal computer (Rivera Cruz 2006). There is only one community radio station, which is based in the town of Adjuntas. This station broadcasts in Puerto Rico's central region and via the Internet, and offers cooperative, participatory, free and alternative content with a nonprofit social management.

Despite this wealth of media sources, residents of poorer communities often complain that Puerto Rico's mainstream news media concentrate on the issues, actions and policies of the elite. Given journalists' propensity to concentrate on conflict and crisis, when less prosperous communities do appear in the news media, the stories take a negative approach and focus on a narrow range of topics such as drugs, violence, poverty and underachievement.

Maximiliano Dueñas Guzmán (2009) notes that current attempts to create alternative communications in Puerto Rico are noteworthy for their goals of supporting economic development and the way that they rely on alliances between different social sectors. He identifies three alternative communications projects as particularly significant. The first involved a coalition of nonprofit organizations, which conducted forums on public policy issues, workshops and other activities involving the mass media and community, leading to greater access for marginalized groups to appear in the news. 'In a limited way, but however significant, there was a change seen in the principal media of the country,' Dueñas Guzmán says (2009: 6). The second is conducted by the Centro de Medios Independientes

(Independent Media Centre), which produces and disseminates news via the Internet as part of the global indymedia movement. Most of its news originates from the contributions of Puerto Rico's most radical political sectors. The third and largest project is *Prensa Comunitaria*. Dueñas Guzmán argues that the key to *Prensa Comunitaria*'s success is its partnerships with other NGOs, universities, associations for media professionals, government, the mass media and businesses that contribute to deepen and broaden the communicative work of marginalized sectors. Dueñas Guzmán emphasizes that these projects can represent the 'others', who are generally excluded from the mainstream media, by virtue of their 'link between vertical and horizon communication, between democracy and hierarchy' (2009: 10).

POOR COMMUNITIES SEEK A VOICE

Prensa Comunitaria was born after a group of professional journalists and other communicators ended a series of workshops, which were organized in early 2003 by the Puerto Rican Public Broadcasting Corporation. The journalists visited communities across the island to train the residents on how to create mini-newspaper-style 'bulletins'. Workshops also ran in other forms of communication, such as video and theatre.

The community residents appreciated the activities, but, in common with many well-intentioned projects worldwide that have attempted to engage citizens in media activities, the workshops had a strictly limited lifespan and impact. Once the professional journalists and communicators had completed the project and left the communities, grave obstacles threatened to obstruct the local people's attempts to use their new skills. The workshop participants received thirty hours of training, and this was not sufficient for them to continue creating any significant media products independently, especially given their varying levels of education and literacy. After the workshops were completed, the trainers also took their equipment with them, and community members rarely had the appropriate technologies for formatting or printing further bulletins. Furthermore, the workshops did not include training about how participants might generate the funds to pay for the printing and other production expenses. There were also unresolved questions about how to liaise between the different districts and villages within the communities to decide upon the formats, agendas and topics for the bulletins.

Due to concerns about the project's sustainability, a group of interested community leaders met at the University of Turabo in Caguas to develop an ongoing, independent media voice for the communities. They incorporated *Prensa Comunitaria* in 2004. Their initial vision was to establish a network of community newspapers to counteract mainstream media images and to help pressure for changes in public policy.

Although the organization started with no resources other than the commitment and labour of its founders and volunteers, five regional community newspapers appeared within a few months and began printing bimonthly. The number of newspapers soon increased to seven, and *Prensa Comunitaria*'s services grew to include four weekly radio programs, a one-hour weekly community television news program, a website and online news portal, a news service that provides stories about community issues to the mainstream media, and production of videos, short films and movies. It also provides communications training and media management services for non-profit organizations. *Prensa Comunitaria* ceased printing the newspapers in 2008 due to production costs, but they have been revived as occasional regional 'bulletins', each covering one issue or theme of importance to the specific region of publication. However, the number of media productions that *Prensa Comunitaria* offers is not as significant as its community-based decision making and production model and its role in organizing and mobilizing communities in the process of deliberation and social change.

COMMUNITY-BASED ORGANIZATION AND CONTENT

Prensa Comunitaria differs dramatically from Puerto Rico's mainstream media in that the organizational structure and workplace operations provide many different avenues for the communities to participate in decisions about what issues are covered, how they are covered, and what type of media are used to cover them. *Prensa Comunitaria* can only do this because its creation and ongoing activities have relied intensely on an important but invisible resource in Puerto Rico's poor communities: social capital. Social capital is the social networks and connections that exist between and across different groups of individuals within communities. It is vital for economic life, as it enables people to work together to satisfy their mutual goals and need for social recognition. These connections enable the type of 'social exchange' required for communities to generate opportunities, motivate members, plan, take tangible actions, and create or cultivate resources (see Adler and Kwon 2002). The social exchanges in *Prensa Comunitaria* are designed to boost 'political capital', or what John Booth and Patricia Richard have described as the 'attitudes and behaviours that actually influence regimes in some way' (1998: 782).

Prensa Comunitaria has an elastic structure that supports and strengthens its community connections. Its president, Samuel Rosario, is one of the original community leaders who founded *Prensa Comunitaria*. The board includes informal Puerto Rican community leaders who have been engaged in organizing community discussions or actions. They have held few meetings since the organization was created, and thus most decisions are made by an extensive team of community leaders who are volunteers, and through consultations with the broader community.

The community leaders who are volunteers are significant because of their extensive networks and strategic positioning as community organizers. The leaders help *Prensa Comunitaria* to locate and activate individuals and groups who assist with formulating the ideas and content for stories, and can also ensure that communities continue to discuss the issues that have been raised. The far-reaching nature of these connections increases the possibility of mobilizing the leadership and concrete resources of potential stakeholders and others interested in the issues, and stimulating synergies within and between communities.

One community organizer and volunteer, Wilfredo López Montañéz, describes this as empowering for both the leaders and the communities:

> The programmes and projects have enabled us to deepen and broaden the public arena where we discuss the issues and problems of the poorest and most marginalized of Puerto Rican society. It puts tools in the hands of community leaders for us to be ourselves the ones who put forward our initiatives and proposals for change (Morales 2008: 20).

Prensa Comunitaria's organizational structure can be envisaged as four concentric but interdependent circles. At its centre are three ongoing professional/administrative staff responsible for management and strategic planning. These are an executive director, a position that is currently filled by a seasoned journalist from a mainstream commercial television background, and two supervisors.

The second circle comprises another thirty full-time staff with specific professional skills. They are paid an allowance through AmeriCorps*VISTA, a United States government program that supports nonprofit and local government organizations in conducting community service activities to fight poverty in the United States and incorporated territories.

The third circle comprises more than 200 professional and community volunteers who contribute their time, knowledge and labour to *Prensa Comunitaria*. The professionals fall mainly into two groups. The first are journalists and other media people who help train staff and other volunteers. The second are students undertaking work experience, who assist in liaising with community leaders, editing and graphic design of the website, and a range of other functions. Community volunteers are provided with skills and knowhow through training courses in content creation and the concept of community social enterprise. When there are insufficient numbers of volunteers to warrant running a training course, *Prensa Comunitaria* partners the new volunteers with an experienced and established mentor.

The largest, outermost circle comprises the wider communities of Puerto Rico. The circles are porous, with the potential of people to shift from one circle to another. Members of the circles constantly communicate with each other and regularly link with some (although not necessarily all) of the board.

Organizational planning follows an inclusive model that allows *Prensa Comunitaria*'s senior figures to lead deliberative processes that include the board, the different levels of staff and volunteers, and the wider community. The president and executive director talk regularly with leaders in the communities that *Prensa Comunitaria* serves, undertake strategic planning about which media or projects will operate in particular areas, and assess the success of those initiatives. While some ideas are initiated by the president and executive director, many are instigated by community leaders or volunteers. This occurred in 2009, when *Prensa Comunitaria* produced three weekly radio programs—one in the capital, San Juan, one in the southern city of Ponce, and one in the mountainous municipality of Adjuntas in the island's central mid-west. Following the success of these radio programs, leaders and volunteers of the other communities that *Prensa Comunitaria* serves have called for local radio programs to be created and broadcast in their areas. The president and executive director evaluate these kinds of proposals and, if they are viable, work with the boards and community leaders in the relevant areas to develop and implement the projects.

Community consultation also drives the media content, although the nature and extent of community input varies according to the type of media. *Prensa Comunitaria* manages the website and online news portal's contents alone, shares editorial control of the short films and television programs with the communities, and has handed almost complete control of the radio programs and the former newspaper operations to the communities.

When the newspapers were initially established, *Prensa Comunitaria*'s founders went to the communities and held gatherings that loosely followed the structure of focus groups and town hall meetings to set the editorial agenda. Following that, regional groups managed the content, distribution and sales of the local newspapers that served their communities. The newspapers ceased operations in 2008, but a plan has been mooted for communities to initiate and print occasional newspapers on an *ad hoc* basis when issues of particular local concern arise.

With the website and online news portal, *Prensa Comunitaria* staff obtain ideas and information from the nonprofit sector. These are used to create stories targeted primarily at nonprofit organizations, educational institutions and the mainstream media. The centralized nature of these decisions is appropriate given that these activities are run mainly in the central office in San Juan by paid staff and student volunteers with very specific professional skills. These activities are also an important funding source for *Prensa Comunitaria*, helping it to maintain the quality of operations and expand its initiatives. The portal and media management activities also help to promote and sustain the activities of the nonprofit sector more broadly, which in itself might be considered a community or public.

In broadcast, there are a range of approaches. *Prensa Comunitaria* staff manage the production and editing of the television programs. Although some of the story topics on its 'Neighbourhood TV' program are initiated from the contacts of *Prensa Comunitaria* staff within the nonprofit sector and other connections, the television programs feature the community leaders as reporters. The leaders thus have considerable autonomy over the topics that are presented. By contrast, in the case of short films, the theme, script and production for each film are chosen, written and produced by the community with coaching and training from *Prensa Comunitaria* staff. In radio, people from poor communities control and create the program content themselves, with some production assistance from AmeriCorps*VISTA service people. This independence arises partly because radio technologies are easier to access and master.

The main foundations of *Prensa Comunitaria*'s strategy for creating media that are in the hands of the community thus lie in the flexible management structure, shared decision making with communities, and production partnerships between professionals and volunteers. Community control is not absolute, and varies considerably depending on the nature of the media involved. However, because professionals coordinate and oversee the volunteers and the organization's management, this overcomes the limitations that stymied the attempts in 2003 by community members to create their own bulletins, such as lack of time, resources or skills to coordinate and conduct all the requisite tasks by themselves. The system allows community members the scope to build their level of participation and competence in media production with time.

The system also creates risks. Such a loosely structured system may create an unaccountable, unresponsive and unproductive organization, unless it attracts staff and volunteers with the diligence, persistence and leadership qualities required to seek input from disparate community voices and embed those contributions into the organization's core plans, operational strategies and actions. The organization may be overrun by dominating personalities or vested interests within communities, unless it maintains systems and routines for finding, incorporating and balancing diverse voices within communities.

DELIBERATIVE JOURNALISM

As Chapter 2 discusses, there is no single, definitive model for how journalists should support community deliberation. Despite this, it is possible to distinguish elements within *Prensa Comunitaria* that position journalists as leaders in the deliberation process and/or provide resources for deliberative talk and action within communities.

Prensa Comunitaria states that it keeps 'a healthy balance between positive information about initiatives from community based projects, and information that showcases their problems and proposes solutions.'[2] In doing this, *Prensa Comunitaria* sets up ordinary community members as key stakeholders with an identity and voice in identifying issues and problems, naming them on their own terms, and framing the approach that is taken. For example, when *Prensa Comunitaria*'s founders first talked with communities in 2004 to set the agenda for the new newspapers, community members determined that they did not want to cover standard politics and political meetings. They also rejected a framing of issues such as violence and drug dealing from the perspective of statistics—how many victims, how much crime, or how much damage. Instead they wanted to publish stories that discussed strategies and attempts to fix problems.

One community leader and *Prensa Comunitaria* volunteer, Justina Diaz Bisbal, attests that these processes have revitalized communities and their leadership:

> It has revealed the ability, determination and preparation of many leaders, helping them gain recognition and respect. Ours is a vivid testimony about what can be achieved with faith. We have always believed that the rich and powerful are the owners of the world and we are there vassals. Now we know it doesn't have to be like that (Morales 2008: 20).

It is challenging for media professionals to monitor whether their stories have informed people, let alone measure whether those stories have promoted any kind of self-determination. *Prensa Comunitaria* usually relies on the assumption that its stories will publicize issues, perspectives and possibilities, and that communities will use that momentum as a basis for finding strategies or resources for planning and reaching goals. However, in recent times, *Prensa Comunitaria* has been making increasing efforts to not just be a venue for talk but to also to support decision making and action.

The degree to which deliberation is consciously promoted varies from media to media. This can be seen by comparing *Prensa Comunitaria*'s television and radio programs. The television stories adopt the same storytelling style as mainstream television, which is to simply present the facts of an issue, although they do also follow longer term processes and attempt to trace how issues develop over a period of time. While the continued spotlight on issues and stakeholders may create impetus for action, it is an indirect way of promoting a deliberation and differs little from mainstream journalism. In radio, if a program reports that government official or other stakeholders are proposing particular solutions, then the programs in subsequent weeks or months will check whether and how action was taken. If the expected action has not occurred, then the target communities will organize a response. The radio station in Ponce also takes its staff and production team outside the station to develop the programs within the community itself, often inviting politicians and bureaucrats to participate. In several programs, a community issue has been resolved as a result of the conversations that have been brokered between community members and other stakeholders.

In such cases, the media are a forum in which parties can share information and negotiate. To a lesser degree, *Prensa Comunitaria* has also adopted an active role as an organizer of community consensus and action. One example was when it organized deliberative forums that brought together public housing residents and others from economically disadvantaged communities. Discussion at this meeting initially focussed on disputes about which communities suffered the worst poverty and the different levels and types of assistance that the government provided to communities. *Prensa Comunitaria* could easily have simply reported the conflicts and grievances. Instead it sustained the discussion until a consensus was reached about mutual goals and how the participants could work together. *Prensa Comunitaria* then created radio programs, television programs and short films that sought to expose how Puerto Rico's government and media institutions had framed poverty as an experience that is different in each community setting, and how an understanding of similarities could lead to a united approach to addressing collective problems.

Prensa Comunitaria extends its involvement in deliberation process even further through its short film projects which address social themes, such as domestic violence. In addition to engaging the community in formulating the topic, drafting the script and producing the film, *Prensa Comunitaria* organizes public screenings which are followed by deliberative discussions. Discussion participants suggest, evaluate and select possible solutions. *Prensa Comunitaria* helps the participants by developing work plans, which detail the steps and provide other information necessary to implement those solutions.

The most noteworthy of these initiatives to date has been the movie about poverty, 'Better do it together', which was created from a six-month process of community deliberations. In the first mass gathering of its type in Puerto Rico, its screening in February 2009 attracted more than 1,000 community leaders, citizens, government officials and academics from across the island. The attendance figure alone indicated the degree to which the community had already been mobilized in their concern about the issue. After the screening, there were several deliberative regional forums and meetings, mostly with the groups that participated in the film's production. During these encounters, participants agreed on several courses of action. This has led to the creation of a national work plan, with a breakdown of tasks to be implemented by different residential neighbourhoods, subcommunities and community-based organizations.

There are differences of opinion within *Prensa Comunitaria* as to how far the organization should extend its role as an organizer of deliberative conversation and action. Some argue that the communities need to be encouraged to initiate their own solution-seeking processes after stories have been published, broadcast or screened, rather than relying on *Prensa Comunitaria* to instigate or organize such processes.

Deliberations about how *Prensa Comunitaria* should itself operate have also led to strong differences of opinion, resulting in some rifts and divisions.

For example, although most community leaders have been reconciled to the closure of the newspapers, several have left *Prensa Comunitaria* due to the belief that the print media should have been the paramount priority.

The screening of *Prensa Comunitaria*'s 'Neighbourhood TV' program on Channel 13, known locally as TeleOro, also raised internal issues. Tele-Oro is owned by Puerto Rico's Roman Catholic Church, which offered *Prensa Comunitaria* a timeslot to screen a program, but stipulated that certain topics were not suitable for airing on a Catholic station. Some *Prensa Comunitaria* staff and affiliated community leaders argued that this was unacceptable censorship. Others took the view that it would be better to find ways to discuss topics that might be deemed contentious—such as a potential story on abortion or condoms—in ways that would not raise sensitivity or seem threatening, rather than lose the opportunity to air community voices on television altogether. The programs commenced in August 2007 and have gained in popularity, although not all staff and leaders feel that their concerns about potential restrictions have been laid to rest.

SOCIAL AND ECONOMIC DEVELOPMENT

Prensa Comunitaria aims to support both social and economic rejuvenation. Its achievements in the social sphere are easier to identify and are arguably more substantial than in the economic arena.

While *Prensa Comunitaria* has not conducted any formal measurements of its outcomes and does not even have a system for recording audience levels, the organization receives a lot of feedback from community members via email and other forms of communications. Community feedback indicates satisfaction that *Prensa Comunitaria* has created opportunities to sound out voices, issues and agendas that would not otherwise be heard in the public arena. *Prensa Comunitaria* staff believe that the communications style promotes 'hope, empowerment and values and such as solidarity, inclusion, tolerance, respect for differences and diversity' and has increased the self-esteem within the target communities by providing a 'different way of looking at disadvantaged groups of society' (Morales 2008: 19). Even the mainstream media has sometimes followed up these stories, in addition to circulating stories from *Prensa Comunitaria*'s news service.

Maria Santiago, one community leader who volunteers with *Prensa Comunitaria*, describes the personal satisfaction she feels 'from being able to help, guiding communities and celebrating their achievements' as her 'greatest gain'. 'In my personal life, it has been a school of constant learning to fight for the community,' she says (Morales 2008: 20). Many other citizens engaged in civic development work have also said that prior to the media presenting their stories, they were unable to see the impact of their work. The stories had helped them to better visualize both the outcomes of their own labours as well as the bigger picture of how they and other communities could improve their circumstances. The Miranda Foundation has also recognized *Prensa Comunitaria* with its Prize for Solidarity, an award presented annually to a nonprofit or community-based organization that has united and mobilized citizens to act for the common good and resolve social challenges.

Prensa Comunitaria faces greater challenges in its goal of promoting economic development. It aims to generate capital for communities through a solidarity-based model that involves agreements and partnerships with the private, community and non-government sectors. This vision matches the recommendations of María Enchautegue and Richard Freeman (2006: 182) that 'non-government organisations could combine their services to low-income populations with efforts to increase employment' in Puerto Rico. However, *Prensa Comunitaria* is yet to achieve its plans for the different media outlets to become self-sustaining enterprises with their own revenue base, which can create jobs and contribute to the economic life of the communities that host them.

The rise and fall of *Prensa Comunitaria*'s newspapers indicate the difficulties involved. When the newspapers commenced, the production and layout was done at no cost on Samuel Rosario's home computer. The money for printing was gathered from community leaders, community fundraising, support from like-minded nonprofit sector organizations, and donations from foundations and corporations. When *Prensa Comunitaria*'s central office coordinated the newspapers, it struggled to attract advertising from a national base. More than 80 per cent of Puerto Rico's newspaper market is owned by one major conglomerate which proves too strong a competitor for advertising resources. *Prensa Comunitaria* closed the newspapers after weighing the financial costs and effort involved in publishing the newspapers against the benefits of placing resources in radio, television, film production and online media. *Prensa Comunitaria* plans to train communities to seek a local advertising and other financing so that they can print occasional mini-newspapers about regional themes.

Prensa Comunitaria's other media activities provide stronger revenue streams, although these too need further development. Costs for the *Prensa Comunitaria*'s radio and television programs are relatively low because they are broadcast by existing stations in times that are dedicated to public service announcements. Radio programs are cheap to create, and advertisements can be sold through the programs. The short films are also produced on minimal budgets, since the communities provide the 'talent' and locations. If travel is required, the production team stay in community leaders' homes. *Prensa Comunitaria* also earns a small revenue stream by selling copies of the films at conferences and similar events. The cameras, recording equipment and other tools have been purchased mainly with funds raised by grants from foundations and corporations. However, most of the funding comes from selling professional services, such as media management workshops, graphic design, photography and promotional corporate-style films for non-government, community and nonprofit organizations.

The financial activities have thus been small-scale and piecemeal, as opportunities present themselves. The largest difficulty arises arguably because its staff members' expertise lies in supporting media content and community engagement rather than in financial expansion or commercial entrepreneurship.

COMMUNICATIONS FOR DEVELOPMENT

The Puerto Rican media has long been a vehicle for promoting nationhood and development. Autonomy from Spain was achieved in the late nineteenth century after 'a strong and persistent effort' by Puerto Ricans both at home and in the United States, with newspapers being 'as an important element in the struggle for independence' (Fitzpatrick 1987: 304). When the United States took possession of the island in 1898, the press struggled for a political status acceptable to Puerto Ricans (Fitzpatrick 1987: 304).

The establishment of the Commonwealth of Puerto Rico in 1952 occurred at a time in which developmentalism (*desarrollismo*) became a dominant ideology in Latin America. Developmentalism promoted the idea that traditional societies would develop urbanized, free-market oriented, entrepreneurial and 'modern' culture, by applying Western scientific and technical knowledge under the guidance of technocratic governments. Unsurprisingly, 'the development model that has prevailed in Latin America has stimulated top-down, unilateral, message-oriented communication approaches' (Quarry and Ramirez 2007: NP).

In recent decades, ideologies of consumerism have largely replaced or overlapped with developmentalist logic in Latin America. Development communicators Wendy Quarry and Ricardo Ramirez (2007) argue that what is needed instead 'is an alternative development model that is centred on pluralism and dialogue, where communication is seen as a basic right and as a tool for citizen engagement. In this perspective, there is no development without communication'. *Prensa Comunitaria* represents a unique effort to use the mass media to offer such an alternative in Puerto Rico. It surpasses the traditions of development and commercial liberalism through its community social enterprise model that aims not just to provide an alternative voice in society but also opportunities for personal fulfilment and collective action.

Mainstream media editors have primarily viewed Puerto Ricans in economically disadvantaged communities as either passive consumers of media products, or the subject for stories about drugs, violence, deprivation and failure. By contrast, *Prensa Comunitaria* attempts to create a social and political forum to help communities to influence public understandings and outcomes. It creates and communicates messages from and for disadvantaged communities, to provide people with a resource that might stimulate and support social and economic change, and recognize and celebrate assets/achievements.

CONCLUSION: SOLIDARITY AND SUSTAINABILITY

According to its promotional material, *Prensa Comunitaria* is a nonprofit organization that assists residents of underprivileged towns to create community media enterprises that promote social development by disseminating constructive information and creating jobs. Video production, radio shows, news and general information articles, newspapers and a website portal are some of the outlets that *Prensa Comunitaria* has identified that can provide marginalized people, left out from public debate, a voice in their own development. *Prensa Comunitaria* aims to keep a healthy balance between positive information about initiatives from community-based projects, and information that showcases their problems and proposes solutions. *Prensa Comunitaria*'s business structure has been designed so that solidarity becomes a fundamental aspect of the project, as evidenced in the Community Newspaper Network, in which newspapers were entities that operated as individual but collaborated as an integrated unit.

The effectiveness of this model depends on the system of linking community leaders with professional and volunteer collaborators. It draws from the extensive networks and social capital of community leaders, without allowing the dominant personalities and vested interests among such leaders and their constituencies so much influence that their perspectives might skew the organization's operations. Volunteers and the broader community are supported by technical and administrative professionals to identify topics and create stories aimed at asserting their identities and transforming their communities. This collaboration allows even those community members with low levels of literacy, education and technological skill to be engaged in publications and broadcasts which are of consistent quality and are circulated on a regular basis.

In contrast to the effective elasticity of *Prensa Comunitaria*'s organizational model, its economic model is rubbery. Despite its aspirations to create jobs and viable economic enterprises, *Prensa Comunitaria* depends on labour that is unpaid (volunteers) or externally funded (AmeriCorps*VISTA). The scope of *Prensa Comunitaria*'s activities is heavily limited by funding constraints. While the stories and deliberative forums created by *Prensa Comunitaria* may help to stimulate the economy by bringing people together and helping them to plan community improvements, the challenge will be to determine whether and how the organization will develop a model of financial self-sustainability for its own enterprises.

NOTES

1. Anette Sofia Ruiz Morales worked for three years in *Prensa Comunitaria*, first as an AmeriCorps*VISTA member and later as a supervisor. The views presented in this chapter are those of the authors, and do not necessarily reflect the perspectives or policies of *Prensa Comunitaria*, its staff or volunteers.

2. This is the standard statement that *Prensa Comunitaria* uses in advertisements for recruiting AmeriCorps*VISTA service people.

BIBLIOGRAPHY

Adler, P.S. and Kwon, S.-W. (2002) 'Social capital: Prospects for a new concept' *The Academy of Management Review*, 27(1): 17–40.

Bauman, K.J. and Graf, N.L. (2003) *Educational Attainment: 2000*, Washington DC: US Census Bureau, US Department of Commerce.

Bigshaw, A. and Semega, J. (2008) *Income, Earnings, and Poverty Data from the 2007 American Community Survey*, Washington, DC: US Census Bureau ACS-09, US Government Printing Office.

Booth, J.A. and Richard, P.B. (1998) 'Civil society, political capital, and democratization in Central America', *Journal of Politics*, 60(3): 780–800.

Caribbean Business (2006) *2006 Business Directory*, San Juan, Puerto Rico: Casiano Communications.

CIA World Factbook (2009) 'Puerto Rico. Available at https://www.cia.gov/library/publications/the-world-factbook/geos/rq.html (Accessed 1 September 2009).

Dueñas Guzmán, M. (2009) *Puerto Rico ante el Desafío por Democratizar la Comunicación de Masas* (Puerto Rico and the Challenge for Democratization of Mass Communication), unpublished manuscript: School of Communication, University of Puerto Rico, Humacao.

Enchautegue, M.E. and Freeman, R.B. (2006) 'Why don't more Puerto Rican men work?', in S.M. Collins, B.P. Bosworth, M.A. Soto-Class (eds) *The Economy of Puerto Rico: Restoring Growth*, Washington, DC: Brookings Institution Press and San Juan: Center for the New Economy, pp. 152–82.

Fitzpatrick, J. (1987) 'The Puerto Rican press', in S.M. Miller (ed.) *The Ethnic Press in the United States: A Historical Analysis and Handbook*, New York: Greenwood Press, pp. 303–14.

Ladd, H.F. and Rivera-Batiz, F.L. (2006) 'Education and economic development', in S.M. Collins, B.P. Bosworth, M.A. Soto-Class (eds) *The Economy of Puerto Rico: Restoring Growth*, Washington, DC: Brookings Institution Press and San Juan: Center for the New Economy, pp. 189–238.

Morales, A.S.R. (2008) 'Poor communities find their own voices: Citizen-run media as a tool for community empowerment in Puerto Rico', *Southern Peace-Building Review*, September: 17–20.

Quarry, W. and Ramirez, R. (2007) 'Compendium of regional perspectives in communication for development', *Glocal Times*, (7). Available at http://www.glocaltimes.k3.mah.se/viewarticle.aspx?articleID=108&issueID=10 (Accessed 1 September 2009).

Red de Fundaciones (2007) *Estudio sobre las Necesidades Sociales en Puerto Rico, 2007 (Social Needs Survey of Puerto Rico, 2007)*, Puerto Rico: Estudios Técnicos.

Rivera Cruz, Y. (2006). 'Establece metas SME para achicar la brecha digital' (SME sets goals for narrowing the digital divide), *El Nuevo Día*, 6 November. Available at http://www.adendi.com/ResultsByDate.asp?page=1&dtrange=day&category=noticias&mon0=11&day0=06&year0=2006 (Accessed 12 July 2008).

Sotomayor, O. (2004) 'Development and income distribution: The case of Puerto Rico', *World Development*, 32(8): 1395–406.

16 Viração Magazine
Consciousness-Raising Media for Young Brazilians

Paulo Lima and Izabel Leão
(Translation by Angela Romano and Alice Baroni)

Viração Magazine is a social project that runs with the goal of stimulating, reasoning with and conciliating with young people as active protagonists in Brazilian society. *Viração* is operated by the Association for the Support of Girls and Boys, a non-government organization in Sé Region, São Paulo. It produces news and information 'about', 'for' and 'with' the *jovem*—young people—at a national level, becoming a forum of reflection and debates on Brazilian and worldwide realities. *Viração*'s publishing line promotes humanistic values, such as education for peace and nonviolence, solidarity between the people, respect for diversity of ethnic/racial, cultural, religious and other backgrounds. The magazine affirms and promotes the rights of young people and valorizes Brazilian culture.

This chapter describes *Viração*'s goal to represent and extend a social dialogue with Brazil's young people, and the strategies that are used to achieve that mission. The chapter draws from Paulo Lima's experience as *Viração*'s founder and director, and Maria Izabel Leão's academic study with Cláudia Lago of the magazine.

ANOTHER STEP IN THE PATHWAY TO ACTIVATING YOUNG PEOPLE

The creation of *Viração* is just one step in a number of progressive initiatives that have attempted to use communications to build recognition and respect for the perspectives of communities that lack a voice in Brazilian society and to support their participation in public life and decision making. Prior to establishing *Viração* in 2003, Lima had worked on many activities aimed at making different communications media available to youth and the common people. Lima, himself born and raised in a *favela* (shantytown or slum), developed links as a teenager with youth groups that tried to improve the lives of poor people through education and community communication. As a youth, he also contributed to community radio, a local magazine and community art. Later, as a journalist with *Without*

Boundaries, he directed a number of initiatives that led to the magazine winning a prize for human rights and an award for himself that recognized his defence of children and adolescents. Lima established a weekly political newspaper, *Brasil de Fato* in 2002, which frames its stories about social and political events in terms of the need for social change in Brazil. Lima founded *Viração* in the following year as a partnership involving the University of São Paulo's School of Communication and Art and the Association for the Support of Girls and Boys.

The word *viração* is rich in meaning. First, the word *virar* means to turn and *ação* means action. From the beginning, *Viração*'s founders intended that the collaborative production of content and reading of the magazine would encourage young people to take action. The final section of the magazine, which tries to mobilize young readers, was initially entitled *Viração Social* (Turn to Social Action), although the name was changed to *Parada Social* (Social Parade) in 2007 on the suggestion of one of the magazine's Youth Councils. *Viração* also draws from the slang of 'street kids' in São Paulo, who use the expression *se virar* to talk about surviving in the face of difficulties. Such survival is a turning to oneself, a form of self-sufficiency. Viração is also a fresh wind from the seaside on Brazil's northeast, where Lima was born. Wind is movement. It is never still. So too is the mobilization that is proposed through the magazine.

Most of Brazil's publications—regardless of whether they target youth audience or a general readership—do not reflect the lives of young Brazilians. Brazil is one of the most economically unequal countries in the world, with the wealthiest 10 per cent of the population earning 46.9 per cent of the national income, and the poorest 10 per cent receiving only 0.7 per cent (UNDP 2005: 56). A third of the population lives below the poverty line, at least one in five people live in the *favelas*, and the majority lack formal education past primary (elementary) school level. Regardless of their socioeconomic status, few young Brazilians have the training or access that would enable them to contribute to media debates. The media that is directed towards a youth audience is focussed on lifestyle issues and promotes a consumer society. The mainstream media for the general public present topics that lack relevance or are written in a style and language that is inaccessible for young people.

Viração is a communitarian media organization that listens to young people across a full range of socioeconomic backgrounds, from the *favela* to the sophisticated urban centres, and enables them to set the editorial agenda. The magazine boosts the esteem and sense of social inclusion of both the creators and readers by providing a platform for young people to identify, describe and explore solutions for their own issues. *Viração* does not confine itself to the lighter topics that are normally the fare of youth magazines. While some of the topics might be seen as exclusively 'youth issues', many of the issues have a major bearing on Brazilian society as a whole, such HIV/AIDS, poverty, corruption, exploitation of resources, and intense traffic congestion.

Style is as important as content in these communications. The editorial team recognizes the importance of communicating in an accessible style and engaging young people through a visually attractive and dynamic layout. *Viração* communicates important messages through graphic design, photo-essays, comics, humorous commentary, poems, and creative work as well as traditional 'serious' stories about significant themes and topics.

Following *Viração*'s success, more initiatives are being promoted by the team. These include 'wall journals', or newspapers that can be created by schoolchildren and other community members and posted on walls in public places, such as schools or city plazas. Training is also being conducted with a variety of youth organizations to build communications skills with the aim that they will develop their own communications media and/or content.

EDU-COMMUNICATION

Viração magazine is regarded as a tool of reflection and debates in classrooms. It is used to progress the fundamental principles of the Brazilian Ministry of Education, with the goals of:

- consolidating and deepening the knowledge acquired in Fundamental High School Education;
- providing a basic preparation for the workforce and marketplace;
- educating young people about citizenship; and
- developing humanity, including ethical instruction and advancing intellectual autonomy, critical thinking and understanding of the scientific/technological foundations of production processes, relating the theory with the practice.

Another concern of the *Viração* team is the pedagogical aim to renew an understanding of language as a means for social action and a medium to influence how people take action in their world. In other words, when young people think, write, take photographs, draw, illustrate and speak out, they engage in an act of social interaction that uses language to construct the understandings, knowledge and social identities that make up our social life.

With this goal, *Viração*'s editorial strategy is to adopt the theoretical framework used in social education called 'edu-communication'. Ismar de Oliveira Soares, a member of *Viração*'s Editorial Council, defines 'edu-communication' as 'the set of the inherent actions involved in planning, implementing and evaluating the processes, programs and products that are meant to create and fortify open, democratic and participatory communications ecosystems. The intention is to extend the spaces for expression in society via the democratic management of communications resources'.

In this way, *Viração* Magazine's social practice is based on a theory of communicative action that privileges the concept of dialogical communication. In other words, it aims to provide opportunities for the key stakeholders to influence both the processes and the topics of the communications. This approach demands ethical responsibility on the part of the cultural producers, and promotes active and creative reception on the part of the audience. The politics of dialogical communications demands that information resources and communication processes serve people with opposing poles of interest and on all sides of an issue, especially the interests of preadolescents, adolescents and young adults. Finally, *Viração*'s political approach promotes the education and development of people as members of a society, especially the professors and students of Brazilian schools. It represents an exercise in their rights to produce messages through all available resources and technologies.

From the time of its launch, the magazine has offered a significant alternative to the mainstream media for young Brazilians. Lago and Leão's study of *Viração* finds that the magazine represents a quantitative and qualitative improvement on how the media normally covers young people. Furthermore, they observed that the magazine's activities acted as a catalyst for the creation of many other projects that place children and adolescents in the centre of media production, not only as media consumers but as agents of the media's creation (Lago and Leão 2007). These projects need to gain social recognition in order to secure the magazine's existence in the publishing market and so that it does not simply rely on public funding to stay afloat.

This chapter points to the possibilities and challenges involved in appropriating journalism to serve young people and transform it into an instrument for rescuing them as citizens. *Viração* performs a function in civil society to appropriate and intervene in the processes of media creation that previously had exclusively been the right of legitimated professionals within the journalistic field.

Lago and Leão (2007) argue that via its Youth Councils (*ViraJovens*), *Viração* magazine gives young people a presence not just in suggesting the editorial guidelines and story topics, but also engages them in all the process of production, since they define the approach and the framing for issues. There is a Youth Council in twenty-one of Brazil's twenty-six state capitals.

Lago and Leão (2007) argue that although there is little systematic research on the magazine's relationship with its target population, *Viração* acts as an appropriate instrument for the valuation of the young and as a forum for building consciousness among the citizenry as individuals, capable of self-reflection. Lago and Leão (2007) emphasize that to operate effectively as a media for young people with applied outcomes, *Viração* and other vehicles like it must operate inside the parameters of radical protagonism. 'Such a possibility, still under construction, is already confronted with some impediments, such as the conception, widely defended (even by the cadre with a leftist political orientation), that journalism is a social enterprise which must be conducted exclusively by professionals formed from the *métier* [professional class]' (Lago and Leão 2007: 111).

The perspective of radical protagonism sees collective action as the starting point for building the autonomy of young people's action. The model does not presume to generate the leadership of specific individuals, but instead develops participation through social cooperation. The protagonism of young people is developed through a pedagogic/political model of educational action that views the person as a subject who can create a process of sociocultural intervention. The United Nation's Convention of the Rights of the Child embraces the whole youth population, from birth to eighteen years of age, and establishes two fundamental precepts for education about citizenship. These are children and adolescents' right to have their opinion taken into account in subjects for which they should be due respect and the concept of progressive autonomy (Muñoz N.D.).

MANAGEMENT

In *Viração*, like all publications, questions arise about how to manage the wide range of processes and activities involved in creating the magazine. To oversee these processes, *Viração* has adopted a general coordinator, who is responsible for the management of resources, the legal representation and facilitation of strategic decisions. The coordinator also participates in meetings of the different staff teams, whose areas cover Youth Administration, Content, Advice (*ViraJovens*), School and Community. In common with mainstream publications, *Viração* also has an Editorial Council. This Council comprises professionals with expertise in the fields of communication and social education, who help to make strategic publishing decisions. However, the Youth Council has as much—or even more—importance for *Viração* than the traditional Editorial Council, due to its power to make decisions and constantly suggest changes. *Viração* also has a Pedagogical Council, a multidisciplinary team that collaborates with the writing team in São Paulo in creating educationally sound proposals for the magazine's content.

PRODUCTION

The production dynamics in *Viração* differ considerably from those in most other publications that are directed toward adolescents and children. The main axle of activity is the Youth Councils. Each Youth Council is mounted to a base of volunteers, comprising mobilized citizens from diverse social backgrounds who establish their own social movements that work in collaboration with the Councils. Because many members belong to other youth networks, the Youth Councils engage in dialogue and cooperation with a wide array of grassroots organizations across Brazil. The formation and ongoing development of the Youth Councils occurs via personal meeting with the writing team in São Paulo, frequent telephone contacts and Internet communication (email or exchange of simultaneous messages). To assist this process of establishing and consolidating of the Youth Councils, there is an instruction guide that shows step-by-step how the set-up process occurs.

Beyond the stories produced by the *ViraJovem*, the magazine also publishes text sent by readers and adult correspondents. Among the adult contributors are cinema critic Sergio Rizzo, and the doctors and psychologists who collaborate in the creation of the 'Sex' and 'Health' sections.

The *ViraJovem* rely on the support of non-government organizations, and they convene meetings at least once a month in the headquarters of the partner institutions, which are centrally located for easy access. In these meetings, the communitarian character of *Viração*'s production becomes evident. The meetings involve the constant participation of adolescents and children in suggesting guidelines, checking facts, writing articles and creating images, as well as providing advice on the magazine's administration, production, sales and distribution. The participants' collaboration has created a new journalistic language about and for youth. The *ViraJovem* meetings also include writing workshops, discussion of magazine's editorial themes and topics, as well as debates, lectures or background briefings on specific subjects. These enable the *ViraJovem* to function effectively and autonomously.

The partner institutions in each state also support the Youth Councils by providing a facilitator, social educator or communications expert, who is responsible for mobilizing the core Council members, organizing logistics, facilitating meetings, and helping to train and mentor the young people. The partner institution signs a cooperation agreement in which *Viração* promises to provide, among others things, the technical support and knowledge needed for the Youth Councils to function effectively. This includes 300 copies of *Viração* per year to each Council (thirty copies of ten editions) plus posters, folders and adhesives. It also includes *cartilhas* (instructional or informational booklets) produced by *Viração* or its partners on themes such as how to create a 'wall journal' or communication for gender, sexual and ethnic/racial diversity. *Viração* also provides weekly backup at a distance via new communications technologies such as instant message systems, discussion lists, and telephone calls via VoIP (Voice over Internet Protocol) system. In return for their contributions, the partner institutions receive advertising space in the magazine, which increases their visibility. Twenty per cent of the income received from *Viração*'s subscriptions also goes to the partner institutions to help to cover the costs of facilitating the Youth Councils.

DISTRIBUTION

It is important to the *Viração* team to reach as many readers as possible, in order to serve the magazine's goal of providing leadership and information that will help increase the education and sociopolitical participation of young

Brazilians. A hard copy version of *Viração* is published monthly, with an average print run of 5,000 copies of each edition. Copies are distributed to subscribers and the Youth Councils, and free copies are circulated at venues for cultural activities or social mobilization, such as community festivals, schools and public libraries. *Viração* is also published via an online portal at www.revistaviracao.org.br. The virtual version is updated daily and includes a discussion forum for readers, writers and editors to exchange ideas.

CONCLUSION

Viração represents the interests and agendas of young people to counterbalance the limited and stereotypical representations in the mainstream media. It helps Brazilians to acknowledge, understand and respect young people's sociopolitical agendas and perspectives. However, *Viração* goes far beyond a simple attempt to create a platform for youth to express themselves or to improve public understanding of young people. The *Viração* team attempts to influence the young readers themselves, by engaging youth with relevant and meaningful information and discussions and encouraging them to participate more actively in their communities. The magazine is also used by schools and other educational and social institutions as a teaching tool that helps to promote awareness of public issues, critical thinking and humanistic values in young people. The *Viração* team furthermore empowers young people through training that provides the knowledge and practical skills to formulate effective messages, and with an organizational network and infrastructure that provides a venue for them to express those messages. Those involved in *Viração* believe that the magazine, as well as the community initiatives that support and feed into it, offer a new way to promote citizenship and community participation among young people.

BIBLIOGRAPHY

Lago, C. and Leão, M.I. (2007) '*Revista Viração*: um projeto social impress' (*Viração Magazine*: A social publication project), *Comunicação & Educação*, 12(3): 103–111.

Lago, C. (2003) *O Romantismo Morreu? Viva o Romantismo. Ethos Romântico no Jornalismo* (*Did Romanticism die? Viva romanticism. Romantic Ethos in Journalism*), unpublished doctoral thesis, ECA/USP, São Paulo.

Lima, P. (2003) *Projeto Editorial da Revista Viração* (*The Editorial Project of Viração Magazine*), unpublished report: São Paulo.

Muñoz, C. (N.D.) 'Otras ciudades posibles' base de ese '*Otro Mundo Posible*' ('Other possible cities' based on '*Another Possible World*'). Available at http://www.intersindical.org/stepv/peirp/participacio/articles/cesar_munoz.pdf (Accessed 1 September 2009).

United Nations Development Programme (UNDP) (2005) *Human Development Report 2005*, New York: UNDP.

Part IV
Conclusions

17 Ongoing Issues for Deliberative Journalism

Angela Romano

The case studies in this book indicate how the mass media have great potential to assist and sometimes even drive the progress of public deliberation in modern societies. Deliberative journalism relies on the journalists' ability to imagine how citizens might play a role in setting news agendas and acting upon the information that the media provides. Jay Rosen sums this up when he memorably comments that from this standpoint, the citizen 'is not a victim, spectator, quote machine, ventilator of steam or cute adornment of the news, but an informed participant in socio-political processes' (1997: 17). The concluding chapter of this book investigates some of the ongoing issues for the various models of deliberative journalism.

OBJECTIVITY, DELIBERATION AND MOBILIZATION

As Chapter 2 makes clear, one of the most common criticisms of deliberative journalism models is that they potentially threaten journalists' standards of objectivity. However, deliberative journalism does not require an absolute abandonment of the concept of objectivity. Instead, it requires a reflection on how high standards of objectivity might be balanced with fairness and ethical considerations. The problems of applying the principle of objectivity in an ethical vacuum can be seen in the issues that arose from the 'neutrality' of Swiss bankers during World War II, when they continued dealing with the German Reichsbank and handling stolen money and gold (see, for example, LeBor 1997). Similarly, objective but unreflective journalists may feel that that they are professionally justified or even obliged to equally represent 'both sides' of a case, even when the merits of the case do not warrant it, or to circulate information that may distract or destabilize the populace in its search for options to resolve their problems.

Mainstream journalism often provides technically accurate but knee-jerk reports about the specific facts about any dramatic event or issue that rises to the reporters' attention. Philosophies like public, development and peace journalism encourage greater consideration of the subtle nuances of the visible facts, and how the manifest and obscure details fit into a bigger

picture of ongoing trends and issues. Journalists also need to be sophisticated in understanding the consequences of their work: how people might
potentially use information from the media and other sources to make sense
of their circumstances and deal with the situations that they face.

Many public journalism proponents argue that public journalists do
remain objective because they are attached to the process of democratic
deliberation, and pursue topics of public importance rather than any particular 'side' or outcome (e.g., Levine 1996). However, there is no universal
acceptance of the principle that public journalists are simply facilitators of
a democratic process. Some public journalism projects have required journalists to play a mobilizing role in their communities by promoting or even
actively coordinating and implementing certain solutions to problems.

Mobilization activities occurred in the first media venture to be recognized as public journalism in the United States. The 'Columbus Beyond
2000' project was run in 1987–88 by the *Ledger-Enquirer* newspaper in
Columbus, Georgia, as an eight-part series of articles that examined the
city's future, its challenges and residents' fears and concerns. This initiative
experimented with many of the public listening and engagement strategies
that subsequently became common elements of American public journalism. The project included a telephone survey with Columbus residents, a
written questionnaire of eighty-five influential citizens, as well as in-depth
interviews with residents, government officials and scholars. When the
thirteen-month project drew a muted response, editor Jack Swift moved
from deliberative to mobilizing activities. He organized a town hall meeting and had newspaper staff trained in moderating public discussion. He
helped to establish and lead a citizen's organization to progress the concerns identified in the discussions, as well as a range of other assemblies,
events and taskforces to maintain the momentum. Swift describes it as a
decision 'to leap across the chasm that normally separates journalism from
the community' (Rosen 1991: 271).

Despite some praise from community leaders and journalism scholars,
the project also prompted many of the questions that commonly arise about
public journalism. Many journalists and media observers are uncomfort-
able with the implications of the media playing such a direct mobilizing
role in social affairs. Many *Ledger-Enquirer* journalists, for example,
reportedly felt unclear about the project's nature and goals, concerned that
the newspaper was trying to manufacture news to cover, exhausted by the
long hours involved, and frustrated that the focus on the project diminished
resources for regular journalism (Waddell 1997: 94–5). Much of this disaffection doubtlessly resulted from insufficient communication within the
Ledger-Enquirer itself. However, it also reflects the division between supporters of deliberative journalism about whether the media should simply
provide the raw materials for communities to deliberate with or whether
they should take the further step to become actively involved in ensuring
that particular outcomes are achieved.

In citizen journalism and the community media, these questions take a different complexion. If such citizen-driven journalism offers us 'random acts of journalism', as Lasica suggests, then obvious acts of deliberative journalism will be even more sporadic. The strength of citizen-driven journalism often does not arise from the citizen-creators' objectivity or their reflection on the consequences of their work. Instead, it stems from the articulation of alternative voices, the formation and strengthening of identities of a multiplicity of social groups that may have previously lacked means of political expression and participation, and the possibilities for cross-referencing multitudinous mainstream and minority perspectives.

In considering questions of partisanship, objectivity and the extent to which journalists should not just support deliberation but promote particular causes or policies, it should be remembered that such issues are problematic in conventional journalism too. For example, numerous texts show that mainstream American journalism has always taken political stands, from hiding the weaknesses of presidents—such as Roosevelt's polio, Kennedy's prolific affairs or Johnson's public drunkenness—to the partisan coverage of the wars in Iraq (e.g., Barnett 2002: 403; Page 1996: 35–7, 109–16).

LEVELS AND LAYERS OF DELIBERATIVE JOURNALISM

Editors and reporters who practise deliberative journalism are paradoxically urged by some quarters of the community to be more local, while others argue that they cannot be effective until they extend their horizons. In community journalism, for example, the local is often celebrated. Clemencia Rodríguez says she has often heard community media people longing to become bigger and more powerful in order to have greater visibility and reach wider audiences. However, she believes that media outlets lose their ability to articulate the local issues and identities if their coverage and audiences expand. 'The capacity to articulate the local constitutes a crucial component of the political potential of citizens' media,' she says (Rodríguez 2001: 155).

Many supporters of public journalism also believe that it is best practised by smaller, local media. James Carey applauds the perceived commitment to reawakening a tradition of journalism and politics that 'emphasizes local democracy, the community of locale, and citizenship as against the distant forces that would overwhelm it' (1999: 63). Research suggests that in the United States, more small- to medium-sized newspapers have engaged in public journalism projects compared to large newspapers (e.g., Arant and Meyer 1998: 209). Community-oriented values associated with public journalism have also been found to be much higher among journalists in small newspapers than medium-sized newspapers, who in turn held these values much more than journalists at large ones (Arant and Meyer 1998: 210).

By contrast, Peter Parisi suggests that public journalism is too greatly focussed on local issues and is hampered by an 'optimistic sense that all problems will yield if local folks just roll up their sleeves' (1997: 680). He suggests that with its focus on volunteerism and personal initiative, public journalism steers away from social and economic facts, particularly those that may result from forces well beyond the bounds of local community control (Parisi 1997: 677).

In response to Parisi's critique, it becomes clear that deliberative journalists need to have a nuanced awareness of whether issues are purely local, or whether they have dimensions beyond the local. Similarly, journalists need to contemplate whether citizen politics can deal with issues, or whether other levels of economic and political action may be needed. The chapters in this book on countries as far afield as Australia, Colombia, Finland and Japan indicate that public journalism can work equally effectively at the local, state and national level, although the practices and techniques may vary to suit differing circumstances. In talking about the public journalism-style projects of *The Australian* newspaper, former editor David Armstrong recognized that a national newspaper could not appeal to small geographic communities but 'had to think more in terms of communities of interest' (2002: pers. comm.). *The Australian* still managed to inject local inflections from both geographically based communities and well as communities of interest as part of the newspaper's ongoing process of exploring the multiple dimensions of nationally significant issues with complex social, economic and political roots.

UNLEASHING CREATIVITY

Much of what passes as deliberative journalism is worthy but dull. Deliberative journalism requires a curious combination of skills. Journalists need proficiencies that are commonly associated with the stereotype of a nerdish bespectacled scientist, such as rigorous observation, data-gathering and intelligent analysis. They also need talents that are associated with a bohemian artist, such as imagination, talent and flair to creatively package the data.

It is a duality that promoters of development journalism have been grappling with for decades. Jakob Oetama, the founding editor of Indonesia's leading daily newspaper, noted this when he said that the problem was 'how to give substance to a development-oriented press. This involves knowledge of development problems and technical or vocational ability to communicate them in stimulating writings' (Oetama 1978: 83). Images and visual design are important elements in this communication process. Dynamic visual portrayals in the media of conflict, adversity or need have often provoked a humanitarian or political response where other forms of communication have failed. Deliberative journalism should ideally engage all verbal and non-verbal elements that can stimulate a sense of connection and understanding among audiences.

Another problem is journalists' propensity to overlook topics until they reach the scorching point of crisis. For example, in many countries, hunger and starvation do not become big media issues until there is a famine (see, for example, Sainath 1996). Even inept journalists can turn disasters and conflicts into interesting reports, because they have so many dramatic elements. Reporters can also easily find numerous examples of past reports about similar disasters or conflicts, and use these as models for structuring their current stories. It is usually harder to write compelling reports about issues that are simmering. It requires more talent and effort to recognize the issues that may be leading to a potential calamity, to find the compelling features of the story, and to be inventive in developing new storytelling strategies to best tell these tales.

DIVERSITY AND DELIBERATIVE JOURNALISM

Many studies of mainstream journalism suggest that the propensity of journalists to gather most of their information from the leading political and economic institutions has disadvantaged women and a range of ethnic and other minorities, who tend to be overlooked and underutilized as the sources of information or topics for stories. In Australia, for example, it has been noted that because 'women are less likely than men to hold the positions of economic and political leadership, they are not only less likely to be invited by journalists to comment on news issues, they are also less likely to be able to influence or initiate news agendas' (Romano and De Ponte 2002: 152). There have been relatively few studies that attempt to identify the impact of deliberative journalism practices on representation of women and other minorities. Of the research studies that have been done, most tend to concentrate on relatively simplistic quantitative analyses of the numbers of nonelite or people from minority backgrounds who 'make' the news as the sources, topics or reporters of information. Despite the limitations of such research, they provide some insight into whether and how much deliberative journalism might improve representation of such groups.

Public journalism aims to facilitate the potential of ordinary people to influence news and political agendas, therefore it should help to redress the imbalanced representation of women and other minorities. Research in the United States and Australia has found mixed results about how well public journalism has improved the position of minority and nonelite sources. Studies of certain American public journalism projects have found that the coverage used substantial percentages of female, minority and nonelite sources such as citizens and citizen organizations (e.g., Blazier and Lemert 2000, Kennamer and South 2001, Kurpius 2002, McMillan et al. 1998). However, studies of other projects in the United States and Australia found that those particular projects did not represent women and ethnic minorities more frequently than the mainstream media (e.g., Ewart 2002, Massey

1999). When considering these research results together, it is useful to remember that public journalism is a relatively new philosophy, and media organizations that attempt to adopt that philosophy may not necessarily have the knowledge, skills or resources to ensure that public journalism ideals are materialized in newsroom practice. The research on public journalism that was practised well—as represented by the kind of stories that would be entered into awards—showed more promising results.

The citizen journalism movement proclaims that all citizens are welcome to join. However, there is little chance for participation for the billions of people who do not have access to reliable electricity, computers or modern telecommunications systems let alone the literacy and technological skills required to use the Internet. There have been many attempts to rectify this imbalance. One example is the etuktuk project in Kothmale, Sri Lanka, that blends Internet and radio technologies. The project team uses the tuktuk—the motorized rickshaws that are commonly used as taxis in the region—to transport a mobile telecentre and radio production studio to villages where the locals create programs about their lives, cultures and issues. The programs are broadcast via loudspeakers mounted on the etuktuk's roof and over the radio via the telephone line in surrounding villages, helping to build harmony between the region's ethnically diverse communities. The project's coordinator describes the etuktuk as being a 'modern day, internet-connected drum', which extends Sri Lankan traditions of messengers who would beat out news on drums as they moved from village to village (Nightingale 2008). The etuktuk and similar projects are admirable but are almost always small in scale. Sometimes this is because they need to be very small and localized to achieve their goals, but in other cases it is because of funding and limitations of resources. Either way, it means that they reach only a small proportion of the world's needy populations.

Participation may be uneven even in wealthy, technologically advanced, democratic societies where all citizens should theoretically have opportunities to engage. This can be seen in the figures from the *OhmyNews* (*OMN*) citizen journalism website about its massive corps of tens of thousands of citizen reporters. Despite its heavy promotion of the perspective that every citizen can be a journalist, *OMN* reported in 2005 that 77 per cent of its citizen reporters were male (Kim and Hamilton 2006: 546). *OMN*'s gender imbalance indicates that further research is needed on whether and how citizen journalism platforms can adequately represent and include public diversity.

ISSUES IN ONLINE DELIBERATION

In addition to these concerns about diversity in citizen journalism, societies are still grappling with questions of how to ensure that online technologies are used for deliberation rather than disorder. The degree to which citizen journalism websites support deliberation is inherently connected to their policies for managing an inclusive environment that encourages users to express themselves while also tolerating or engaging with other opinions and experiences. One of the most common systems is to rely on moderators who may (a) set the ground rules for communication, (b) solicit, monitor, edit, or censor the content that is uploaded, and/or (c) discipline or veto users who behave disruptively. Many also use 'reputations systems that try to capture the somewhat transitive nature of trust' (Bowman and Willis 2003: 43).

One of the best known reputation systems can be seen in the Slashdot technology-related news website, whose model has been adopted by thousands of other sites. Negative behaviours are not banned or censored. Slashdot's three strategies for sustaining trust and a civil dialogue generally mean that negative behaviours are so lowly ranked among the millions of entries that they rapidly disappear from sight. Slashdot's first strategy is moderation. It has a pool of members in good standing, who rank all postings according to their quality. The second is the meta-moderators, who ensure that the moderators do not overexert their control. The third is a karma rating for all users, which allows them to increase their status via constructive contributions and behaviours. Slashdot's founder, Rob 'CmdrTaco' Malda, advises that in order to develop positive karma, site users need to:

- post intelligently (interesting, insightful, and thought provoking comments);
- post calmly (no flaming);
- post early (once the number of posts on a particular article has reached a certain level, moderators are less likely to moderate further posts);
- post often (the site seeks 'lively discussion in an open forum');
- stick to the topic;
- be original;
- check their messages before they post for spelling and grammar, and to ensure that they convey the intended meaning;
- log in as a registered user ('"Anonymous Coward" does not have a karma rating. . . . Have pride in your work and take credit for it.');
- read Slashdot regularly ('You can't possibly contribute to the discussion if you're not in the room. Come to the party and play.') (abridged from Malda 1999)

The problems of this approach are illustrated by the experiences of the Kuro5hin site for technology-related news and opinion, which initially relied on mojo, a principle similar to karma. Kuro5hin's founder Rusty Foster radically revised this system in 2003, claiming that thoughtful but quiet users never gained enough mojo to become moderators, 'while the battle was being waged among a small number of very prolific posters, with wildly differing views of what an appropriate comment looked like' (Foster

2003). The system was changed twice again in the following years because of offensive postings and trolls (users who post offensive, controversial or off-topic messages aimed specifically at disrupting conversation, inflaming emotions or provoking a disciplinary response). It can clearly be a time consuming and complicated exercise to create a citizen journalism site that provides a public sphere in which participants exercise a high degree of both freedom and responsibility, let alone engage in deliberation.

Howard Rheingold (2002) also argues that netizens are increasingly acting as 'smart mobs', with both positive and negative consequences. In contrast to the unruly behaviour of traditional mobs, 'smart mobs' are intelligent and efficient because the Internet provides them a multiplicity of opportunities to connect and coordinate with networks of other people and information. Enormous benefits may accrue from this. However, as David Ronfeldt and Ron Arquilla observe, the Internet is not the exclusive province of 'good guys' who do 'the right thing. . . . The cutting edge in the early rise of a new form is just as often found among malcontents, ne'er-do-wells, and clever opportunists, all eager to take advantage of new ways to maneuver, exploit, and dominate' (Ronfeldt and Arquilla 2001: N.P.). Rheingold (2002) describes how this can aid human networks with malevolent goals, such to coordinate terrorist or criminal organizations, breach individual privacy and organizational security, or instigate bloodshed and other abuses.

OUTCOMES: TOO EARLY TO TELL?

Raymond Williams pointed out more than four decades ago that the process of translating a new democratic model for journalism into practice 'will obviously be long and difficult' (Williams 1966: 128). Chapter 2 presents a range of models for deliberation, including public journalism, citizen journalism, community journalism, development journalism and peace journalism. This book does not put these new democratic models forward as examples of categorical success. If I was asked whether or not these or other deliberative journalism models are achieving their goals, I would paraphrase Zhou Enlai, the former Premier of the People's Republic of China. When asked by US Secretary of State Henry Kissinger in the 1970s for his assessment of the 1789 French Revolution, Zhou famously replied was that it was 'too early to tell'.

The types of deliberative journalism that are discussed in this book have existed for only a few decades at most, with the exception of community journalism, which has a somewhat longer history. It is useful to remember that modern Anglo-American media systems evolved progressively from the experiences and philosophical principles of liberalism in sixteenth- and seventeenth-century Europe. The media only shifted from their initial, predominantly authoritarian model to a more libertarian one in the eighteenth century (Siebert 1956: 44). Thus the reporters, editors and proprietors of Anglo-American mass media have spent approximately two centuries exploring and developing the types of reporting and editing practices that work effectively within the expectations, opportunities and confines of the social, legal, economic and political structures of liberal societies. Arguably it is too early for deliberative journalism practitioners to have established a distinctive set of new journalistic practices that provide a comprehensive, viable and effective way of promoting or serving deliberative democracy.

Journalism mirrors the conflicting social conventions, ideologies, rules, laws and constitutional provisions of the cultures in which it operates. Studies of how audiences across the world receive and use media messages have also long indicated that the audiences' social cultures and historical contexts strongly shape the ways in which they will 'read' and respond to those messages (e.g., Alasuutari 1999; Hagen and Wasko 2000; Martín-Barbero 1993). Therefore, those journalists who step too far from existing conventions may face indifferent or even hostile responses from audiences and other social forces. They might be ridiculed or demonized, just as American journalists who were accused of following 'communist' models were harassed during the McCarthy era. They might be detained, tortured or executed, just as Soviet journalists were in the Stalinist era if they were deemed to be too liberal. In most cases, when journalists' operations do not match the surrounding sociopolitical systems and beliefs, the fate will be less dire. They are more likely to be ignored by audiences or the journalistic cadre. This means that their stories and the journalistic techniques will not gain and maintain sufficient currency for them to become embedded in society or newsroom cultures.

Unless there is a political revolution or other major upheaval, then attempts to alter media practices—such as a shift to a deliberative journalism model—will generally occur only incrementally within the spaces allowed by the current system. Similarly, introduction of deliberative media practices will only have incremental effects on a community's life unless other social forces compel more rapid change. The examples presented in this book suggest that those media people who practise public journalism and other deliberative forms of journalism sometimes conduct large and splashy projects. However, most of them are conducting small but significant modifications of mainstream journalism practice within their societies. Many of the chapters in this book indicate how the success of these deliberative journalism initiatives has often depended on the support of government bodies, non-government organizations, community groups, and other sociopolitical actors and institutions that seek to progress the notions, practices and institutions for deliberative democracy.

SUSTAINABILITY AND THE FUTURE

Further questions have been asked about how to sustain deliberative practices, both financially and in terms of altering newsroom cultures. The experiences of public journalism in America indicate the importance of leadership in introducing and preserving changes in newsroom cultures. Media companies are usually more committed to public journalism when their news executives express greater concern for social responsibility than profits (Loomis and Meyer 2000). The support of editors and newsroom leaders is also an important factor, although attempts by editors to embed public journalism philosophies have achieved mixed results (see Chapter 5). There are indications that this leadership has a more long-lasting impact when public journalism philosophies are interlaced with an organizational development strategy and team-based newsroom structures (Gade and Perry 2003).

Public journalism activities often tend to be one-off projects, which may not have long-lasting effects on newsroom practices. Public journalism activities are also often expensive, as they generally require more labour and incur more costs than mainstream reporting (see Chapter 5). After years in which cost-cutting has been the constant mantra within newsrooms, public journalism proponents struggle to gain endorsement for such strategies, let alone support for the concept that audiences should be viewed as citizens rather than consumers.

Funding limitations should not be a complete disincentive to public journalism. Civic mapping strategies, such as those discussed in Chapter 3, can often be implemented cheaply and without disrupting bread-and-butter newsroom activities. The case study of larger projects by two large Australian newsrooms in Chapter 5 also demonstrates how editors can take pragmatic steps to reallocate budgets and staff from areas that may have less need for the newsroom's creative energies and then dedicating those resources to public journalism-style activities.

There is no clear model for how citizen journalists might develop a sustainable, citizen-based economic structure. This is exemplified by the financial struggles of *OMN*, even though it is one of the world's best-known citizen journalism sites. After *OMN* sustained losses in 2008 of 700 million won (approx US$550,000), its founder Oh Yeon-ho acknowledged that only a miniscule proportion of readers made voluntary financial contributions. These comprised only 5 per cent of *OMN*'s revenue, compared to his target of 50 per cent. 'OhmyNews has succeeded in creating a revolutionary model for news production and consumption, but only if we can also create a new revolutionary revenue model, then can we call ourselves a true citizen participatory new media,' he says (Oh 2009).

Financial stresses also plague the community media. The community media commonly have little priority on financial management compared to the emphasis on their content and community connections. However, financial limitations often thwart the aspirations of staff in community-based media worldwide to expand the number, variety, style or outreach of the activities they run. For example, Anette Ruiz Morales, the former supervisor of *Prensa Comunitaria* community media group in Puerto Rico, believes that the organization's greatest challenge and stress is budget (see Chapter 15). She expresses acute awareness that *Prensa Comunitaria*'s economic development activities lag behind its social development achievements, and that *Prensa Comunitaria* might achieve far more if there were funds to expand its operations (2009: pers. comm.). Even a profit-oriented community media organization, like Britain's *Big Issue* magazine and other street papers, face dilemmas about how to build their commercial concerns sufficiently to fulfil social-service goals but without obstructing their prime purpose (see Chapter 11).

More thought is also needed about what factors are required to encourage journalists and editors to adopt deliberative journalism practices in contexts where they might enrich the stories that newsrooms create. Further research is needed also to examine whether, when and how deliberative journalism practices are effective in empowering ordinary people to participate in economic, cultural and political decision making and development. It is one thing to innovate with different journalistic practices but another to have any grounded understanding of their outcomes for newsrooms or the communities they serve.

BIBLIOGRAPHY

Alasuutari, P. (ed.) (1999) *Rethinking the Media Audience: The New Agenda*, London: Sage.

Arant, M.D. and Meyer, P. (1998) 'Public journalism and traditional journalism: A shift in values?', *Journal of Mass Media Ethics*, 13(4): 205–18.

Barnett, S. (2002) 'Will a crisis of journalism provoke a crisis in democracy?', *Political Quarterly*, 73(4): 400–8.

Blazier, T.F. and Lemert, J.B. (2000) 'Public journalism and changes in content of the Seattle Times', *Newspaper Research Journal*, 21(3): 69–80.

Bowman, S. and Willis, C. (2003) *We Media: How Audiences are Shaping the Future of News and Information*, The Media Center at the American Press Institute. Available at http://www.hypergene.net/wemedia/download/we_media.pdf (Accessed 1 September 2009).

Carey, J. (1999) 'In defence of public journalism', in T.L. Glasser (ed.) *The Idea of Public Journalism*, New York: Guildford Press, pp. 49–66.

Ewart, J. (2002) 'Overlooked and underused: How Australia's first public journalism project treated women and Indigenous people', *Australian Journalism Review*, 24(1): 61–81.

Foster, R. (2003) 'Comment rating changes: Mojo, jojo', *Kuro5hin*. Available at http://www.kuro5hin.org/story/2003/10/6/172738/261 (Accessed 1 September 2009).

Gade, P.J. and Perry, E.L. (2003) 'Changing the newsroom culture: A four-year case study of organizational development at the *St Louis Post-Dispatch*, *Journalism and Mass Communication Quarterly*, 80(2): 327–47.

Hagen, I. and Wasko, J. (eds) (2000) *Consuming Audiences? Production and Reception in Media Research*, Cresskill, NJ: Hampton Press.

Kennamer, D. and South, J. (2001) 'Civic Journalism in the 2000 U.S. Senate Race in Virginia', a paper submitted to the Civic Journalism Interest Group of the 2001 AEJMC Conference, Washington, DC, September.

Kim, E.G., and Hamilton, J. (2006) 'Capitulation to capital? OhmyNews as alternative media', *Media, Culture and Society*, 28(4): 541–57.

Kurpius, D.D. (2002) 'Sources and civic journalism' *Journalism and Mass Communication Quarterly*, 79(4): 853–66.

LeBor, A. (1997) *Hitler's Secret Bankers: The Myth of Swiss Neutrality during the Holocaust*, Secaucus, NJ: Carol Publishing Group.

Levine, P. (1996) 'Public journalism and deliberation', *Report from the Institute for Philosophy and Public Policy*, 16(1): 1–9.

Loomis, D. and Meyer, P. (2000) 'Opinion without polls: Finding a link between corporate culture and public journalism', *International Journal of Public Opinion Research*, 12(3): 273–84.

McMillan, S.J., Guppy, M., Kunz, W. and Reis, R. (1998) 'Public journalism: What difference does it make to editorial content?' in E. Lambeth, P. Myer and E. Thorson (eds) *Assessing Public Journalism*, Columbia, MO: University of Missouri Press, pp. 178–90.

Malda, R. (1999) 'Slashdot Moderation'. Available at http://slashdot.org/moderation.shtml (Accessed 1 September 2009).

Martín-Barbero, J. (1993) *Communication, Culture, and Hegemony: From the Media to Mediations*, Newbury Park, CA: Sage.

Massey, B.L. (1999) 'Civic journalism and gender diversity in news-story sourcing', Paper presented to the Civic Journalism Interest Group of the 1999 AEJMC Conference, September. Available at http://list.msu.edu/cgi-bin/wa?A2=ind9909D&L=aejmc&T=0&F=&S=&P=180 (Accessed 1 September 2009).

Nightingale, K. (2008) 'Pod-ready: Podcasting for the developing world', *SciDev.net*, 19 June. Available at http://scidev.net/es/new-technologies/icts/features/el-mundo-en-desarrollo-listo-para-el-podcast.html (Accessed 1September 2009).

Oetama, J. (1978) 'Mass media in Indonesia', *Media Asia*, 5(2): 82–5.

Oh Y.-H. (2009) 'What does OhmyNews mean to you?', *OhmyNews*, 8 July. Available at http://english.ohmynews.com/ArticleView/article_view.asp?menu=A11100&no=385441&rel_no=1&back_url= (Accessed 1 September 2009).

Page, B.I. (1996) *Who Deliberates? Mass Media in Modern Democracy*, Chicago, IL: Chicago University Press.

Parisi, P. (1997) 'Toward a "philosophy of framing": news narratives for public journalism', *Journalism & Mass Communication Quarterly*, 74(4): 673–86.

Rheingold, H. (2002) *Smart Mobs: The Next Social Revolution*. Cambridge, MA: Perseus Publishing.

Rodríguez, C. (2001) *Fissures in the Mediascape: An International Study of Citizens' Media*, Cresskill, NJ: Hampton Press.

Romano, A. and De Ponte, M. (2002) 'Changing representations of women: *The Courier-Mail* over four decades', *Australian Journalism Review*, 24(2): 151–70.

Ronfeldt, D. and Arquilla, J. (2001) 'Networks, netwars and the fight for the future', *First Monday*, 6(10). Available at http://firstmonday.org/htbin/cgiwrap/bin/ojs/index.php/fm/article/view/889/798

Rosen, J. (1991) 'Making journalism more public', *Communication*, 12(2): 267–84.

Rosen, J. (1997) 'Public journalism as a democratic art', in C. Gibbs (ed.), *Public Journalism Theory and Practice: Lessons from Experience*, Dayton, OH: Kettering Foundation, pp. 3–24.

Sainath, P. (1996) *Everybody Loves a Good Drought*, New York: Penguin.

Siebert, F.S. (1956) 'The libertarian theory', in F.S. Siebert, T. Peterson and W. Schramm (eds) *Four Theories of the Press*, 2nd edition, Urbana, IL: University of Illinois Press, pp. 39–71.

Waddell, L. (1997) 'Voices: In the beginning there was Columbus', in J. Black (ed.) *Mixed News: The Public/Civic/Communitarian Journalism Debate*, Mahwah, NJ: Lawrence Erlbaum, pp. 94–5.

Williams, R. (1966) *Communications*, 2nd edn, London: Chatto & Windus.

Contributors

Laura Ahva is a researcher and a doctoral student in the Department of Journalism and Mass Communication at the University of Tampere in Finland. Her PhD research focuses on the practices and interpretations of public journalism in the Finnish press. She has also acted as an educator for students, teachers and journalists on public journalism and related topics. She is currently working on an audience research project that focuses on the relevance of newspapers in the everyday life of the readers.

Tokunbo (Tokz) Awoshakin is a journalist and communications researcher. He started his journalism career with *The News/Tempo Magazine*, a national publication that fought against military dictatorship in Nigeria in the in the early 1990s. He also worked as a news editor with the *Sunday Concord* newspaper and as regional editor and supervisor for *ThisDay* newspaper's operations in the Niger Delta region. He moved to the United States in 1998 as the newspaper's pioneer Washington, DC, Bureau Chief, also covering the United Nations, the US Congress and the White House. He trained at the Poynter Media Institute in the United States with Roy Peter Clark and Christopher "Chip" Scalan. Awoshakin was the Katharine W. Fanning International Fellow for Journalism and Democracy at the Kettering Foundation in 2003. He is a contributing writer for the *Dayton Daily News,* and a doctoral student at Antioch University's PhD program in Leadership and Change.

Jiannu Bao is a senior lecturer in the Department of International Journalism and Communication, Beijing Foreign Studies University, China. She worked as a journalist for the Chinese state Xinhua (New China) news agency from 1992 to 2001. Bao completed her PhD in media and communication from Queensland University of Technology, Australia, in 2006.

Maria Alice Lima Baroni is a journalist at Universidade Veiga de Almeida's Experimental Agency of News in Brazil. She is associated with the

'Thought and Experience' research group at Universidade Estadual do Rio de Janeiro and the 'Theories and Practices in Journalism' research group at Pontifíca Universidade Católica do Rio de Janeiro (PUC-Rio). She completed a Social Communication degree with Universidade Católica de Brasilia and specialized with a Master's of Business Economics, International Analyst, from Universidade Federal do Rio de Janeiro and a Master's in Communication from PUC-Rio. Her specialties are the study of the effects of truth, discourse, power and strategy in journalism and literature.

Margie Comrie is an Associate Professor in the Department of Communication, Journalism and Marketing at Massey University in New Zealand, where she teaches journalism studies and public relations. She joined the University after seventeen years in the news media. With Dr Judy McGregor, she has coedited two foundation books on the New Zealand media. Her research interests centre on citizen empowerment and include publications on public service broadcasting, political communication, public journalism, consultation and adult literacy.

Brett Davidson has an MA in journalism and media studies from Rhodes University. He is based in Cape Town, South Africa, and works throughout eastern and southern Africa as an independent media consultant, assisting non-government organizations to develop communications and advocacy strategies, as well as practical and effective ways of working with the media. He has worked as a radio journalist, presenter, producer and trainer. He also has experience in senior management in the NGO sector.

Klaus Forster wrote his dissertation about public journalism and received his doctoral degree in 2006 at the Ludwig Maximilian University of Munich. He teaches communication studies at the Munich campuses of the Media Academy and the Macromedia University for Applied Sciences of Media and Communication. Beyond that, Forster works as a freelance market and media researcher. His areas of study include quality in journalism, multimedia and computer-aided learning, as well as visual communication.

Yohtaro Hamada is an assistant editor for the *Asahi Shimbun*, one of Japan's leading daily newspapers. During the last ten years, he has been covering public policy related to the provision of social services such as healthcare and the pension system. From 2001–02 he was a Fulbright Scholar in the United States, studying journalism at the University of Minnesota. He won a Japan Agricultural Journalist Award in 1994 for his reporting on rice farming. Hamada graduated from Hitotsubashi University (Tokyo) in 1990 with a BA.

Maria Izabel de Araújo Leão is a journalist with the Newspaper of Universidade de São Paulo (USP) and an edu-communicator in Brazil. She has a Master's in Communications Science and a specialization in Management of Communications Processes from USP's Escola de Comunicações e Artes (ECA). She tutors the distance education program, 'Media in Education', which has been developed by the Ministry of Education in partnership with the Centre of Communication and Education in the ECA/USP, and in association with the *Viração* Magazine Editorial Council.

Paulo Pereira Lima is from Ceará, Fortaleza, in Brazil. He is a journalist and edu-communicator, director of the *Viração* Magazine project and a social entrepreneur with the Ashoka Foundation. He is a graduate in philosophy, theology and journalism, and has specialization in Communication from Paolino International Studio of Social Communication in Rome. Lima was director of the *Sem Fronteiras* magazine and edited the *Brasil de Fato* newspaper, which he also helped found in March 2003. He is a consultant on youth issues for UNESCO, UNICEF, the Mundial Organization of Health and many Brazilian government ministries. Lima has written one book and coauthored three others. Lima was awarded the title of 'Journalistic Friend of Children' (*Jornalista Amigo da Criança*) in 2002 by UNICEF, the Abrinq Foundation for Children and Adolescent's Rights, and the Agency of News of Childhood Rights (ANDI) for his defence of children and adolescent's rights through popular communication. He won the international Don Mario Pasini Communication Prize in 2004 from the Italian Misna News Agency and Cuore Amigo Association.

Ana Maria Miralles is a professor and researcher of Public Opinion at the Communication Department in the Universidad Pontificia Bolivariana, Medellín, Colombia. She has been the Director of the Citizen Voices project since its creation in November 1998. Miralles has written five books and is an international consultant in the field of communication, politics and democracy for institutions like UNESCO, Radio Nederland, GTZ, International Development Consultant, International Media Support, Comunidad Andina de Naciones, Interamerican Bank, and others.

Anette Sofía Ruiz Morales' career has mainly developed in Puerto Rico's nonprofit sector and communities with high rates of poverty, where she has worked as research assistant, coordinator of media management workshops, supervisor of a national volunteer project and journalist for a TV news show, several radio programs and print media. In 2008 she was finalist of the *Spirit of Service Award* and participated in the Delegation of Anthropology and Archaeology to China by invitation of the Golden Key International Honour Society. She has a BA in journalism and a minor in anthropology. Currently she is in enrolled in graduate studies of communications, with a specialty in media and culture, and is a member of the international network of the Kettering Foundation.

Angela Romano teaches journalism at the Queensland University of Technology, Brisbane, Australia. Romano conducts research on a wide range of issues relating to journalism and the media, including democracy and politics, corruption, gender, ethnic and cultural diversity, refugees and asylum seekers, and media education. Her major publications include *Politics and the Press in Indonesia* and *Journalism and Democracy in Asia* (coedited with Michael Bromley). She engages in ongoing applied research projects in journalism, such as a series of documentary-style deliberative radio programs that won the Best Radio category of the 2005 Media Peace Awards, organized by the United Nations Association of Australia.

Gita Widya Laksmini Soerjoatmodjo is a researcher for the Institute for Study of Press and Development (LSPP) in Jakarta. Prior to joining LSPP, Gita worked as a journalist for Indonesia's best-known news weekly magazine, *Tempo*, and she was awarded a Young and Talented Media People award by *Pantau* magazine in 2002. She has a Master's degree in human rights from the University of London, which she completed with the support of a British Chevening Award. She writes, cowrites and edits books about freedom of expression and information.

Pradip Thomas is an Associate Professor at the School of Journalism and Communications, University of Queensland, Brisbane. His research interests include the political economy of communications, religion and media and communication and social change. His most recent writings include the volume, *Strong Religion, Zealous Media: Christian Fundamentalism and Communication in India* (Sage, 2008) and the article, 'Selling God/Saving Souls: Religious Commodities, Spiritual Markets and the Media', in the journal *Global Media and Communication*, April 2009.

David Venables is the former head of the Journalism Programme at Massey University in New Zealand and has ten years' tertiary teaching experience in the subject. He has also worked as a reporter at Radio New Zealand and has been chief reporter for a network of community newspapers. He is currently Communications Manager at New Zealand's Ministry for the Environment.

Index

A

Aamulehti (Finland), 124–132
Aboriginal and Torres Strait Islander people and the media, 23, 70
Al Jazeera, 21, 29
Aliansi Jurnalis Independen (Alliance of Independent Journalists, Indonesia), 188, 189, 190, 192
alternative media, 9, 22–4, 153, 154, 159–60, 163, 209–10. *See also* Independent Media Center *and* Prensa Comunitaria (Puerto Rico)
Ambon Ekspres (Indonesia), 184, 191
America. *See* United States of America
AmeriCorps*VISTA, 212, 214, 220, 221
Armstrong, David, 69–70, 71, 72–4, 234
Asahi Shimbun (Japan), 91–102
Australia, 13, 23, 63–74, 83, 164, 234, 235, 240
Australian, 69–70, 72, 73–4, 234
Australian Broadcasting Corporation, 65, 67

B

balance. *See* objectivity of journalists
Big Issue (Britain), 153–65, 241
Big Issue (United States), 162
Bird, John, 154–5, 156, 157, 161–3, 164
blogs, 20, 21, 36, 56–7, 112–117, 133, 205, 206. *See also* citizen journalism *and* social networking via the Internet
Brazil, 13, 148, 222–8
Britain, 49, 50, 153–65, 188, 198, 241

C

Campbell, Cole, 16–17, 64
Charity, Arthur, 18, 55, 73, 108

children. *See* young people and the media
China, 13, 166–78, 238
China Business, 173, 175
China Central Radio Station, 168, 172, 176
China Central Television Station, 172
China Youth Daily, 172, 173, 175, 176
Chinese Communist Party, 166, 170, 177
citizen journalism, 12, 13, 19–22, 29, 35, 111–17, 233, 238, 240
City Voice (New Zealand), 80
civic journalism. *See* public journalism
civic mapping, 12, 18, 37–9, 63, 240
collective learning. *See* public learning
Colombia, 13, 136–150, 234
Communist Party of China. *See* Chinese Communist Party
Courier-Mail (Australia), 65–7, 70–1, 72–3
community: community and politics, 4; definition of community, 5; difference of a community from a public, 5; communities of interest versus geographic communities, 5, 20, 234
community leadership. *See* leadership
community media, 12, 22–4, 29, 35–47, 57–8, 68–9, 80, 148, 153, 154, 159–60, 208–20, 222–8, 233, 238, 240–1
community mobilization. *See* mobilization
community social enterprise. *See* social entrepreneurs and enterprises
conscientization. *See* critical consciousness
conflict reporting, 13, 21, 26–9, 54–55, 180–1, 183–192
costs of deliberative journalism. *See* sustainability of deliberative journalism

creativity in deliberative journalism, 138, 167, 224, 234–5
crime reporting, 81, 87–8, 113, 136, 215
critical consciousness, 6–7, 25–6, 51, 189, 191, 199, 204, 217–8, 224–5. *See also* myths and public consciousness
cultural difference. *See* diversity

D

De Tocqueville, Alexis, 4, 10
deliberation: definition of, 3; difference from other forms of conversation, 3; difference from mobilization, 4–5; inclusion of diverse opinions in deliberation, 3–4; deliberation and substantive democracy, 10. *See also* diversity and deliberation
deliberative forums, 6, 216
deliberative journalism (definition of), 10–11. *See also* alternative journalism; community journalism; citizen journalism; development journalism; peace journalism; public journalism; *and* sustainability of deliberative journalism
Denmark, 106
development journalism,13, 24–6, 37, 29, 53–4, 61, 122, 218–220, 203–4, 208, 219–20, 231–2, 234, 238, 241
Dewey, John, 3, 5
diversity and deliberation, 3–4, 7–10, 70
diversity and journalism, 22–3, 25, 28, 65, 122, 180–1, 185–92, 201–3, 204, 217, 222, 226, 227, 235–6. *See also* gender and journalism
Dominion and *Dominion Post* (New Zealand), 79–82, 84–88
Dujiangyan dam proposal, 166, 171–3

E

edu-communication, 224–6. *See also* educational function of journalism
educational function of journalism, 6–7, 10, 16–17, 18, 24, 25–6, 28, 49, 54, 74, 76, 84, 163, 166, 168, 177, 196, 197, 198, 199, 202, 222, 224–8
El Colombiano (Colombia), 142, 145

emotion versus rationality in deliberation, 8–9, 28, 168, 238
environmental journalism, 13, 53–5, 71, 73, 76, 77, 93, 94, 100, 156, 157, 166–78, 198–9
Ethiopia, 164
etuktuk (Sri Lanka), 236
Evening Post (New Zealand), 79
Evening Standard. See Manawatu Evening Standard (New Zealand)

F

Facebook, 20, 56
Fagan, David, 70–1, 72–4
financial costs of deliberative journalism. *See* sustainability of deliberative journalism
Finland, 13, 106, 121–134, 234
focus groups conducted by/for journalists, 18, 38, 64, 213
forums in deliberative journalism. *See* public forums
France, 158
Freire, Paulo, 6, 13, 25

G

Galtung, Johan, 24, 25, 29, 185–6
Gandhi, Mahatma, 7, 10, 13, 197–9
gender and journalism, 53–4, 57, 66, 83, 93, 159, 186, 189, 199, 201–3, 206, 227, 235–6. *See also* diversity and journalism
Germany, 13, 105–117, 121, 231
Gillmor, Dan, 20, 105, 112, 114
government–journalist relations, 12, 18, 24, 26, 28–9, 37, 38, 39–42, 49, 50–1, 54–6, 57–9, 69, 76–7, 93, 94–5, 96, 101, 111, 116, 125, 137, 141–2, 143–4, 166–7, 169–70, 174–5, 177, 194, 201
'green' issues. *See* environment and journalism
Guardian (Nigeria), 53, 55–6,
guerrilla journalism, 50

H

Habermas, Jürgen, 8, 11, 107, 112, 149
Hartley, John, 159
Harvey, John, 76, 77, 79, 80
Helsingin Sanomat (Finland), 124–32
Hippocrates, Cratis, 65, 67, 71
HIV/AIDS, 36, 52, 57, 223,
homelessness and the media, 13, 71, 153–64, 241

Howard, Ross, 26–7, 187

I

Idasa, 35–6, 37, 39, 41
independence of journalists. *See* objectivity of journalists
Independent Media Center , 20, 210
India, 13, 164, 194–206
indigenous communities and journalism, 23, 70, 199–200
Indonesia, 13, 24, 28–9, 180–192, 234
indymedia. *See* Independent Media Center
Institute for Press and Development Studies (Lembaga Studi Pers dan Pembangunan, LSPP), 180, 188
Inter Press Service (IPS), 24, 25, 26
Internet, 19–22, 29, 36, 38, 47, 56–7, 111–17, 122, 133, 148, 174, 194–7, 200, 205–6, 209, 211, 212, 213, 220, 236–8
interviews as tools for deliberative journalism, 18, 26, 39, 55–6, 64, 70, 79–80, 92, 94, 96–7, 113, 114, 124, 126, 128, 130, 132, 137, 140, 141, 143, 144, 145, 146, 155, 156–7, 162, 176, 232
Israel, 21
issue-driven versus event-driven journalism, 11, 25, 108–10, 114–6
Itä-Häme (Finland), 124–32

J

Japan, 13, 91–103, 164, 234
journalistic objectivity. *See* objectivity of journalists

K

Kenya, 164
Kettering Foundation, xii, 36, 37, 42, 243, 246
Khabar Lhariya (India), 201–3
Kuro5hin, 237–8

L

Lasica, J.D., 20, 233
Laskar Jihad, 182, 185
Latin America, 6, 106, 148–9, 219. *See also* Brazil, Colombia *and* Puerto Rico
Latrobe Valley Express (Australia), 68–9
leadership, 27, 38, 50, 59–60, 63, 69, 72, 74, 100, 177, 208, 211–2,

214, 215, 217–18, 220, 226, 227, 235, 239–40
learning organizations, 18, 46–7, 58, 65, 67, 68, 71, 73, 100, 190, 201–2
Ledger-Enquirer (USA), 232
listening across difference, 8–9
listening in deliberation and journalism. *See* public listening *and* listening across difference
localism versus mass communities in deliberative journalism, 36, 53, 64, 66, 72, 114, 195–6, 233–4
Lynch, Jake, 26–9, 187, 188

M

Malawi, 164
Maluku conflicts, 180–92
Manawatu Evening Standard (New Zealand), 76–80, 85
McGoldrick, Annabel, 26–9, 187, 188
Mathews, David, 3, 6, 29, 59
Merritt, Davis (Buzz), 97, 98, 108
Mexico, 106
minority groups. *See* diversity and deliberation
Mitchell, Chris, 67, 70–1
Miura, Akihiko, 92–3
mobilization of communities, 3–5, 16, 51, 108–10, 116, 126, 128, 139–40, 172, 195, 198, 199, 200, 211, 212, 215–6, 218, 219, 223, 226, 228, 232
multiculturalism. *See* diversity and deliberation
Münchner Merkur (Germany), 109–11, 112
myths and public consciousness, 6–7, 17, 22, 27, 201, 209, 215. *See also* critical consciousness

N

Namibia, 122, 164
Netherlands, 158
netizens, 112, 197, 238
New Zealand, 12–13, 64, 72, 75–89
New Zealand Herald, 80–2, 85–6
news sources, 11, 18, 20, 21, 24–5, 26, 27, 28, 29, 37
newspaper and magazine journalism, 3, 10, 16, 19, 36–7, 40, 42, 47, 50, 53–6, 65–71, 75–89, 91–102, 106, 108–10, 121–33, 137, 139, 142, 145, 153–64, 167, 172–5,

183–5, 194–7, 198–202, 204, 206, 209, 210–11, 213, 214, 215, 217, 218, 220, 222–8
newsroom leaders and leadership. *See* leadership
Nigeria, 12

O

objectivity of journalists, 3, 18–19, 22, 23, 26, 27, 28, 108–10, 146, 176, 185, 197, 201, 231–3
Oh Yeon-ho, 20, 240
OhmyNews, 20, 211, 236, 240
online journalism. *See* citizen journalism *and* internet
opinion polls. *See* surveys, questionnaires and polls in deliberative journalism
organic politics, 6
Otago Daily Times (New Zealand), 80–3, 85–6

P

Page, Warren, 76, 80
Pakistan, 164
Palestinian–Israeli conflict, 21
Pankhurst, Tim, 77, 80, 81, 83, 85, 88
participatory journalism. *See* citizen journalism
peace journalism, 13, 26–9, 180–1, 185–92, 222, 231–2, 238
Pinontoan, Novi, 180, 191
polls. *See* surveys, questionnaires and polls in deliberative journalism
political capital, 211. *See also*, social capital
politics: definition, 4
politics of presence, 7–8
Prabhat Khabar (India), 199–200
process reporting. *See* issue-driven versus event-driven journalism
print media. *See* newspaper and magazine journalism
public: definition of a public, 5; weaknesses of publics, 5; formation of publics, 5–6. *See also* public sphere
public forums, 6, 43, 51, 52, 54, 63, 65–6, 71
public journalism, 12–13, 16–19, 35–47, 49–61, 63–74, 75–89, 91–103, 117, 121–34, 136–150, 231–2, 233–4, 235–6, 238, 239–40

public knowledge, 17. *See also* public learning *and* public reason
public learning, 6–7, 18, 51, 84
public listening, 18, 58, 63, 66, 93–4, 98, 99, 143, 232
public reason, 4. *See also* public knowledge *and* public reason
public sphere, 7, 20, 22, 35, 107, 136, 138, 154, 159, 197, 199–200, 204, 238
Prensa Comunitaria (Puerto Rico), 208, 210–21, 240–1
Press (New Zealand), 76–87
Puerto Rico, 13, 208–21, 240–1

Q

questionnaire. *See* surveys, questionnaires and polls in deliberative journalism

R

radio, 3, 35, 36–7, 39, 42–7, 52, 57–8, 65, 67, 68, 73, 75, 142, 148, 167, 168, 172, 176, 180, 182, 183–5, 188, 209, 211, 213–14, 215–6, 218, 222
race relations. *See* diversity
Rawls, John, 4
Readers Edition (Germany), 112–17
religious diversity. *See* diversity
reputation systems of websites, 237–8
Reynolds, Anna, 65–7, 71
Richmond Times Dispatch (USA), 108–10
Rosen, Jay, 11–12, 59, 88, 97, 98, 103, 108, 112, 121, 149, 231
Rwanda, 3–4

S

Schudson, Michael, 19, 148
self-governance of communities, 4, 7, 60, 215
Sherson, Venetia, 80, 84, 87
Slashdot, 237
social capital, 21, 23–4, 25, 142, 211, 220
social entrepreneurs and enterprises, 13, 153–4, 155, 160, 161–4, 218–20
social exchange, 211. *See also* social capital
social networking via the Internet, 20, 21, 56–7, 205
South Africa, 12, 35–48, 164
South Korea, 20–1

sources. *See* news sources
Southern Metropolitan News (China), 173, 174
Sowetan (South Africa), 36
Sri Lanka, 236
stakeholders in deliberation, 4, 6, 11, 25, 54–5, 58, 68, 94. 95, 154, 157, 159, 160, 167, 182, 212, 214, 215, 225
street press, 13, 153–64, 241
St Louis Post Dispatch (USA), 64
Suara Maluku (Indonesia), 183, 184, 191
Sunday Times (South Africa), 36
surveys, questionnaires and polls in deliberative journalism, 18, 41, 52, 64, 65, 76, 77–8, 79, 80, 81, 83–6, 87, 92, 109, 114, 124, 133, 232
sustainability of deliberative journalism, 63–74, 88–9, 121, 123, 155, 163, 164, 169, 191–2, 197, 218–9, 220, 225, 239–41
Sweden, 106, 122
Swift, Jack, 232
Switzerland, 121, 148, 231

T
talk shows and talkback radio, 42–5, 46, 52, 65, 67, 68
Tehelka (India), 194–7, 200, 206
television, 35, 47, 65, 73, 75, 137, 142, 148, 167, 172, 180, 183–4, 194, 204, 209, 211, 213–4, 215, 216, 217, 218
town hall meetings, 18, 54, 58–9, 64, 66, 70, 213, 232
weblogs. *See* blogs
ThisDay (Nigeria), 54–5, 58–9,
Tocqueville, Alexis de. *See* De Tocqueville, Alexis
Twitter, 20, 21

U
UNESCO, 57, 171, 172

United States of America, 4, 6, 11–12, 16–19, 35, 37, 49, 51, 58, 59, 63, 64, 88, 91–2, 97, 101, 103, 106, 108, 121, 148–9, 154, 156, 157, 158, 162, 208, 212, 219, 232, 233, 235, 238–9
United Kingdom. *See* Britain

V
Valley FM (South Africa), 42–5
Vanguard (Nigeria) 54–5
Viração (Brazil), 222–8
Virginian-Pilot (USA), 64, 108–10

W
Waikato Times (New Zealand), 76–86
Wang Yongchen, 168, 172, 176
women as journalists and sources. *See* gender and journalism
Wisudo, Bambang, 183, 190, 191
Witt, Leonard, 105, 112

X
Xiamen Evening News (China), 174, 175
Xiamen Paraxylene (PX) project, 166, 171, 173–6,
Xinhua News Agency (China), 167, 172

Y
Yomiuri Shimbun (Japan), 98
Yoshida, Shin-ichi, 91–3, 98–99, 100, 102,
Young, Iris Marion, 8–9
young people and the media, 13, 38, 42–5, 53, 68, 69, 87–8, 95–7, 157, 186, 189, 222–8

Z
Zhang Keija, 172, 176